Keeping Slug Woman Alive

Keeping Slug Woman Alive

A Holistic Approach to
American Indian Texts

Greg Sarris

UNIVERSITY OF CALIFORNIA PRESS
Berkeley · *Los Angeles* · *Oxford*

The following essays in this book have been previously published in slightly different form:

"The Verbal Art of Mabel McKay: Talk as Culture Contact and Cultural Critique," *MELUS* 16, no. 1 (Spring 1991).

"The Woman Who Loved a Snake: Orality in Mabel McKay's Stories," *American Indian Quarterly* 15, no. 2 (Spring 1991).

"A Culture under Glass: The Pomo Basket," *In Writing* (Spring 1987).

"Telling Dreams and Keeping Secrets: The Bole Maru as American Indian Religious Resistance," *The American Indian Culture and Research Journal* 16, no. 1 (Spring 1992).

"Hearing the Old Ones Talk: Reading Narrated American Indian Lives in Elizabeth Colson's *Autobiographies of Three Pomo Women*," in *New Voices in Native American Literary Criticism*, ed. Arnold Krupat (Washington, D.C.: Smithsonian Institution Press, forthcoming).

"Storytelling in the Classroom: Crossing Vexed Chasms," *College English* 52, no. 2 (February 1990). Copyright 1990 by the National Council of Teachers of English. Reprinted with permission.

"Keeping Slug Woman Alive: The Challenge of Reading in a Reservation Classroom," in *The Ethnography of Reading*, ed. Jonathan Boyarin (Berkeley and Los Angeles: University of California Press, forthcoming 1993).

University of California Press
Berkeley and Los Angeles, California

University of California Press, Ltd.
Oxford, England

Cataloging-in-Publication data follows the index to this book.

Printed in the United States of America
9 8 7 6 5 4 3 2

The paper used in this publication meets the minimum requirements of American National Standard for Information Sciences—Permanence of Paper for Printed Library Materials, ANSI Z39.48-1984. ∞

Contents

Prologue:
Peeling Potatoes

"Here Greg," Auntie Violet said. "You can peel some potatoes." She placed a paper towel, a small sharp knife, and three potatoes on the table. She plunked the potatoes down just as she had spoken. Now do something, she seemed to be saying. Make yourself useful.

I was sitting at the kitchen table listening to Mabel McKay tell about a man she had known when she was a young girl, around ten or so. It was Mabel's eighty-second birthday, and I had driven Auntie Violet Chappell to Mabel's place so we could visit and celebrate. Despite her recent trouble with arthritis, Mabel looked bright, alert. She sat in her wooden chair, its seat neatly padded with colorful cushions, the arms wrapped with towels so she could rest her arms comfortably. She was near the head of the table, as always. I was sitting next to her, busy taking notes. I was a graduate student at Stanford University preparing a dissertation on the life story of Mabel McKay, renowned Cache Creek Pomo Indian basketweaver and medicine woman, whom I had known since childhood. No part of the project had been easy. Mabel didn't present her stories in chronological sequence. Her stories moved in and out of different time frames and often implicated me as a listener. Of course this was always my experience with Mabel. Still, I wanted to get the pieces of her life in some order so that I might grasp it for others, and when she started talking about this old medicine man, or Indian doctor, who followed her around, I quickly found a pencil and paper. It was something I hadn't heard before.

But just then I picked up the knife and began peeling one of the potatoes.

1

I watched Violet, who sat across from me with three potatoes of her own. I felt self-conscious; usually I did not help prepare food. I volunteered with the dishes afterwards, and the women could count on me for yardwork and trips to the grocery store. Alone, in my own home, I cooked, but here with Mabel and with relatives I did not. Auntie Violet upset routine. She was a tease, and I suspected some antic.

Her first potato looked smooth as an egg. The objective, I thought: get the potatoes smooth, perfectly rounded. I could tell she was watching me.

Frances McDaniel, Mabel's younger sister, came to the table and began working on potatoes also. The conversation turned to gossip, centering on a local man's wife, who was white. Violet bobbed her head around and rolled her eyes, mocking the woman's air of superiority. "Shoot, why did she marry an Indian if she wants to be Princess Diana?" Violet asked.

Often when whites are discussed, particularly in a derogatory way, I become uneasy. I think of my mother, who was white, of the fact that I am a mixed blood. I wanted to hear more about the medicine man Mabel knew. I pictured him in trousers and suspenders; perhaps he wore a hat, a Stetson typical of the time. Mabel said he came in the evenings and wandered outside the yard of the white woman's home where Mabel was staying at the time. What did he want? Did he know she was destined to be a doctor? Was he going to help her? Hurt her? I looked to Mabel, but she was distracted, chuckling to herself and listening to Violet.

Frances's potatoes too were smooth, egg-like. She held the potato and knife in front of her just as she might a basket and awl, as if she were weaving. I hardly had the grace, but to my satisfaction my potatoes were smooth; I'd even gone back and planed any rough edges. And I was finished before Violet.

I set my knife down and leaned back in my chair, just for a moment, just to let Violet know I was finished. But she was not moving. Her face was tight, swollen, blushed with color, her eyes set on her pile of peelings where she held her knife, pointing. The peelings, something I hadn't thought of . . . Her peelings were paper thin, shards of skin, thinner than carrot peelings, almost transparent. I felt the thick, coarse lumps under my hand. I lifted my eyes just in time to catch Auntie Violet hiss. "Just like a white man," she managed to say, exploding with laughter. "So wasteful!"

The entire room was laughing, and in the midst of the loud hysteria,

Mabel stopped for a moment, and turning to me, said ever so matter-of-factly, "My life is like that."[1]

I learned a lesson. It was a lesson Mabel reminded me of again and again, every time we talked about her life stories. It was a simple lesson: things aren't always what they seem. Not the way I saw two women peeling potatoes. Not Mabel.

As simple as this lesson is, it provokes and informs current critical discussion about literature and art and other elements of culture. It becomes particularly relevant as the critical discussion engages questions regarding reading in cross-cultural contexts. Specifically, how do people read across cultures? What are the aims and consequences of their readings? How are the readings located in a certain history, say that of American Indian and Euro-American interrelations? Is there a way that people can read across cultures so that intercultural communication is opened rather than closed, so that people see more than just what things seem to be?

In each of the eight essays collected in this book, I explore answers to these questions and demonstrate that people can see more than just what things seem to be. The essays are concerned with American Indian texts, oral and written, as well as with other American Indian cultural phenomena, such as basketry and religion. They cover a range of topics around American Indian studies that include orality, art, literary criticism, and pedagogy. I often focus on texts and other cultural phenomena associated specifically with Pomo culture, yet I always locate my work in broader discussions of the topics considered and cross-cultural communication. And as diverse as these essays may be in terms of the texts and topics considered, each essay is predicated on, and inspired by, what I have learned from Mabel McKay about seeing beyond what things seem to be.

That day in the kitchen I learned that I did not see a potato the way Frances McDaniel, Mabel McKay, and Auntie Violet Chappell did. My interaction with these women demonstrated as much, exposing the differences between us that constituted the different ways we saw potatoes. For example, I came to terms with the fact that I am a man and have never had to worry about feeding a family, making ends meet. And

---

1. Here and throughout these essays I have written from memory my conversations with Mabel McKay and her conversations with others that I have witnessed. Sometimes I use recorded material, in which case I note the time and date of recording. Quotations from family members, such as Violet Chappell, are likewise written from memory unless otherwise indicated.

writing about this interaction in a way that reveals my limits and expectations becomes a means for me to extend to readers what made for the exchange at hand. It is the way I learned to write Mabel's life stories, so that the written text becomes the story of my hearing her stories.

Storytelling is a fundamental aspect of culture, and stories are used in a number of ways and for a multitude of purposes. Stories can work as cultural indexes for appropriate or inappropriate behavior. They can work to oppress or to liberate, to confuse or to enlighten. So much depends on who is telling the story and who is listening and the specific circumstances of the exchange. Mabel McKay tells me some stories that have certain narrative properties, say a beginning, middle, and end, and she may have certain intentions at times for telling me the stories, even if I cannot always be clear about her intentions. But it is not just these stories that I am referring to and representing in specific ways, but what I might simply call her talk, which includes responses to questions, gossip, idle chitchat, and any stories that can become a basis for intercultural and interpersonal communication and understanding. Of course nonverbal interaction, as in the case of the potatoes, can work in the same way as a basis for intercultural and interpersonal communication and understanding. This interaction with Mabel, verbal and nonverbal, serves as the basis for dialogue within and between people that can expose boundaries that shape and constitute different cultural and personal worlds. It is the kind of dialogue I will attempt to have and represent in these eight essays.

Dialogue in the most general sense is understood as conversation between two or more people, people talking back and forth with one another. M. M. Bakhtin sees dialogue as an essential characteristic of the novel, which for Bakhtin is comprised of a diversity of voices. *Heteroglossia* is Bakhtin's term, or major trope, for the multitude of voices that comprise not only the novel but all forms and elements of communication. He observes that "at any given moment of its historical existence, language is heteroglot from top to bottom: it represents the co-existence of sociological contradictions between the present and the past, between differing epochs of the past, between different socio-ideological groups in the present, between tendencies, schools, circles and so forth, all given a bodily form. These 'languages' of heteroglossia intersect each other in a variety of ways, forming new socially typifying 'languages'" (291). Thus, a unit or system of language, say the novel, can be seen as a representative of dialogue and interaction between a number of languages and voices. But as David Bleich notes about the novel, and I would add all other units of language activity, it is not just a *representation* of interaction but also the *occasion* for interaction (418). A reader's intermingling internal voices hold dialogue with the intermingling voices of the novel. Still, the definition of dialogue here remains general, vague. Dialogue, like stories, can work to oppress or to liberate, to confuse or to enlighten. Just because we are conversing with one another does not mean we are understanding one another. Think of the teacher who converses with a student only to convince the student that a certain method or definition is absolute and correct. Think of the reader who assimilates what he or she reads so that the text's many "other" voices are ignored or silenced. What Mabel provokes and what I explore in my essays is a specific kind of dialogue, or conversation, that can open the intermingling of the multiple voices within and between people and the texts they encounter, enabling people to see and hear the ways various voices intersect and overlap, the ways they have been repressed or held down because of certain social and political circumstances, and the ways they can be talked about and explored.

In general, Mabel has suggested to me in our various encounters over the past thirty years that, as David Murray said so plainly, "description cannot be separated and made prior to interpretation" (147). Readers, for instance, cannot be separate from the history of their reading, of all that makes for their encounter with and response to that which they read. Mabel once said: "Don't ask me what it means, the story. Life will teach you about it, the way it teaches you about life." It is important that I remember my life, my presence and history, as I attempt to understand Mabel. As I learn more about Mabel, I learn more about myself. In this way, using much of what Mabel has taught me, I show in these essays myself and others learning, seeing beyond what things seem to be. I chart dialogues that open and explore interpersonal and intercultural territories.

Of course, much of what Mabel McKay has suggested to me in terms of reading others and writing about them is echoed by contemporary social scientists. Stephen Tyler (1986) describes a way of writing cross-cultural experience where all facets of the encounter are revealed for the reader—the different persons with different cultural perspectives, the nature and consequences of their interaction in the encounter, and the ways each is responsible for and contributes to some kind of understanding about the encounter and the writing of their experience. Tyler and many other contemporary social scientists, most notably Renato Rosaldo, George E. Marcus, and Michael M. J. Fischer, stress the importance of polyvocality in the written document, the presence of multiple voices. They call for reflexivity, asking ethnographers to account for their conclusions, for their notions of truth and knowledge, and for the political and historical consequences of their work. They argue that for cross-cultural communication to be open and effective, interlocutors must be aware of their boundaries, both personal and cultural, so that they might know the limits on and possibilities for understanding one another in the exchange. That is, in understanding another person and culture you must simultaneously understand yourself. The process is ongoing, an endeavor aimed not at a final transparent understanding of the Other or of the self, but at continued communication, at an ever-widening understanding of both.

The work of literary theorists interested in reading practices converges with the work of these social scientists. Specifically, Stanley Fish and a host of other literary scholars question how readers read written texts. They see the reader as subjective, as positioned by his or her historical, cultural, and gender-based background. David Bleich argues that readers, literary critics in particular, must historicize their positions as readers, come to terms with their biases, so that they might better understand the text they are reading and their relationship to it. My work draws upon the discussions of both these literary theorists and the aforementioned social scientists and bridges the respective fields of study. But I write quite differently from these scholars. They tend to employ conventional argumentative narratives, the forms of which usually undermine not only a record of a scholar's interaction with a text or whatever but also the scholar's autobiography, which is a necessary component of the reading and writing practices these scholars call for.[2]

Keeping Slug Woman Alive tells stories about relationships. In each of the essays I interweave a myriad of voices with autobiography and theoretical discourse to create a document representing exchanges that open the world people share with each other. As such, the essays collapse the dichotomy between personal narrative and scholarly argument. Many scholars still see criticism as a meta-discourse that works in the hands of scholars to distance itself from the texts and subjects it studies. I not only take issue with this sense of criticism but also work to demonstrate how criticism might be other than these scholars understand it. I

2. The use of conventional argumentative narratives is particularly common among literary theorists. Some social scientists, anthropologists in particular, including Michael M. J. Fischer, are calling for and creating texts that convey multiple voices and narrative forms. I mention some of these writers in my first essay.

use a myriad of voices and narrative forms to show how criticism can move closer to that which it studies. My mode of expression is performative as well as expository; I tell stories not only to show how they might be used in critical discussions but specifically to place them in the contexts of those critical discussions in order to inform, often by means of their different narrative forms, the content and nature of the discussions. A meta-discourse would not allow me the latitude I need given my purposes. This does not mean in any way that I am privileging personal narrative over scholarly argument, or subjective modes over objective modes, as a way of understanding that which we consider in our work. Rather, the point is to see these methods and modes not as dichotomous and oppositional, but as interrelated and relational, as different voices capable of communicating with and informing one another.

This book does not develop a single idea or argument in a linear fashion from chapter to chapter. It is a collection of essays, each essay exemplifying ideas and arguments in the manner described above. *Keeping Slug Woman Alive* starts with essays about experiences with Mabel McKay so that readers might be able to see how I use what I have learned from her in my discussions of orality, basketry, religion, literature, and pedagogy. Again, because of the wide range of texts and topics pertaining to American Indian studies that I consider, this collection of essays should prove interesting and informative to many people interested in American Indians—folklorists, art historians, literary critics, anthropologists, teachers, tribal scholars. I hoped to write these essays in a manner that many people could read and enjoy.

The book should not be taken simply as an insider's record of things "Indian." I am not privileging an Indian's point of view regarding the texts and topics considered. I am not interested in pitting Indians against non-Indians, insiders against outsiders, or in showing that any one group of people is necessarily privileged or better or worse than another. Instead, these essays try to show that all of us can and should talk to one another, that each group can inform and be informed by the other.

I occupy a somewhat unusual and awkward position as a mixed-blood Indian and university scholar. As a scholar I work from the borders of different cultures and traditions, talking about the ways these cultures and traditions intersect in time and place. My father, Emilio Hilario, was Kashaya Pomo, Coast Miwok, and Filipino. My mother, Bunny Hartman, was Jewish, German, and Irish. But before I tell more about myself, I must say something about the Pomo and Miwok Indians so that readers have a better understanding not only of me as a writer but also of the people and social setting I write about.

Pomo is the name given by ethnographers to several tribes of north central California natives, speaking different but related languages and residing in Lake, Mendocino, and Sonoma counties. Before European contact, over a hundred Pomo villages existed along the coast, inland valleys, and foothills of this region. Today the Pomo still exist in relatively large numbers on about a dozen reservations, locally known as rancherias, and in many of the local towns and cities. Miwok is also a name given by ethnographers to tribes of native people speaking different but related languages.[3] Coast Miwok territory, which borders southern Pomo territory, extends south from the Russian River to the San Francisco Bay and includes much of southern Sonoma County and all of Marin County. The Coast Miwok, like the Pomo, had numerous villages. Unlike the Pomo, none of the Coast Miwok tribes is federally acknowledged, and as a result, there is today not one reservation or Miwok land base, even while Miwok people exist in significant numbers in the towns and cities and rural areas throughout the region.

The Pomo and Miwok tribes always interacted and traded with one another. Intermarriage was common. The native people didn't classify themselves as distinct from one another in the same manner that the ethnographers and linguists have. They didn't see one tribe belonging, say, to a "Miwok" language family and another to a "Pomo" language family. People of one tribe, or even one village, saw themselves as distinct from people of another tribe or village in terms of local customs, histories, stories, and local language whether ethnographers classified them as Pomo or Miwok. In fact, from what I have heard in my family, the Kashaya, or southwestern Pomo along the coast, got along better with the Miwok immediately south of them than they did with the south central Pomo tribes to the east. People along the coast, whether Pomo or Miwok, gathered mussels, clams, abalone, and seaweed from the ocean, hunted small game, and gathered acorns, edible bulbs, berries and the like from the coastal hills. Tribes that lived inland in the drier, hotter valleys and foothills also hunted game and gathered acorns and edible bulbs and fruit. They depended more on the lakes and rivers for fish. Each tribe once had small permanent and semipermanent settlements throughout their respective territories. All features of the landscape were

3. There are also "Miwok" tribes around Clear Lake and areas east of the Sacramento valley, but here I am referring to Coast Miwok tribes of Marin and Sonoma counties.

named and stories were associated with each of them. People moved from place to place within their home territories during the summer months to hunt and gather. During summer they also traveled to other tribal territories to visit and trade. In the winter, they returned to permanent settlements.

The histories of the different Pomo and Miwok tribes vary, particularly since European contact, and account for local differences today. Generally the tribes in the southern areas—Miwok and southern Pomo—experienced the earliest contact with Europeans, and, as a result, suffered disease, enslavement, and cultural disruption much sooner than many of the northern tribes. In 1817 the Spanish padres and military established Mission San Rafael in central Coast Miwok territory. The padres, with the help of the military, forced Miwok and southern Pomo people into the mission. The natives were converted, forced to work for the padres, and forbidden to practice their religion. In 1835 Mexicans secularized Mission San Rafael and occupied Miwok and Pomo territories. They established an elaborate system for raiding and trading slaves and took Miwok and Pomo people as far as Mexico. In 1812 the Russians established a colony they called Fort Ross at the Kashaya coastal village of Metini in the heart of Kashaya territory. Like their European and Mexican counterparts, the Russians came to colonize the land and its people. They virtually enslaved the Kashaya, forcing them to work the land to grow crops the Russians in turn sent to their Alaskan colony. But the Russians were not interested in converting the Kashaya, and they protected them against the Spanish and Mexicans. As a result, the Kashaya Pomo were able to retain most of their religious and cultural traditions with little difficulty. In 1838 a smallpox epidemic swept through Miwok and Pomo territories, killing over ninety percent of the remaining Miwok and southern Pomo and over eighty percent of the northern Pomo. In 1842 the Russians abandoned Fort Ross after depleting the coast sea otters and left the Kashaya at the mercy of the Mexicans and the ever-growing numbers of American "squatters." From the late 1840's until around the turn of the century, when the U.S. Government began allotting small parcels of land to (Pomo) Indians that the U.S. Government recognized as tribes, Miwok and Pomo people lived wherever they could, usually exchanging labor on the settlers' ranches for a place to live on the ranches.[4] By 1900 disease, slave raiding,

4. California became a state in 1850 and in that same year enacted the Act for the Government and Protection of Indians which stipulated that Indians were the rightful property of the owner on whose land they resided. This law was not repealed until 1868.

and starvation had reduced Pomo and Miwok people to a small fraction of their pre-contact numbers. Many tribes had only a handful of survivors. Many tribes had none.

Indian resistance to cultural domination by non-Indians was significant, however, and some tribes, most notably among the Pomo, retained their languages and cultures. In the winter of 1871–1872 the revivalistic Bole Maru (Dream Dance) cult started and spread throughout Pomo and Miwok territory. Local cult leaders, known as Dreamers, organized their respective tribes around this one cult. Dreamers were guided by their dreams, and they inculcated an impassioned Indian nationalism in the homes and roundhouses. (In the chapter "Telling Dreams and Keeping Secrets" I describe the cult in more detail.) Here again the Kashaya, who survived in relatively large numbers, were somewhat distinctive.[5] They produced exceptionally strong cult leaders. Annie Jarvis, as religious head, or Dreamer, from 1912 to 1943, continued the Bole Maru doctrine of Indian nationalism and isolationism even as its influence faded within the neighboring groups of Pomo and Coast Miwok. She outlawed intermarriage with non-Indians, forbade gambling and drinking, halted attempts by government officials to take Indian children to boarding schools, and demanded the Kashaya restrict their interactions with whites to work-related situations. Essie Parrish, the last Kashaya Pomo Dreamer, held sway from 1943 until her death in 1979. While she insisted that the Kashaya maintain Kashaya beliefs and participate in ceremonials, she favored open relations with non-Indian communities. She was particularly interested in education and felt schooling could help the Kashaya defend and further their interests. Since the mid-fifties, Mormons and others, particularly Pentecostals, converted many tribal members, and the Kashaya began to splinter. Still, at the time of Parrish's death, many Kashaya remained faithful to her teachings. Many still sang the old songs and participated in her ceremonials. Several people spoke Kashaya fluently. At the same time, there was

---

Ranchers set aside "rancherias" on their ranches where Indians could live in exchange for work. Most Indians stayed on these "rancherias" long after 1868. The term "rancheria" is used interchangeably with "reservation" today.

5. While the Kashaya were one of the smaller pre-contact tribes, numbering perhaps 500 to 1,000 individuals, they were one of the larger tribes at the turn of the century with close to one hundred individuals. Robert Oswalt notes: "Any figure given for the aboriginal population of the Kashaya can only be a rough guess; Kniffen (1939:388) suggests 550; Stewart (1943:51) quotes an Indian's estimate of 800" (3). Undoubtedly, their history with the Russians had much to do with their survival as a distinct and sizable group.

not one fluent speaker of any of the Coast Miwok languages. Miwok dances had not been performed for over fifty years.

Today Mabel McKay is the last Bole Maru Dreamer. But Mabel never had a tribal congregation of her own people. When she was born in 1907, only six of her Long Valley Cache Creek Pomo tribe from the foothills east of Clear Lake in Lake County were alive. Today she is the last. When she was in her mid-forties, she was taken into the Kashaya Pomo tribe by Essie Parrish, and the two women worked together until Essie's death. Mabel serves as Dreamer and spiritual consultant for those Kashaya faithful to Essie's teachings.

Today the overwhelming majority of people identified as Pomo or Coast Miwok are of mixed heritage. Intermarriage with other Indians (i.e., Pomo with Miwok, Pomo with Wintun) and with Mexicans, Filipinos, and many European groups, particularly Spanish and Portuguese, is common. For example, my grandmother, Evelyn Hilario, whom I never knew, was Kashaya Pomo and Coast Miwok. She grew up in Marin County, San Francisco, and Los Angeles and married a Filipino, my grandfather, Emilio Hilario. I was born so-called illegitimate, and my mother's family put me up for adoption. I was adopted by George and Mary Sarris, who thought they could not have children of their own. They did eventually have children, and when George became abusive, Mary allowed me to live with different families on farms and ranches around Santa Rosa. From an early age, about six or seven, I lived with many different families, some of whom were Indian. Some I later discovered were my own relatives, though growing up I was never sure of my family lines. Mabel McKay was one of the people who took me in, and from her I learned what is most important to me today.

I was not always bent on becoming a scholar. I did not always do well in school. In junior high school and high school, I took up with Indian and Mexican kids. I learned bits and pieces of the Kashaya language and of Spanish. I also roamed the streets with my gang, drank, sniffed glue, smoked pot, and beat up "white" kids. People always ask what caused me to turn around. I don't have clear answers, but it was probably lots of things. I bought an old Ford when I was sixteen, and to support the car I took a job as a busboy in a local restaurant. Because of work, I was separated from my peers. A friend's father was a dishwasher in the same restaurant and another friend's mother was a banquet waitress. I remember thinking, this job is the end of the road for me too. Then I began to imagine myself differently, as someone doing something besides working as a busboy or dishwasher.

And there was Mabel.

Perhaps what happened in that restaurant was that I began to gain a critical perspective about myself and my world. I began to consider my limits and possibilities. I began to think about who I was and what I was doing. Mabel always forced me to think about who I was and what I was doing, whether it was when I was a young kid in trouble or a Ph.D. candidate wanting to record and write her life stories. She said things and told stories that reminded me I wasn't alone in the world. She reminded me that there were other people, other stories. She laughed with others as I discovered something about peeling potatoes. She cared.

When I began to trace my mother's and father's families, Mabel was supportive, but she reminded me that no matter what I found I could never deny or forget my own life experiences. My mother died shortly after she had me. When I located her family, they accepted me but generally did not, I felt, encourage a close relationship. Many members of my father's family lived on the Kashaya Reservation, and they were extremely warm and receptive. I embraced many old friends, people I had known growing up. As it turns out, some of my closest relatives at Kashaya, second and third cousins, do not follow the teachings of Essie Parrish and Mabel McKay, and while I am friendly with these cousins, I find I spend most of my time with members of the Parrish family who, for the most part, are not as closely related to me. Together we pray and continue the ceremonies of Essie and Mabel. I refer to the Parrish family as my cousins also, as my family, my aunties and uncles. (My great-grandfather, Tom Smith, was married to Essie Parrish's grandmother, Rosie Jarvis.) Auntie Violet Chappell, for instance, is Essie's daughter. It seems Mabel is always bringing me home, and home is an interesting, often confusing place.

So many of us are a mixed-up lot, a chorus of intermingling voices and histories, and I write to tell you of that mixing, of the sounds of that chorus.

I kept thinking about the man Mabel started talking about on her eighty-second birthday. The potato incident didn't make me forget. I asked Mabel about the man on another occasion, and now in the writing of this introduction to my book, what she told me comes back and makes a certain kind of sense here and now.

The second time she talked more about how the man followed her wherever she lived, first with her grandmother and then with the white woman who owned a large ranch where many Indians lived and worked.

He always showed up in the evenings. He watched for her, always waiting at a safe distance, sometimes hidden behind a tree or somewhere in the nearby garden. This went on for a long time. What did he want? Did he know Mabel was destined to be a great doctor? Was he going to help her? Hurt her?

We were driving along the backroads, on our way to Mabel's home on the Rumsey Reservation. She saw something out the window and began telling another story. In my mind her story about the old man was not complete. She was leading to something and didn't get there. She mentioned the man had powers, that he was a medicine man, a doctor. I felt there had to be a point or conclusion to the story.

I began firing my questions at Mabel, if only to bring her back on track. She looked annoyed. Then she crossed her hands resolutely over the black patent leather purse on her lap.

"What did the guy want?" I asked.

"Oh," she said, as if hearing my question for the first time. She looked at me and said, "Nothing. He was just seeing I done OK. He wanted me to remember, I guess. I don't know. He was a friend of Grandma's brother, Doctor Richard Taylor. Anyway, I remember that so I tell it."

She looked back out the window and was quiet. I wasn't satisfied with her answer. There had to be more to the story. But I knew enough not to ask then.

And there is more to the story.

I can see the way certain images linger in the mind. I keep remembering the story, too. It teaches me in ways that I keep learning. I keep seeing Mabel and hope that in these essays I've done OK, for Mabel and for you.

The story is now yours too.

PART ONE

Lessons from Mabel McKay: The Oral Experience

CHAPTER ONE

The Verbal Art of Mabel McKay

Talk as Culture Contact and
Cultural Critique

For years Mabel McKay has been pursued by countless people who want to know about her world. As the only surviving member of the Long Valley Cache Creek Pomo tribe and the last of the Bole Maru Dreamers, she is seen as a repository of valuable information: anthropologists seek ethnographic data; linguists want to record her language; and still others want to know about shamanism and the dream world. Yet her responses to questions are maddening.

"What do you do for poison oak?" a student once asked in a large auditorium where Mabel was being interviewed as a native healer. "Calamine lotion," Mabel answered.

In another instance Mabel was asked to speak before a group of Stanford medical students who wanted to know about "ethnic medicine" and how they might work cooperatively with native healers. She smoked a cigarette on stage while waiting to be introduced. Once she was introduced she rubbed out her cigarette in the tin ashtray a student found for her, set the ashtray on the floor, stood up and said, "I have to pray first." She prayed and sang a song, all of which lasted about five minutes, then sat down and talked somewhat in a trance about the dictates of her spirit and her doctoring. Then suddenly she stopped and looked up, out to the audience. "OK," she said, "now who can tell me what I just said?" Her audience was quiet, stunned. "Ain't nobody got a word for me?" she asked finally and laughed. "I thought you wanted to know about healers." One student spoke up and paraphrased a portion of Mabel's presentation, reinforcing Mabel's legitimate claim to be teacher rather than naive informant. Then another student challenged the dynamic Mabel had established by asking how she became a doctor. "Like you," she said, "long time studying!"

In the first instance Mabel answered the question (about poison oak) but, at the same time, renegotiated the representation of reality that the question presented. In answering the student's question, she acknowledged that she is Indian but, at the same time, introduced the fact that she is a contemporary American, which redefined the student's notion of "Indian." In the latter instance she challenged the assumption that the students could take information without having to account for it. The students were prepared to take notes and get answers, but could they say what those answers meant, as Mabel understood them and wanted them understood? Here she interrupted the classic participant-observation method.

While Mabel may not give so-called straight answers, she continues to answer. Until a recent bout with arthritis, she traveled regularly, demonstrating basketry and talking about her art and culture. She enjoyed interviews and told stories about the "ancient times" and about her life and people and places she has known. Always she insisted that it "is important for people to know." If her interlocutors find themselves baffled by her talk, it must have something to do with knowing or, more precisely, how people are to know. Again, by talk I include all speech categories—responses to questions, gossip, idle chitchat, stories—that Mabel may use in conversation with others, since, as I hope to demonstrate, the various categories engender the same effect. The talk establishes the premises on which an understanding of her world can begin, and an examination of this talk reveals, I think, just how those premises are established and in what ways they are significant.

Talk as such raises the question of talk as performance, specifically in terms of Richard Bauman's notion of performance as a distinct communicative phenomenon whereby "performance sets up, or represents, an interpretive frame within which the messages being communicated are to be understood [so that] this frame contrasts with at least one other frame, the literal" (9). The frame is in this sense metacommunicative; the speaker's use of a special code, perhaps the attribution of an archaism or special formula (e.g., "Once upon a time"), keys the nature of the event or performance (genre) and how the interlocutor is to respond. Hence the interlocutor knows "this is a story" or "this is a joke" and subsequently has expectations associated with the respective keyed speech event. For the ethnographer or folklorist Bauman suggests "the essential task in the ethnography of performance is to determine the culture-specific constellations of communicative means that serve to key performance in particular communities" (22). Ideally, fieldworkers would acquire keys to the "entire domain, viewing speaking and performing as a cultural system and indicating how the whole range of performance is keyed" (22–23). Yet Bauman is quick to point out that such perfect, standardized ethnographies—where certain keys always indicate certain speech events—cannot account for the individuality of each speech event or, more important for my discussion here, for how the speaker may manipulate certain frames given the context in which she is speaking, particularly if that context is new or unusual in some way. I am thinking of what Dell Hymes (1981) calls *metaphrasis*, where a speaker can use "the structural, conventional performance system itself as a resource for creative manipulation, as a base on which a range of communicative transformations can be wrought" (34). The structure of performance events can change, or new structures may emerge, depending on particular contextual conditions.[1] If one considers the presence of a fieldworker as real, and thus a variable, in the so-called native domain, what constitutes a frame in the speech event the fieldworker records and describes is likely to depend on and to emerge from that specific context. The fieldworker cannot know about frames independent of his or her presence. What the fieldworker sees is not so much how the entire community keys speech events for its members but rather how it keys them for the fieldworker specifically.

If Mabel is performing in ways that are specific to the Cache Creek Pomo, there is little way of knowing. The fact that she is using English may necessarily preclude the presence of a native form as such. What is known is that her speech activities, at least in what I have related thus far, point to the frames her interlocutors are using to understand her. It is difficult to discern the extent to which Mabel is performing, or if and to what degree her activity is intentional, because she forces her interlocutors to examine presuppositions that shaped and are embedded in their questions.

To illustrate how a fieldworker's presence can generate emergent forms of framing activity on the part of the informant, and to further

1. Bauman observes "the emergent structure of performance events is of special interest under conditions of change, as participants adopt established patterns of performance to new circumstances" (42). He adds that "one would expect aspects of the social structure of the [contextual] interaction to be emergent from the interaction itself, as in any other situation" (43). See Bauman's "The Emergent Quality of Performance" in *Verbal Art as Performance*.

discuss Mabel's talk, I want to take a cursory glance at Robert Oswalt's *Kashaya Texts*. Perhaps along with S. A. Barrett's *Pomo Myths, Kashaya Texts* is the most complete collection of Pomo literature in one text. Of interest is the fact that the book is primarily a study in linguistics and includes the Pomo text with the English translation. Also the text comprises stories from one tribe of Pomo (Kashaya) told largely by just two informants, Herman James and Essie Parrish. Perhaps the most notable feature of all the speech events, regardless of Oswalt's categories (i.e., Myth, The Supernatural, Folk History, Miscellany) or how James and Parrish might themselves categorize a story they are telling (e.g., "This is a story from the old days" or "Now I am going to tell about something I did"), is James's and Parrish's use of formal frames to open and close their talk.

In the first text, titled by Oswalt "The Creation of the Ocean," Herman James begins: "This is something from ancient times—I am going to tell about the creation" (37). James concludes the narrative stating, "This is the end of my account of the start of the world in the old days and the making of the ocean—that is what I have been telling about. This is finally the end" (41). In another story titled by Oswalt "The Flood," Essie Parrish begins, "I am now going to tell about people turning into trees at the time of destruction" (129) and concludes with "This is all" (131). Oswalt observes that the narratives told by James and Parrish differ most notably in the endings: "Essie Parrish usually terminates a story rather abruptly with a phrase like 'This is the end.' Herman James employs such phrases but typically precedes them with often-repeated protestations of the truth of the story" (10). In concluding his telling of a long story associated with "The Flood" and titled by Oswalt "The Whale in the Creek," James, for example, declares:

> This is also a true story. It really happened. This is what my grandmother said when she told it. I listened when she told me. "It is true," she said. That is why we believe it and tell it too. This is a true story. This is the end.
>
> (129)

It seems though that Essie Parrish, too, often repeats protestations of the truth, albeit more subtly, as in the case of "The Flood," where she says before closing with "This is all" that "Our old people used to tell us about it, saying that's the way it was [and why] that mountain is taboo" (131). Still, in the case of either James or Parrish, the use of formal frames is standard. Sometimes Parrish or James might open by setting the scene, perhaps by giving the location of the action. But even short descriptions of activities, such as "Preparing Buckeye," end abruptly. Parrish begins, "I am going to talk about preparing buckeyes"|*bahsa dutatoc e a dici duwan k'e*|, and after a brief description of the process says, "this is all"|*mu ma a e me p i*| (305), just as she does when closing a mythic story. Here myth and description of daily activity—indeed all genres of speech—meet on common ground. We may find terms such as *duwi dici du* (telling about Coyote or Coyote stories), which might be said to serve as special codes keying genre (i.e., Coyote stories), but these terms, often occurring at the beginning of the narrative, do not affect the formal frames opening and closing the texts.

This framing activity had something to do with the context in which the stories were produced. Oswalt's "original purpose in collecting the texts was to provide a corpus for the study of languages" (10). He wanted language, linguistic units that he could study and translate, and that is exactly what he got—stories that are rendered as separate and complete units, framed so that Oswalt has the story but no context beyond the story in which to understand it. He has information, but it is not engaged with the world from which the information comes. I doubt that Mrs. Parrish would use the same abrupt frames when telling family members about preparing buckeyes. In my entire experience with Mrs. Parrish and among the Kashaya Pomo—nearly thirty years—I have never heard such frames used in English or Kashaya, except in very formal situations, where Mrs. Parrish was preaching to a large Kashaya congregation, and then the situation was again quite different. And just recently when I asked her daughter, Violet Parrish Chappell, about these texts and their frames, she replied, "Mom just did it that way, for the language. He [Oswalt] wanted language. I heard those stories different—when Mom used to tell them when we kids were in bed."

But one must also consider the possibility that such framing devices, emergent in this context, are also convenient for James and Parrish. Information regarding formalized or "traditional" Pomo storytelling is scanty. Both Mabel McKay and Essie Parrish have talked about listening to old-time storytellers where "you had to sit on the floor and listen." Parrish told Oswalt, "they [old-time storytellers] say that it is dangerous to relate Coyote stories while sitting up" (Oswalt 119). Any attempt on the part of fieldworkers to recreate the "native scene" risks the danger of denying the present, of displacing the significance of the fieldworkers' presence and how it affects the speakers' and ultimately the fieldworkers' re-creation of the text. In this instance with James and Parrish, we might examine rules and ethics of behavior that are still endemic to the Pomo, particularly as they might affect how a story is told. Mabel, for instance, mentions regularly that she cannot tell Coyote stories during the summer months. "It is forbidden," she says. "It's an old-time rule. Us old people know that." Equally significant is the pervasive notion of privacy among the Pomo, particularly in terms of sacred objects, songs, and stories. A person's songs and stories are considered valuable property not to be shared openly with strangers. Sacred objects are never handled or touched except by their owners. Given just these strictures we might imagine why James and Parrish presented the stories the way they did to Oswalt, who did virtually all of his fieldwork in the summer months. James and Parrish, as elders and religious people, were in the position of being asked to break taboo and disregard an invasion of privacy. What resulted was a text that reflected, at least to some degree, that situation; the texts, as already suggested, are framed so that they are closed ("This is all"), thus inviting neither further storytelling nor inquiry into their world.[2]

While Bauman and others acknowledge the possibility of emergent forms, particularly in new situations, or, as Bauman notes, "under conditions of change" (42), they still tacitly assume, somehow discounting their presence as recorders/interpreters, that a "true structure" (Hymes 1981) can be discerned. Dell Hymes's "major purpose is to argue for the systematic study of variation in performance" (86) whereby he can compare various textualized forms of the same tale to discover the true, or "authoritative," text. Dan Ben-Amos argues for a kind of holism where fieldworkers should examine "the set of contrastive attributes (thematic, behavioral) [that] represent the structure of relations between distinct genres in the system of folklore communication" (235). Yet if Hymes were to study the variations in performance as discerned solely in the textualized narratives of James and Parrish, what would emerge as an authoritative text would not be a text native to the Kashaya Pomo but to the Kashaya Pomo and a fieldworker, in this case James or Parrish and Oswalt. The contrastive elements that Ben-Amos would discover to determine Kashaya genres of speech would be those predicated on the presence of Oswalt. What we are given by James and Parrish is some-

2. One might question why Parrish and James told stories in the summer at all. Unfortunately, both Parrish and James have passed away. Their motives, I am sure, were many and complex. Parrish was interested in having a dictionary of the Kashaya Pomo language for future generations of Kashaya. The ways in which these recorded tales vary in form and so forth from the ways they have been told in other contexts could be the subject of another paper or book. Suffice it to say, the stories took a given form in the given context with Oswalt.

thing like a note on a door describing what is inside, although the door itself is closed.

If, in this instance, James and Parrish close discourse about their world, Mabel does something quite different. Where James and Parrish present stories as isolated pieces of information devoid of meaningful contexts in which we might understand them, including the opportunity to question, Mabel McKay, as pointed out, makes the interlocutor immediately aware of the present context and of the ways the interlocutor may be framing her world, which does not close the discourse but exposes the chasms between two interpretive worlds over which the discourse must continue. Whether the interlocutor is a student, friend, ethnographer, or myself, the dynamic of Mabel's talk remains characteristically the same. Granted we are left to *read* textualized versions of James's and Parrish's texts, and there my analogy may appear shaky in its attempt to illustrate the difference here, but perhaps that is precisely why Mabel will not allow herself to be recorded—she will not be absent from any discussion of her world.[3] Consider again some examples of her talk.

Mabel has just finished talking about dreaming to a group of non-Indian, Marin County people interested in Pomo culture. A middle-aged woman asks if it is the spirit that keeps Mabel young-looking and what tips Mabel or the spirit might have for maintaining a youthful appearance. "You could try dyeing your hair," Mabel answers. After Mabel had explained how she met Essie Parrish in a dream twenty years before she had met her in person, Mabel was asked if she recognized Mrs. Parrish when Mrs. Parrish walked into the room. "Yes," Mabel answered, "but I think she cut her hair a little." In another instance, where she is talking to a group of social scientists, Mabel tells about a famous Indian doctor who was notorious for escaping from the Lake County jail. Many people claimed he turned into a horsefly and flew through the cell bars. "Do you believe that?" a psychiatrist asked. "No," Mabel says with a laugh before adding earnestly, "I believe he went down the toilet." In a basket-weaving demonstration at Stanford University, Mabel talks about how she must pray for all the materials she gathers (for basket making), and a student asks if she talks to plants. "Yes, if I have to use them," she answers.

3. Here an irony appears. I am recording her talk for the reader of this book, and obviously I am the one doing the textualizing and critical (interpretive) discussion of her talk. Several years ago she asked me to do a book about her life. So much in this essay has been an attempt to understand fundamental principles of such an undertaking. I feel any textualization of her talk should reflect as much as possible the reflexivity her presence as a speaker engenders.

"Do plants talk to one another?"

"I suppose."

"What do they say [to one another]?"

Mabel laughs. "How do I know? Why would I be listening?"

Any discussion of frames and keying brings to mind Irving Goffman's *Frame Analysis,* in which he discusses the ways in which a particular strip of activity can be keyed and rekeyed. I am thinking specifically of what Goffman calls a fabrication, or "the intentional effort of one or more individuals to manage activity so that a party of one or more others will be induced to have a false belief about what it is that is going on. Those taken in can be said to be contained" (83). Goffman continues "that for those in on a deception, what is going on is fabrication; for those contained what is going on is what is being fabricated" (84). What is essential here is that both parties operate in terms of the rules and premises of a primary framework. And that is the point Mabel elucidates—that she and her interlocutors are not operating from the rules and premises of the same primary framework.[4] Again, questions regarding Mabel's intentionality are difficult, and, I would argue, unnecessary, to answer. But she is not tricking or fabricating; her talk points to what constitutes difference. In the above examples of her talk, as with the examples I cited at the start of this essay, Mabel is responding to questions, and her responses expose that which is embedded in the question that accounts for the rifts between her world and that of her interlocutors.

What happens with longer forms of talk, say the stories Mabel tells?. Here for purposes of my discussion I am arbitrarily separating longer forms—stories and extended conversations—from other forms—idle chitchat and responses to questions—since in reality they are often integral to one another in a variety of ways. Concerning a tale or anecdote, or what he calls "a replaying," Goffman claims it "will be something that listeners emphatically insert themselves into, vicariously reexperiencing what took place" (247). If the longer speech events are associated with, and engender the same effects as, the shorter ones, as I am suggesting, it is not emphatic identification and vicarious reexperiencing that Mabel's tales and anecdotes elicit but rather the limits of such.

As mentioned, I have heard her stories since I was a child, since that

4. Goffman observes "a strip of activity will be perceived by its participants in terms of the rules or premises of a primary framework, whether social or natural, and that activity so perceived provides the model for two basic kinds of transformations—keying and fabrication" (247).

first day I walked into her home with Marshall, her adopted son, and heard her talking to some woman about a sacred mountain. But it wasn't until one winter evening during a visit home from college that I began thinking seriously about Mabel and the nature of her talk. I think the story of that visit can illustrate how the longer and shorter speech events resemble one another and, at the same time, further my exploration of Mabel McKay's talk.

First a story.

What happened, a man poisoned.

See, them girls' grandmother, ——'s mother, she got fixed that way. How it happened, a man poisoned her.

He wanted her, this man. She was beautiful, but she would do like this: doctor somebody, then get up and leave her equipment. If she liked a man she would do like that: get up and go out that way. Maybe not come back until the next day.

Well, this man, he wanted her. But she was already married to another man, ——. She said, "I don't want you." See, he was old at that time already. He was an old man and I guess she liked the younger men, I don't know [chuckling].

He got mad then. He told her, don't be fooling around no more, no leaving your doctoring here and there.

Then I don't know what it happened, but she got pregnant AGAIN. Some older man, not her husband, I understand.

Then HE got mad. He got REAL mad. Then he got sick, the old man. Send for ——, he was saying: I'm dying and I need her to pray, he was telling somebody.

So she went there. And that's how it happened, they say. He tricked her, took something of hers while she was singing—I don't know what, maybe a pipe, cocoon, something anyway—and fixed her with it. And that's how they found her in the morning. She was already dead with that baby, frozen they say. And he's the one cursed all them with that man-wild business. For generations, he was saying.

Anyone familiar with Pomo lore and ethnography might discern recognizable features in this story. E. W. Aginsky noted that "there is no phase of Pomo life that [he] could discover which did not have some taboos connected with it" (321) and "that every death and misfortune was the result of indirect or direct retaliation from (1) the 'supernaturals' or (2) from some individual" (319). According to Bean and Theodoratus, "illness could be caused by ghosts but was most often caused by poisoning" (297). Depending on the different ethnographic descriptions used and how the story is viewed in terms of those descriptions, the typical and atypical Pomo features can be discussed endlessly. Likewise, a closer reading of the text might suggest ways that elements of language and narrative format determine meaning. Deconstruction would unveil Mabel's hidden agenda.

Mabel told me this story about the man who poisoned the beautiful woman doctor when I was trying to solicit answers from her to questions raised by a professor of mine. He had "done some work on the Pomo"— we read his article in an introductory anthropology course—and he was impressed that I knew Mabel McKay, whom he deemed "impossible to crack." He gave me a list of questions about doctoring and the use of crystals and herbs. Mabel promptly circumvented the questions. It must have appeared odd to her that I was suddenly interested in such things. Then again she knew I had been to the university, and now seeing me at home for the first time, she may not have been so surprised. After all, she had had more experience with college than I. She had been answering student and faculty questions for over forty years.

I remember it was quite late. I looked at the clock above her head on the kitchen wall. It was raining too, and though I lived only a couple of miles up the road, I wanted to get on.

"Now what was I saying? Oh, yeah. About the laundry. Do you know ——?"

Thinking of going home, I had not been following. For the last hour I had contented myself with this same idle chitchat about people and daily routine. I was tired. "Yes," I said, finally catching up with her. I told her how I knew the woman's daughters in high school. Marshall and I both had known the girls.

"Oh, yes?" Mabel took a sip of her coffee, then set her cup carefully on the table. "Hmmm," she said. "Well, I seen her for the first time today, first time since she was a girl. At the laundromat I seen her. She said to me, 'Are you Mabel?' I said, 'Yes.' Then I seen who it was.

"It happened I seen her coming. I seen her in the car with those grand-kids, the black ones. She was trying to hide them from me, even yet. Keeping them in the car when she was talking to me. Looking around to see if they jumped out. It was funny the way she did that.

"After while Marshall says, 'Who is that, Mama?' I say it's relatives, some kind. He says, 'Oh, do we have to claim them too?' I start up laughing [chuckling]. 'Yeah,' I said, 'we do.'

"Well, not relatives that way, but way her mother, ——, took in Grandma dancing up there by that place they call Rattlesnake Island."

I tried to explain why Marshall might feel the way he did. I made a few derogatory remarks about the woman's loose daughters and about the woman's sister, the girls' aunt, who got stuck between the bars in the county jail while reaching for a man in another cell.

Mabel looked up, over her glasses, admonishing. "You don't know the whole story," she said. "What happened, a man poisoned . . ."

Paul Ricoeur suggests "the absolute here and now" of the dialogical "we" is "shattered by writing" (35). By inserting the context of the storytelling event here, which, granted, the reader must accept second-hand, I feel I can at least produce a representation of the dialogical "we."[5] This representation helps to illustrate how the story, like the shorter speech events cited earlier, interrupts preconceived notions on the part of the interlocutor. The story was not a response to a question but rather a response to a statement made about the subject of a conversation. Intentional or not, the story commented on a specific statement about the subject and simultaneously pointed beyond the statement and immediate subject. If I had to reconsider *how* I saw the girls in the story, I would also have to reconsider *how* I saw other things—doctoring, crystals, and herbs. The story opens dialogue about two personal and cultural worlds, exposing what makes for the "we" in "the absolute here and now."

Here I am not simply indicating the limits of a text-centered approach nor extolling the virtues of contextual studies.[6] It is the dynamic of the speech event in context that I am talking about, not as it may be geared to a particular person or persons, say, with a specific moral in tow, but as it works to establish a premise from which a moral or ethic emerges.

5. James Clifford and others (e.g., Stephen Tyler 1986:122–140) suggest that any textualized dialogue between individuals, say between a fieldworker and an informant, in a cross-cultural context will remain a representation of that dialogue as rendered by the textualizer. However, Clifford offers that fieldworkers "can resist [the] pull toward authoritative representation of the other [depending] on their ability fictionally to maintain the strangeness of the other voice and to hold in view the specific contingencies of the exchange" (135). I have attempted to make "the strangeness of the other voice" as it reveals "the specific contingencies of the exchange" a central subject in this essay. Thus I must present (or represent) Mabel McKay as she presents herself to me.

6. Many others, notably Tedlock, Toelken and Scott, and Basso, have demonstrated the importance of the story-telling context in the study of oral literature. Tedlock, for instance, notes that "the speaking storyteller is not merely addressing a hypothetical future audience, unlike the writer. The world evidenced by the audible text, considered in its entirety, includes not only the world projected by the story proper but the world of the performer and audience" (10).

Anyone with whom Mabel is speaking can experience this dynamic. The speech event can interrupt and simultaneously expose the interlocutor's presuppositions at any point—in a single response to a question, in a story, or at some point in a conversation—and such interruption and exposure will be generated by the particular experiences and presuppositions of both the interlocutor and Mabel. For me it was a story about people Mabel and I know, people from our community. For someone else it may have been Mabel's response "calamine lotion" to a question about Indians and poison oak.

Of course, interlocutors will not necessarily see themselves as exposed. They may have a completely different interpretation of the situation; Mabel can be seen as odd, crazy, or intentionally obscure to the extent that she is, in the words of my undergraduate professor, "impossible to crack." Then again her interlocutors may be confused or intimidated and for any number of reasons choose not to explore what is perplexing. In these situations the possibility of dialogue that is interruptive is foreclosed. Mabel may stop her interlocutors without challenging them. If some element of the speech event *is* interruptive within the larger exchange between Mabel and the interlocutors, it can be seen as working in two interdependent arenas: in that place where the point of exposure occurs and within the interlocutor's internal talking. In Bakhtin's words, Mabel touches the interlocutor's "inner dialogue" such that her words and ideas become "internally persuasive." This internal activity can continue after the initial interruption.

For days I kept thinking about the girls and their mother. I drove to the little clapboard house at the south end of town where I remembered waiting with a group of friends for the girls to give us a sign that their mother had gone up the street to play cards. The family had long since moved—they had moved several times, living here and there on the fringes of town like many Indian families I knew. The house was painted another color, not the dull off-white I remembered but a bright yellow with sepia trim. I thought of other "strange stories" I heard while growing up.

Back in college, after my visit home, I had a sense of why descriptions and discussions of American Indians felt so incomplete. As Mabel would say, "there is more to the story." Any discussion of shamanism, for instance, brought to mind this entire story, not just how the girls' grandmother was poisoned by a poisoning shaman but about how my own experiences met with those of the family in the story. And this sense that there is more to the story makes me think of something else I feel is missing in the studies of American Indians, indeed in the studies of other cultures in general—not the kinds of personal contact I have had, not even a brief acquaintance with a person from another culture, although any of these things can be helpful, but interruption and risk. How do scholars see beyond the norms they use to frame the experiences of others unless those norms are interrupted and exposed so that scholars are vulnerable, seeing what they think as possibly wrong, or at least limited?

Of course the story does not end, as I discovered one day while Mabel and I were driving up near Clear Lake looking at the various places she remembered as a young woman. We came upon a tract of land just above the lake, near Sulfur Bank, where the woman in the story had been poisoned. Parked alongside the road, gazing at an open lot between two newish ranch-style homes, Mabel began to speak:

"See a priest gave the Indian people this land to live on. They had no place to go during that time, them who was around here down by Sulfur Bank. He let them live here, the priest. See ——'s husband, he was from this place."

"She wasn't?"

"No, she was from the valley, over the mountains there. When they [——'s people] got moved from that place they got split up. Soldiers— white people—marched them to Covelo. Some went to Ukiah. Her father, he went to Santa Rosa, I believe. She come here to this place and married that man.

"See I had a man here too. When they give me in marriage first time. Them girls [mother and aunts of the girls I know] was small yet. Then I left, when I was over with that man. I went back to Rumsey. I never saw but I heard what happened—how that man poisoned. Then I never seen —— until that day at the laundromat, in Santa Rosa.

"Well, I always stick up for her though. She was born there and her mother is the one took Grandma in dancing there after Grandma and them got put off the old place on Cache Creek. Took Grandma in dancing. Adopted Grandma in up there when she had nowhere to go. So that's how I call —— cousin."

The story opened onto a broader, historic context. The earlier stages of European colonization affected, directly and indirectly, the lives of the women in the story and Mabel. I mentioned this idea, and Mabel re- torted: "Yes, them days was hard time. Killing. Raping time, how they [Europeans] done with the women. Starvation. People moving . . . You know about people moving around, different people."

I took these last words as a direct statement about my life, about my living in different homes as I was growing up. In that way I had a small sense, on a personal level, of the displacement our ancestors experienced. And the same history plays itself out in the present with so many I know. Witness the family about whom the story was told. Witness the fact that eighty percent of California Indian school children drop out of school by ninth grade, and that life expectancy is forty-seven years and suicide for teenage Indian males is ten times the state average for that age group. To gather materials to make the baskets art historians and basket specialists admire so, Mabel must search roadside ditches or ask permission to enter private property where her ancestors in large numbers gathered freely to dig sedge root and cut willow and redbud. Clearly, for Mabel a discussion about the material aspects of her basketry cannot be sepa-rate from a discussion of other things, history among them. And this history was not only something which my life experience helped me to understand; it also played an integral role in the constitution of my experience and mixed heritage.

If Mabel's talk initiates in the interlocutors a kind of internal dialogue where the interlocutors examine the nature of their own thinking, that dialogue can be carried over to an ever-widening context of talk in stories and conversations, such that the inner dialogue can inform and be informed by new stories and conversations. Thus a simultaneous open-ing of two worlds continues. The shorter pieces of dialogue I related, mostly responses to questions, illustrate various points where interrup-tive dialogue can begin. The story I told shows how it can continue.

Some might suggest I have been positioned as an initiate learning the rules of entry into another worldview or society. Stories and conversa-tions may open and overlap, thus evoking themes or morals, but my understanding of them will always be tied to my larger experience. I cannot reconstruct Mabel's world independent of my experience of it. The dynamic of her talk undermines the authority I would have to assume to do so. What I can do is reconstruct my relationship to her world, at least to the extent I understand it at this time, and this essay has been just such an attempt. Mabel is not a pedant; her talk is improvisa-tional, emergent, always pointing beyond itself such that it is difficult to see what she says as representing one thing or another. Even as a place or name might suggest certain things (i.e., taboo, a historic occurrence), other talk—a new story or topic of conversation—can affect meaning as the listener has previously constructed it. So while the talk may evoke certain themes and morals, these are presented such that they become themes and morals for a generative understanding of the worlds Mabel and I share. She is not Don Juan and I am not Carlos Castaneda; neither is her talk a drug that plunks me into a separate reality.

Of course, as I have mentioned, my position is unique, as is anyone's, but if my familiarity with aspects of Mabel's world—I am thinking particularly of my knowledge of people and places she talks about— affects anything, it is the texture and not the dynamic of the talk. I refer to Toelken's notion of texture "as *any* coloration given a traditional Item or statement as it is being made" (82).[7] Of course how one determines what is "traditional" is problematic, especially when you consider that Mabel is speaking English. (If Mabel were speaking to someone in Cache Creek Pomo, more than texture might be affected, perhaps even the dynamic of the talk as I have been discussing it. I do not speak Cache Creek Pomo and neither does anyone else.) My familiarity with certain people and places allows Mabel to invoke by allusion the setting of a story or the thematization of an idea, whereas with others who are not familiar with these people and places, through either personal association or other talk, she would have to spell things out. The mere mention of a feature in the landscape, for instance, may bring to mind a story and a notion of taboo associated with the feature. Keith Basso observes that among the Western Apache "geographical features have served for centuries as mnemonic pegs on which to hang the moral teachings of their history" (44), that "narrative events are 'spatially anchored' at points on the land, and that the evocative pictures presented by Western Apache place-names become indispensable resources for the storyteller's craft" (32). This familiarity is not unusual for a community that has shared over millennia the same landscape and various stories associated with the landscape, and often accounts for the paucity of natural description and human motivation typically found in the literature of such a community.[8] But in my case, familiarity with a landscape and certain people

7. Toelken adds to Alan Dundes's notion of texture as the use of particular phonemes, morphemes, rhymes, stresses, tones, pitches, and so forth (Dundes 1964, 251–65). Toelken states: "In narrative it [texture] would certainly include linguistic features, as well as any verbal manipulations which evoke, suggest, and describe, or those which in any way qualify, modify, expand, or focus the rational structure by reference to or suggestion of emotions, mores, traditional customs and associations, aesthetic sensitivities and preferences, and so on" (82).

8. Renato Rosaldo sees that among the Ilongot "hunting stories, and probably annals, can communicate in a telegraphic shorthand because speakers can safely assume their listeners' depth of knowledge about the landscape, hunting practices, the huntsmen's

cannot presume an understanding of the landscape and people, at least not in Mabel's terms. While I might know some things and continue to learn, the dynamic of the talk remains the same.

Certainly Mabel's life has been unique in many ways. As mentioned, only six members of the Cache Creek Pomo were living when she was born, and though she was raised by her maternal grandmother, Sarah Taylor, she was not raised on or near Lolsel, the main Long Valley Cache Creek village at the time of European contact. She grew up among the southwestern Wintun in the Rumsey area of the Sacramento Valley, where Sarah had gone to find work. She traveled with a carnival for a while, dancing the Charleston every night before large crowds; in San Francisco she worked as a maid for the madam of one of the better known houses of ill repute. She tells stories about these aspects of her life. Her experiences as a contemporary American Indian woman are many, and her personal history is complex, varied, multicultural. But it must be remembered, underlined here, that Mabel has never presented herself as a representative of one thing or another. She fights typification; she rebukes the attempts of those who wish to see her in an ahistorical light, as merely a vestige of a prelapserian world.

And it is in this struggle that her talk interferes with any move that would displace history from myth or from any number of things she talks about. A story may be beautiful in and of itself, but it is not timeless. The interlocutor's experience is not displaced either; it is held up, and therefore affirmed, juxtaposed not to show how one experience or world view is better than the other but to expose the tension between them.

Tedlock suggests that "anthropological dialogue creates a world, or understanding of the *differences between* two worlds, that exists between persons who were indeterminately far apart, in all sorts of different ways, when they started out on their conversation" (323). This *betweenness* can become the locus of cultural critique whose aim, as Marcus and Fischer say, is "not the statement and assertion of values [but] the empirical exploration of the historical and cultural conditions for the articulation and implementation of different values" (167). One contemporary technique for cultural critique is a "strategy of defamiliarization" where "disruption of common sense, doing the unexpected,

---

abilities, previous hunts in the area and elsewhere, and so on . . . for Ilongot place names in and of themselves contain myriad associations." See his "Ilongot Hunting as Story and Experience," in *The Anthropology of Experience,* ed. Victor W. Turner and Edward M. Bruner (Urbana and Chicago: University of Illinois Press, 1986), 108.

placing familiar subjects in unfamiliar, or even shocking, contexts are the aims of this strategy to make the reader [or listener] conscious of difference" (Marcus and Fischer 137).[9] This *betweenness*, if jarring to some extent, can expose and challenge presuppositions predicated on cultural and historic conditions that shape the way(s) people think about themselves and others. Mabel's talk provides her interlocutors this opportunity to see the constructedness of their own culture and history as they are confronted by what in her world does not make sense. If Mabel McKay is the last of her tribe, indeed the last of many roles among the Pomo people, she is not simply going to describe what was; she is going to invoke the present that accounts for what is.

Dialogue is essential here, dialogue that interrupts and disrupts preconceived notions, that can open the intermingling of the multiple voices and histories within and between people. To some extent Mabel assumes a teacher's role in the speech activity. She disrupts the kind of dialogue that has been typical between fieldworkers and informants. Yet it must be remembered that the dialogue with Mabel is not necessarily meant to teach a specific rule or idea but to expose something about the relationship between Mabel and her interlocutors and how that is affecting their understanding of one another.

Some of the newer ethnographic endeavors and textual recreations of oral literature seek to reveal, among other things, the different worldviews and interactions among participants—fieldworkers and native scholars—and the problems that arise as a result. Difficulties are likely to surface with the textualizing process and should be made apparent to the reader. Responding to the call for polyvocality, these texts present multiple voices and narrative forms. They are said to be collaborative in nature.[10] For Mabel McKay and her interlocutors, talk itself initiates and sets the groundwork for collaboration. It is an art generating respect for the unknown while illuminating the borders of the known.

What I have written about in this essay immediately reminds me of a story. The context of this storytelling event I do not remember, except

9. Marcus and Fischer add "the defamiliarizing effect is only a springboard for sustained inquiry" and "is a process that should entail a critical reflecting back on the means of defamiliarization itself" (137).

10. Examples of collaborative texts include *Birds of My Kalam Country* by Ian Majnep and Ralph Bulmer (1977), *Pinan Shamanism* by Donald M. Bahr, Juan Gregorio, David I. Lopez, and Albert Alvarez (1974), *Nisa: The Life and Words of a !Kung Woman* by Marjorie Shostak (1983), *Debating Muslims* by Michael M. J. Fischer (1990), and *The Poetics of Military Occupation* by Smadar Lavie (1990).

that Mabel and I were driving, looking at old places Mabel remembered as a child.

"Do you know how babies are born?" she asked.

Of course I knew the facts of life. Mabel had something else on her mind.

"Like this," she said. "The spirit follows the parents for two years before it is born. It follows, watching. It knows everything. Even when it is born it knows everything.

"Until it starts walking, talking. Maybe a year old. Then it forgets, falls apart what it knows.

"Then, you know, it starts learning again. If the person gets old, REAL old, it will be all together again. In between is what you call living."

CHAPTER TWO

The Woman
Who Loved a Snake

Orality in Mabel McKay's Stories

One day I took a colleague of mine from Stanford University to the Rumsey Wintun Reservation to meet Mabel McKay. "I want to meet this famous Pomo medicine woman," my friend said. "I've heard her talk and I've seen her baskets in the Smithsonian." My friend, Jenny, had heard me talk about Mabel also. I had been recording Mabel's stories for a book about her life. As always, Mabel proved a gracious host. She served us hot buttered toast and coffee and, for lunch, tuna fish sandwiches with pickles and lettuce. As Jenny and I ate, Mabel told about the woman who loved a snake.[1]

"See, her husband, he would work at night. 'Lock the door,' he'd tell her. 'Don't let nobody in.' Every night he'd go off saying that: 'Lock the door, keep everything locked up.' She would fix his dinner, then his lunch." Mabel chuckled to herself. "By lunch I mean what he takes to work. That's what I call lunch when I was working nighttime at the cannery.

"Anyway, this woman, she says 'OK.' And sometimes, after he would leave, she'd stay up for a while. She'd clean up around, maybe do the dishes, get things ready for the morning, for the breakfast. I don't know.

"Then ONE TIME she hears a knock on the back door. 'What is that?' she's thinking. First she thought maybe it was her husband; maybe he was coming home early; maybe he got sick or something. 'But then

---

1. This story has been produced from tapes, notes, and my memory of my meeting with Mabel McKay on October 15, 1988. My friend—Jenny—did not want her true name revealed.

why doesn't he just come in?' she was saying. Well, then she thought maybe she was hearing things. She just kept working then.

"But it kept on, this knocking. Then she got scared. See in those days no phones up there. And this was far out, up on some white man's place there, where her husband worked. She could not yell, nothing. Nobody to hear her. Maybe she's thinking this to herself. I don't know.

" 'Who is this?' she is saying. Then I don't know what he said. I forgot. Something, anyway. And she opens the door. Just a little bit. He comes in and she stands there looking at him. But she doesn't recognize him.

"Anyway, she fixes some coffee. I don't know. Gives him something to eat. They're talking around there. I don't know what.

"Next day, her husband comes home. 'What's this?' he is saying. He's standing there—by the bedroom—and he's looking down in some vase. Something there. It was on the table. 'What are you talking about?' she says. Then she goes and looks where he's looking. And she sees it, too: a snake, a little black snake all coiled up. 'What is this?' he says to her. Then he takes it out and puts it in the brush. He lets it out there.

"Next day, same thing it happens. Then the husband, he gets suspicious of that snake. 'What is this?' he is saying. Then she gets worried; now she knows what the snake is. But she don't say nothing. 'I'm going to kill it,' he says, 'chop it to bits out in the brush.' He's testing her, but she don't say nothing. Then she got REAL worried, seeing him go out with that snake.

"But next day same thing it happens. Maybe she tried talking to that man. I don't know. 'Don't stay around here,' she might said to him. But it's there again, that snake. Now her husband, he shakes her; he knows something is going on. 'What is this?' he's saying. But he had an idea about it anyway. 'You come with me,' he says, 'and watch me kill it.' He starts pulling on her arm, shaking her, but she refuses him. She won't go. She's crying by this time.

"He takes the snake out, same way, coiled around his hand. She just sees him go. Then he comes back. She doesn't know what it happened. Maybe this time he DID kill it. She's crying yet. Her husband, he comes in and says nothing. Just goes to bed.

"But he never did chop that snake up. Maybe he did. I don't know. Anyway, it went on like that . . ."

Jenny, a Ph.D. candidate in English, asked what the snake symbolized. Mabel didn't seem to understand the question. She looked at me then turned to Jenny. "Well, it was a problem, I don't know."

"Why didn't he, I mean the husband, just kill the snake?" Jenny asked.

With an incredulous look on her face, Mabel focused on Jenny. "Well, how could he?" she asked. "This is white man days. There's laws against killing people. That man, he would go to jail, or maybe get the electric chair, if he done that."

Jenny's response to the story, that is, her question, prompted in turn a response from Mabel that exposed what was different about their respective worldviews regarding the story. For Jenny the snake was symbolic of something and, in that sense, supernatural. For Mabel the snake/the man was part of one coexistent reality, a reality that is located in historic time and subject to its strictures. Mabel mentioned that she knew the woman, that she often visited her when she lived in the same area north of Clear Lake. "Then one night I seen that man. He was handsome, too," she chuckled. "It was late. Lakeport grocery was closing and I seen him come out with groceries. He didn't take the road. He went the creek way, north. Then, I say to myself, 'I bet I know where he's going.'"

"Maybe he just carried the snake with him and left it in the vase each morning before he left," Jenny offered. "Like a sign."

Mabel laughed out loud. "Like a sign. That's cute. Why he want to do that?" She lit a cigarette and exhaled a cloud of smoke. "See, I knew he was odd. He's moving in cold, late at night. Snakes don't do that."

"Well, was it man or snake? I mean when you were looking at it?" Jenny was desperate now.

"You got funny ideas," Mabel answered. "Aren't I sitting here?" She tapped her cigarette in the aluminum ashtray on the table. "You do crazy things like Greg. And he's Indian! He gets ideas where he wants to know this or that so he can write it all up for the people. Well, it ain't like that what I am saying."

Jenny told me that for weeks she kept thinking about Mabel and the story. "Hearing that story, just hearing Mabel, I thought more and learned more about myself in one sitting than I have with Shakespeare in ten years," Jenny said. "I've been studying Shakespeare and, well, if my ideas change, and they do, at least the text is the same. With Mabel what is the story? There is so much more than just the story and what was said that *is* the story. I wanted to write it, you know, when I was thinking of things, so I could think about it. But it—whatever it is—wouldn't stay put. Mabel was right: 'It ain't like that what I am saying.' Greg, how are you going to write her stories?"

Once again Mabel confounded her interlocutor. She undermined clear-cut, unqualified answers. She opened the context in which the exchange took place, exposing what made for people talking and listening. Jenny, in retelling "The Woman Who Loved a Snake," will remember that for Mabel the snake/the man was not what it was for Jenny and that the difference spoke of the differences between them. I am reminded of the context, of the world Mabel and I share when talking, every time I try to write something she said.

Writing recreates oral experience in given ways. The transcriptions of American Indian oral literatures, for example, sometimes provide nothing about the context in which the literatures were told and recorded or the manner in which they were translated. In the end we have a story as an object devoid of the context that might suggest something about the story beyond our interaction with it as an independent text. The context of the story consists of story and reader. Based on their biases and purposes for writing, writers select and shape what they experience orally. In the example just cited, editors might decide that a certain story is the whole Indian story. Writing then fixes or makes permanent not only oral experience but what is actually an interpretation of that experience. In this sense, Mabel's talk impedes these literate tendencies for closure by continually opening the world in which oral exchange takes place. "The Woman Who Loved a Snake" is a story not only about the woman in the story but about Jenny and, as I will show in this essay, about me.

Jenny's instinct was literate. "I wanted to write it . . . so I could think about it." She thought if she had a written (fixed) text she would be able to sort out what was in her mind from what was on the page. (Of course Stanley Fish and a host of others have been telling us for some time that such sorting is problematic at best with written texts.) It was not just a matter of what was spoken that made writing the oral story problematic but also what was unspoken. The unspoken that was exposed in the verbal exchange, in this case the different worldviews of Mabel and Jenny regarding the story, became part of the story such that a straight version of "The Woman Who Loved a Snake" (Mabel's narrative without Jenny's presence as a listener) would hardly represent Jenny's experience of the story. Even if Jenny were to write a conventional version, and even if she were to include the brief conversation with Mabel about the story, she would not automatically have a clear picture of her experience and the way she negotiates that experience in time. So much of Jenny's verbal encounter—that which might be transcribed from a tape recorder—had life and significance not only in terms of what was unspoken in the immediate context but in the days and weeks ahead as

Jenny kept thinking about the story and her relationship to it. As she
said, the story "wouldn't stay put." She told me: "I began to think of
snakes differently. People too. All kinds of things came up. I went back to
my dissertation on Shakespeare and began to think about Shakespeare's
historical period. How was I understanding that period? How was I
understanding Shakespeare as a result?"

More and more scholars of oral literatures are looking to the broader
contexts in which these literatures live. Specifically, they are considering
what lies beyond the spoken word, beyond their perceptual range as
listeners and readers, and what that larger context says about their
position as literate speakers and writers for and about oral traditions.
Concerns regarding context become particularly significant in cross-
cultural situations. After struggling with the question as to whether
structure or texture generated meaning in Navajo stories, Barre Toelken,
with the help of Tacheeni Scott, a Navajo who knew the stories, resolved
that

> actually both structure and texture unite to provide an excitement of meaning
> which already exists elsewhere, in the shared ideas and customs of people
> raised in an intensely traditional society. . . . Thus, the stories act like 'surface
> structure' in language: by their articulation they touch off a Navajo's deeper
> accumulated sense of reality. . . . They provide culturally enjoyable correla-
> tives to a body of thought so complicated and profound that vicarious
> experience in it through entertainment is one of the only access points avail-
> able to most people.
>
> (110)

Toelken asked the storytellers questions and found that "by seeing the
story in terms of any categories [he] had been taught to recognize, [he]
had missed the point" (73). Dennis Tedlock notes: "The problem of the
mythographer is not merely to present and interpret Zuni myths as if
they were objects from a distant place and time and the mythographer
were a sort of narrow, one-way conduit, but as events taking place
among contemporaries along a frontier that has a long history of cross-
ings" (292). Tedlock is not just talking about Zuni contemporaries. He is
stressing the presence of the mythographer who positions the Zuni
storytellers in certain ways, and whose interpretation of the situation
will partly depend on a subjective interpretation of the stories produced
in the context of his presence. After writing about his experience and
sense of an oral story-telling event, Tedlock says: "Everything that has
been reported here concerning the events of a certain November evening
at Zuni, New Mexico, rests finally on conversational and more broadly

interactional grounds, and it was there, just there, that it was even possible for me—and now, I hope for us—to understand at least a part of what was going on. . . . Here I say, leewi (all), which means it's someone else's turn" (301).[2]

Without ever directly addressing the question about what is oral in an oral exchange, or what constitutes context, Toelken and Tedlock suggest that in an oral exchange there is much that is unspoken—the histories and varying perspectives of speakers and listeners—which may or may not be evoked verbally in the exchange itself or in continued exchange. Mabel's story and conversation with Jenny—Mabel's talk—reminds us that in oral discourse the context of orality covers the personal territory of those involved in the exchange, and because the territory is so wide, extending throughout two or more personal, and often cultural, worlds, no one party has access to the whole of the exchange. One party may write a story, but one party's story is no more the whole story than a cup of water is the river.

While this may seem obvious, it underscores what it is we do when we tell, transcribe, or write about oral texts. Basically, in whatever form or manner we deal with oral texts, whether orally or literally, we continue their life in very specific ways. This is just as true about an oral exchange within a single culture as it is about an oral exchange that is cross-cultural. No two personal worlds are identical anywhere. This does not mean that we are not, or cannot be, distanced or critical, for critical response is part of hearing. We sort out what we hear, unconsciously and consciously, and this sorting has to do with our cultural and personal histories and the situation of our hearing.

My discussion here continues the story of "The Woman Who Loved a

2. Other scholars—linguists and social scientists in particular—have studied differing coherence systems in oral and written communication, an approach that is basically comparative and contrastive and that focuses on the relationship and differences between spoken and written language in human interaction. The works of these scholars, most notably Erickson (1984) and Scollon and Scollon (1984), show that there are different kinds of nonliteracies and that scholars must remember this fact when considering issues of orality and literacy. Scollon and Scollon note: "We feel that this [Northern Athabaskan] oral tradition is strikingly unlike the bard-and-formula oral tradition [i.e., the Homeric tradition studied by Parry and referred to by Ong via Parry] so often advanced as the representative of oral traditions" (182). In Northern Athabaskan storytelling, sense-making is dependent upon audience response as it is for the Chicago-based Afro-American youth (whom Erickson studied) in their general verbal (oral) interactions. Further, Tannen (1982) shows that it is not just a matter of orality vs. literacy but that there is an "interplay in spoken and written discourse in various settings" (4). The work of these scholars focuses primarily on the spoken and written word, and, while this focus is important in a variety of ways, particularly in terms of what it can tell us about different learning styles, their work does not explicitly consider the larger world in which either the oral or the written word lives and is made meaningful as do scholars such as Toelken and Tedlock.

Snake" in specific ways. Mabel's story, characteristic of her talk, opens the vast territory that is oral and, in so doing, not only suggests the extent of the territory but also lets the territory be talked about and explored. The story reminds me of this and in turn of other stories and experiences. While I am Indian and am familiar with certain aspects of Pomo culture, I am, like Jenny, literate and have specific literate expectations, including the urge to fix, when writing, stories and ideas in given ways.[3] Mabel bucks these literate expectations so that neither she nor any aspect of her world is seen as or reduced to anything other than what it is, in all its complexity and difference; and I am never more reminded of how her talk frustrates such expectations than when I write about something she says. "The Woman Who Loved a Snake" then is as much about orality and interpersonal and intercultural discourse as it is about anything else. You may or may not be able to glean this dimension from a mere transcription of Mabel's narrative. You might, for example, look at the husband's interaction with the snake, the wife's interaction with the snake, or the husband's interaction with his wife, as an encounter with an "other" and then project from the nature and outcome of the encounter. But let me continue my story here of "The Woman Who Loved a Snake" by telling you more of it as I heard it and as it became particularly meaningful for me:[4]

Mabel and I were parked along a road on the south side of Clear Lake, where we had a view of the lake and of Elem Rancheria, the old village site and present-day reservation of the Elem tribe of Pomo Indians. Mabel had been talking about her maternal grandmother, Sarah Taylor, and about how the Elem people initiated her into their dances and cult activities after Sarah's people, the Cache Creek Pomo, had been removed from their land and ceremonial grounds by the non-Indian invaders.

" 'You will find a way, a way to go on even after this white people run over the earth like rabbits. They are going to be everywhere,' he was saying. That's Old Man, I forgot his name. He had only Indian name, Taylor's father, Grandma's grandfather. He's the one saying these things."

Mabel opened her purse, pulled out a cigarette. She lit her cigarette and exhaled a cloud of smoke. Below us, on the narrow peninsula of Elem, smoke rose from the rusted chimney tins of the small, dilapidated houses. A lone dog barked in the distance.

"Well, it was over here, below them hills," Mabel said, gesturing

3. Of course a nonliterate audience probably would negotiate Mabel's talk in ways very different from those of us with certain strong literate tendencies.

4. This story has been produced from tapes, notes, and my memory of my meeting with Mabel McKay on November 20, 1988.

south over her shoulder with her chin. "This things, they come over the hill in a trail, long trail. So much that dust is flying up, like smoke wherever they go. And first to see them this people down there, where you are looking. 'What is this?' the people saying. Things with two heads and four legs, bushy tail, standing here on this hill somewhere, looking down at Elem people.

"Lots of people scared, run off, some far as our place, Cache Creek. They tell what they seen then. All Indians, Indians all over, talking about it then. 'What is it?' they is asking. Nobody knows. People is talking about it all over the place. Lot's scared. I don't know. People say different things.

"Some people somewhere seen them things come apart, like part man, then go back together. Then I guess maybe they knew it was people—white people. I don't know," Mabel said and chuckled. "They Indians dance and pray. I don't know. Then they was saying these things mean, killing Indians and taking Indians."

Mabel drew on her cigarette and leisurely exhaled. "But he seen it in his Dream, Old Man. He said what is coming one day, how this would be."

"So they knew what it was coming down this hill," I ventured.

"Hmm," Mabel said, gazing across the lake. "They knew what he meant by 'white man.'"

"So why did they run? Why all the fuss?"

Mabel rubbed out her cigarette and looked at me as if she had not understood what I said. "If they knew from Old Man's prophecy that white people were coming, why didn't they know what was coming down the hill? Why all the fuss?"

Mabel started chuckling, then exploded with loud, uncontrollable laughter. She caught her breath finally and asked, "How can that be? You ever know white people with four legs and two heads? Maybe you do. You're raised around them—your mother's people. I don't know," she said, chuckling again.

She lit another cigarette, then straightened in her seat. "Sometimes takes time for Dream to show itself. Got to be tested. Now we know what he told about, Old Man. He was told . . . He said lots of things: trails, big trails covering the earth, even going into the sky. Man going to be on moon he was saying."

"But how did HE know that?"

"But sometimes Dream forgets, too. Like them snakes. Old Man come in MY Dream, give me rattlesnake song. 'You going to work with this snakes; they help you,' he is saying. Then, after that, I seen them. All over my house I seen them: porch, closet, in my bathtub when it's hot, all over. Then I say to him, to that spirit, 'This is modern times, better take that song out of me . . . I don't want nothing to happen. People around here might call animal control place.

"You know, peoples around here they don't always understand things like that."

Mabel was not merely making a comment about a gap in understanding between two cultures but also, intentionally or not, pointing up what I had just experienced as a result of my interaction with her. I had been implicated: my own understanding, or lack of understanding, had been exposed. The sentence in context, like the story about intercultural contact in context, pointed beyond itself to the present, opening the story of the two people talking and listening. Here I was busy taking notes and tape-recording her stories for a book about her life, as I had been for the past six months, and, as always, she reminded me of my prejudices and point of view, locating me in the present, turning a story she tells into a story of our exchange. Contact narrative became an instance of culture contact and culture contact a story.[5]

Not new news for Mabel.

Not so ironically I was just laughing a month before at Jenny's question about what the snake symbolized. Non-Indians often ask what this or that symbolizes, as if signs and semiotic systems were transcultural. I was used to stories about snakes. I have heard how rattlesnakes were used by certain medicine people for healing the sick. There are stories of rattlesnake cults in which cult members handled the snakes, asking the snakes for special powers, for guidance. And always there is talk of snakes taking the form of human beings and vice versa. It seems to me that the ways snakes are viewed by the Pomo vary from tribe to tribe and even from person to person within a given tribe. So much depends on the situation, who is in the situation, who is telling about it, and who is listening. Jenny was an outsider, a non-Indian from the university. Suddenly I felt the same way.

Presuppositions that predicated my question about Mabel's story

---

5. Here I use the term *culture contact* in the broadest sense, as Gregory Bateson says, "not only [in] those cases in which the contact occurs between two communities with different cultures and results in profound disturbance of the culture of one or both groups; but also in cases of contact within a single community. In these cases the contact is between differentiated groups of individuals, e.g. between the sexes, between the young and old. . . . I would even extend the idea of 'contact' so widely as to include those processes whereby a child is molded and trained to fit the culture into which he was born . . ." (64).

about first contact between natives and non-natives were overturned by her laughter and her question to me, "How can that be? You ever know white people with four legs and two heads?" I had assumed a literal, linear relation between prophecy, or Old Man's Dream, and so-called empirical reality, a relation which posits a kind of fundamental difference between the two states that Mabel may not share. I must begin to consider a worldview in which dream "[g]ot to be tested," as Mabel said later, commenting on both the story and my reaction to it. This difference between Mabel and me is an essential feature of the context in which words are spoken, and that context influences how the words are presented again here, in the way I am now telling the story in this essay.

The contact narrative about what the people of Elem encountered is embedded in the longer narrative about Mabel's grandmother, Sarah Taylor, which in turn is embedded in the conversation about Mabel's life as we sat in a car above Clear Lake, which is embedded in our work over the last six months, and so on. The context is ever widening. Still, a dialogical dynamic can be seen in the straight contact narrative just as easily as within the context in which the narrative is told. Mabel made context within the narrative independent of my interjections by commenting on the narrative. Her remarks about Old Man "see[ing] it in his Dream" were interpretive and reveal a dialogue she had with the text about the coming of those "things with two heads and four legs" such that this dialogue made the story. Old Man "seeing what [was] coming one day" is as integral to Mabel's narrative as what the people of Elem saw coming "over the hill in a trail." The story, or the part of it she told, about what the people of Elem saw is likely to be an interpretation rather than a literal retelling on Mabel's part; therefore, it is a comment on another version of the first contact between the natives and the non-natives, in which case we have a comment on a comment, an endless cycle of text becoming interpretation becoming text.[6] Mabel's dialogical dynamic that might otherwise be interior (unspoken) was exposed in the oral presentation of the story.

While such a dynamic may be present in Mabel's narrative independent of my interjections, and while I may be able to talk about the dynamic, I could only gain a sense of its significance for Mabel and of the

6. Tedlock has illustrated that when listening to a Zuni storyteller listeners are "in the presence of a performing art, all right, but are getting the criticism at the same time from the same person. The interpreter does not merely play the parts, but is the narrator and commentator as well. . . . At times [listeners] may hear direct quotations from that ["original"] text, but they are embedded in a hermeneutics" (236).

limits of my own projections with regard to its significance when we talked about it. Mabel's exchange with me, as with Jenny, opened the narrative to new territories, or, more specifically, to the territory of our meeting together in the instance of my hearing a story.

Of course, scholars can excerpt the contact narrative or any part of it from the larger story. Folklorists, for instance, might want to compare various textualized versions of the same tale and attempt to discover the true, or what Hymes calls "authoritative," tale (Hymes 1981, 79–141). So if they were to determine, let's say, that one text, or tale, of what the people of Elem saw was the authoritative Lake County Pomo contact narrative, they would effectively exclude the larger context in which the narrative was told and still lives for the various Pomo of the area and, subsequently, the means for getting an idea of how the narrative might be meaningful for different Pomo beyond the folklorists' interpretations. "A systematic study of variation in performance" (Hymes 1981, 86) of textualized versions of a given tale might show that the so-called true tale is being used or performed in different ways structurally, but that the significance of the difference is understood only in terms of the folklorists' interpretations. Likewise, if scholars were to consider the text proper as only what Mabel says before my interjections, they may be able to discern the dialogical dynamic that I have seen, but they would not have the opportunity to know any story about the text except that of their own invention. Little, if anything, would inhibit their culture-specific projection, which, in turn, can engender further discussion about the projection and spin the discourse further and further from the Indian narrator and her narration.

Again, as I indicated in the last essay, I am not using Mabel's stories and my interaction with her simply to indicate the limits of a text-centered approach to oral literatures or to extol the virtues of contextual studies. "The Woman Who Loved a Snake" and "What the People of Elem Saw" suggest to me, in the ways they come together as one story for me, the territory of orality and a way that territory is opened with Mabel's talk. When Mabel told Jenny about the snake, I saw how I understood Mabel's world; when she told me what the people of Elem saw, I discovered the limits of my understanding of her world. In both instances, I learned there is so much more than just the story and what was said that *is* the story. Mabel's talk not only reminds me of what is at stake when writing, or textualizing, oral experience but also suggests that the writing, as much as possible, should reflect oral tendencies to engage the larger world in which the spoken word lives so that it is seen for what it might or might not be beyond the page. To answer Jenny's question presented at the start of this essay regarding how this is done, specifically how I write Mabel's stories, I offer this same essay as a model of, though not necessarily a model for, writing what Mabel says. Mabel is saying: Remember that when you hear and tell my stories there is more to me and you that *is* the story. You don't know everything about me and I don't know everything about you. Our knowing is limited. Let our words show us as much so we can learn together about one another. Let us tell stories that help us in this. Let us keep learning.

Naturally stories are told differently in different situations, and tellers often do not suggest much about the situation in which they are told or invite further discourse about the stories or the world of the stories. In the last chapter I discussed how Kashaya Pomo scholars Herman James and Essie Parrish in their work with linguist Robert Oswalt used frames to open and close their stories, a use which is likely to reinforce certain literate tendencies that would diminish the larger world of the stories and their tellers. See the following contact narrative told by Essie Parrish to Robert Oswalt:

> This that I am going to tell is what the people thought when they first saw a boat.
> In the old days, before white people came up here, there was a boat sailing on the ocean from the south. Because before that they had never seen a boat, they said, "Our world must be coming to an end. Couldn't we do something? This big bird floating on the ocean is from somewhere, probably from up high. Let us plan a feast. Let us have a dance." They followed its course with their eyes to see what it would do. Having done so they promised Our Father [a feast] saying destruction was upon them.
> When they had done so, they watched [the ship] sail way up north and disappear. They thought that [the ship] had not done anything but sail northwards because of the feast they had promised. They were saying that nothing had happened to them—because of the promise of a feast; because of that they thought it had not done anything. Consequently they held a feast and a big dance.
> A long time afterwards, when white men had come up and they saw their boats, they then found out what they had thought was a big bird was otherwise. It wasn't a bird they had seen; they had spied a sailboat. From then on we knew that they hadn't seen a big bird.
> This is the end.
>
> (Oswalt, *Kashaya Texts*, 224–47)

The text, as with virtually all of the texts in Oswalt's collection, is effectively framed so that it is closed ("This is the end"), inviting neither further story nor inquiry into the world of the story.

By looking at Mrs. Parrish's contact story, we can further appreciate the ways Mabel does not end or close her story but opens it continually, by the dialogue she has both with it and with the person hearing it. Her story—her talk—counters literate tendencies that would close the vastness of its world and, hence, the complexity of its teller.

In closing I must mention again that Mabel should not be seen as representing a typical Pomo speaker or storyteller. Her talk—her narratives, conversations, responses to questions—seems in many ways unique. I have known other Pomo storytellers who expose internal dialogue they have with a story they are telling. I have also known Pomo storytellers to implicate their listeners in what they are saying. None of the speakers I have known, however, is as consistent in these matters as Mabel. But I have not done a study or comprehensive survey. I have only looked at Mabel's talk in terms of its effect as I have known it, not in terms of the ways it may or may not represent traditional or typical Pomo discourse.

Specifically, I have explored in this essay the ways Mabel's talk counters literate tendencies to close the oral context in which oral communication takes place. Mabel's dynamic is not, I am sure, the only way to break open that immense oral territory, nor is it any guarantee that the territory will be opened. So much depends on the interlocutor. And, as demonstrated with Mrs. Parrish's narrative, some speakers, inadvertently or not, may keep the gates to the territory closed. The territory— all that is oral, spoken and unspoken—is as vast as the culture which it gives life to and from which in turn it takes life. For that reason it is as impossible to generalize about "oral discourse" as it is about "culture." They are inseparable from and specific to particular people, either as the people interact with one another from a shared knowledge base or with groups (or individuals) with a different knowledge base and history. Within a given group or between groups certain kinds of discourse may be aggressive or prompt fear; other kinds may do just the opposite. It depends on the given circumstances in the broadest sense. Mabel's talk, which is oral, provides an opportunity to explore the territory for individuals who may in some ways share her territory, such as myself, and for those who do not at all, such as Jenny. The territory, after all, is not empty, unpeopled.

After Mabel told the story about the people of Elem seeing non-Indian invaders coming "over the hill in a trail," we headed east, back to the Rumsey Reservation. On the way home, Mabel again told the story of "The Woman Who Loved a Snake": "It was across there. Up in them hills where she lived. That time Charlie [Charles McKay, Mabel's husband] running stock up there. By stock I mean the cattle. Charlie always wanted to have the stock. That woman lived there. Sometimes she would come down the road the other side there and talk to me. Anyway, how it happened she was alone at night. Her husband used to go off working, where it was I don't know. I forgot. How it happened she hears this knocking one night, at her door . . ."

I was quieter now, listening.

"Well, you see, I know about them snakes," she said as she finished the story. "They can teach about a lot of things."

Mabel pulled her purse to her lap and began rummaging for her cigarettes. I looked to the cold, damp winter hills. Too cold for snakes, I thought to myself.

"Hmm," she said. "Maybe you'll get some idea about the snakes." I looked at her and she was laughing, holding an unlit cigarette between her fingers. "I know you. You'll . . . you're school way. You'll think about it then write something."

She was right.[7]

7. Portions of this essay have appeared in my "Fieldwork as Cultural Contact and Cultural Critique: Mabel McKay's Model," a paper presented at the 1989 California Indian Conference, Humbolt, California, and in my "Conversations With Mabel McKay: Story as Contact, Contact as Story," a paper presented at the 1989 Association for Study of American Indian Literature (ASAIL) session of the Modern Language Association Convention, Washington, D.C.

PART TWO

About Pomo Baskets
and Secret Cults:
Cultural Phenomena

CHAPTER THREE

A Culture under Glass

The Pomo Basket

Whatever I say—whatever I talk about the baskets—the
white man just turns around and does his own way anyway.

Mabel McKay

Baskets as small as eraserheads. Storage baskets. Cooking baskets. Brightly colored feather baskets. Museums dedicate entire walls to the basketry of Mabel McKay. The Smithsonian and other prominent museums in this country and in Europe retain her work in permanent collections. No wonder people want to know about her baskets.

The Pomo are considered the finest weavers on earth. The variety of design and technique is unequaled among indigenous peoples, and the use of feathers as well as the creation of miniature baskets, some no larger than an eraserhead, cannot be found anywhere but among the Pomo. But for Mabel the questions about her basketry appear repetitive, most often inappropriate, no less so than the questions about "Pomo life" or about her Dreams and doctoring. "Oh how they keep going on with the questions," she once lamented at Berkeley. While a handful of other notable weavers, most of whom are quite old, can talk about design and technique and the process of gathering sedge roots and other materials necessary for the creation of these baskets, Mabel cannot separate a discussion about the material aspects of her basketry from a discussion about Dreams, doctoring, prophecy, and the ancient basket-weaving rules, since for Mabel these things cannot be talked about or understood separately. Mabel is the last "traditional weaver," that is, a weaver whose work is associated with power and prophecy. "Everything is told to me in my Dream. What kind of design, what shape, what I am to do with it—everything about the baskets—is told in my Dream." Often Indian people fear and avoid Mabel because of her reputed power as an "old-time doctor and Dreamer." If she is not feared by scholars, she is, as I have noted before, inscrutable to them and maddening in her replies, which turn scientific discourse about her world on its head. Her seemingly mystifying response must have something to do with the fact that she has become a spectacle in a context (i.e., museum, lecture hall) that is not only somewhat incongruous to her world but also diminishes it to mere artifacts and snippets of disconnected information, so that a basket specialist can talk about design as separate from dream and an anthropologist about shamanism as separate from the craft of basketry. And this inquiry never seems to include a consideration of the history that shapes and maintains a context in which a surviving member of an entire tribe has herself become an object of study. Mabel's situation is peculiarly modern: while museums exhibit basketry and universities offer courses entitled "Prehistoric Peoples of California," enabling the larger dominant culture access to the Pomo world, these same museums and universities inhibit, or at best render incomplete, an understanding of this world and of the history that diminishes it. Yet Mabel still talks.

It is imperative to ask how a fuller sense of the Pomo basket as an integral part of Pomo culture and history has been lost and continues to be obfuscated despite the growing attention Pomo basketry has garnered both in the academy and in the world of popular culture. This current wave of interest is nothing new. When the Russians abandoned Fort Ross in 1842, after having established and maintained the fort since 1812, they took with them large collections of baskets collected over the years from the Kashaya Pomo, the people of Metini, whose village had become the site of Fort Ross. Museums in Russia still exhibit these baskets. Spanish settlers, too, decorated their adobes with baskets, as did the Mexicans and "squatters" who followed the Spanish as occupants of Pomo land. By the end of the nineteenth century, basket collecting had become a popular pastime and even an outright occupation for some, who traded, bought, and sold baskets far beyond the confines of Pomo territory. For example, Mrs. Grace Hudson, who shared an interest with her physician husband in Indian life, gathered an extensive collection that is today exhibited with her paintings of Indians in the Hudson family home, lately transformed into a museum. Of course, Pomo life was affected by this interest. Pomo women suddenly found they could earn money, albeit a scanty amount, for their work, and for the first time baskets were produced not for utilitarian, social, and sacred purposes but for outside income—*white man* money.

Making baskets for outside income renders their production independent of tradition possible, and we can see how they might be received and valued in a nontraditional manner. As Walter Benjamin notes in his "The Work of Art in the Age of Mechanical Reproduction," the work of art is now produced for its "exhibition value" as distinct from its "cult value"; whereas the object's existence was once what mattered, now what matters is its being on view (224). The work of art loses its basis in ritual and in other traditional aspects of Pomo life different from but not without ritual, such as hunting and gathering, storytelling, and the like. The object loses what Benjamin calls *aura*, its "authenticity [as] a thing that is the essence of all that is transmissible from its beginning, ranging from its substantive duration to the history which it has experienced" (221). And "since historical testimony rests on the authenticity, the former, too, is jeopardized by reproduction when substantive duration ceases to matter. And what is really jeopardized when historical testimony is affected is the authority of the subject" (221).

If these baskets were suddenly being produced separate from the domain of tradition, it was perhaps scarcely noticed by, or of little consequence to, a people for whom this separation became inescapable. Separation of a people from their land and age-old way of life and separation of families from tribes and of family members from one another splintered tradition. One might argue that the separation of tradition from the craft of basket making at least gave a cash return. But this is presuming, of course, that all baskets produced for outside income were produced independent of tradition on the part of the weaver, that is, without significance for either the maker or the buyer. Perhaps the most important effect of this shift from "cult value" to "exhibition value," regardless of the degree to which it occurred among the Pomo weavers, was on the spectator—anyone outside Pomo tradition—who never discerned it. Ultimately, interest in Pomo basketry becomes an interest in discourse about baskets, a discourse principally about itself. What kinds of designs were used in twined basketry as opposed to coiled basketry? Are consistent designs found in feather basketry? In the miniatures? What is not asked—perhaps because the answer has been successfully swept into the corners of a political unconsciousness and thus assumed in a vague way—is what happened and continues to happen that allows one group of people to discuss the artifacts of another people separate from the people themselves? I know we often have no living representatives to speak for the artifacts, but is this not further reason to remind ourselves of the question? It seems that this shift from "cult value" to "exhibition value" displaces the basket's historical testimony

and subsequent authority, and this displacement not only maintains a
separation of the spectator from the world and history out of which the
baskets were created but also precipitates a closed cycle of presentation
and discussion about the basketry itself.

I have heard the stories. I have heard the old-timers talk about the
past. Many of their parents and grandparents fought wars and escaped
slavery. Among the Pomo these stories about Kelseyville and Bloody
Island and about Mr. Hildreth and Mr. Shores, both notorious Indian
slaveholders, do not die. From a multitude of sources—personal testimony, county and state records, historical societies—Victoria Kaplan
has collected a number of telling stories in the history of the Pomo
people. In her collection entitled *Sheemi Ke Janu* (*Talk from the Past*),
Kaplan reprints a story of the circumstances preceding the Stone and
Kelsey Massacre on the shores of Clear Lake in 1849. The story was
originally written by William Ralganal, a Pomo, as follows:

> the herders who had large families were . . . starveing, about 20 old people
> died during the winter from starvation. from severe whipping 4 died, a
> nephew of an indian lady who were liveing with Stone was shoot to death by
> Stone. the mother of this young man was sick and starveing. this woman told
> her son to go over to stones wife, the sick woman's sister. tell your aunt that i
> am starveing and sick. tell her that i would like to have a handful of wheat. the
> young man told the aunt what his mother said. the lady then gave the young
> man 5 cups of wheat and tied it up in her apron and the young man started for
> camp. stone came about that time and called the young man back. the young
> man stopped. stone who was horseback rode up to the young man took the
> wheat from him and then shoot him. the young man died two days after. such
> as whipping and tieing their hands together with rope the rope then thrown
> over the limb of a tree and then drawn up. untill the indians barly touchs the
> ground and then let them hang there for hours. this was common punish-
> ment . . .
>
> (Kaplan 77)

Eventually the people revolted. Mr. Stone and Mr. Kelsey were mur-
dered, and the United States Army was called in and carried out a brutal
massacre of the Clear Lake Pomo, most of whom were not associated in
any way with the deaths of Stone and Kelsey. The killing of Pomo people
did not end at Clear Lake. Soldiers, under the command of Captain
Lyons, marched over the mountains and down into the Ukiah Valley
about thirty miles away. Kaplan reprints Captain Lyons's report to his
commanding officer regarding the search for Yokaya Pomo in the valley.

> I found them early on the morning of the 19th [May], on an island formed by
> a slough from the Russian River, which was covered with dense undergrowth,

and in the part where the Indians were mostly concealed were many trees, both dead and alive, in a horizontal position, interwoven with a heavy growth of vines. Their position being entirely surrounded, they were attacked under the most embarrassing circumstances; but as they could not escape, the island soon became a perfect slaughter pen, as they continued to fight with great resolution and vigor till every jungle was routed. Their number killed I confidently report at not less than 75, and I have little doubt it extended to nearly double that number. I estimate their whole number as somewhat greater than those on the island before mentioned. They were bold and confident, making known their position in shouts of encouragement to their men and defiance to us. Two of their shots took effect, wounding somewhat severely Corporal Kerry and Private Patrick Coughlin, Company "G," the former in the shoulder and the latter in the thigh.

(Kaplan 79)

"The raping time," says Mabel McKay, noting the period of war and its aftermath: "They took the girls and raped them that way—tying them with ropes, like cattle. A lot it happened that way."

I can't help but think of Mrs. Grace Hudson and her interest in Pomo baskets. Her family was among the first permanent settlers in the Ukiah Valley, and certainly she must have heard some stories too, however they may have been told to her. Of course, for the Pomo, the wars continue today; born of the old wars and subsequent separation, their wars are the wars of the dispossessed taken away from their ancient lands, cut off from many of their traditions, and relegated to the margins of society where their struggles against invisibility are undermined by poverty, disease, and inadequate education. If Mrs. Hudson sympathized with the people who created these beautiful baskets, it is virtually impossible for the spectator today, viewing the baskets in state and local museums quite removed from the Pomo themselves, to see them as much more than autonomous pieces of art. This autonomy eclipses the possibility of understanding the forces—those in which the spectator is immanently involved—of history.

For Benjamin, the work of art devoid of aura has emancipatory potential. When a work of art becomes reproducible and accessible to the masses, it simultaneously loses its aura, that is, its authenticity and authority in the eyes of the beholder; however, it also allows for a type of rational discourse with it which was impossible before it became "emancipated from its parasitical dependence on ritual" (224). At the same time, Benjamin warned that this discourse might be impeded by a passive public and by the creation of movie stars produced by moviemakers' capital, which set the fashion: "The film makes the cult value recede into the background not only by putting the public in the position of the critic, but also by the fact that at the movies this position requires no attention. The public is an examiner, but an absent minded one" (240–41). The emancipatory potential of reproducible art may, in fact, be used to recreate "aura" for the purposes of exploitation and terror. Benjamin did not overlook the use of film by the Fascists and the Fuehrer himself. Likewise, Leo Loewenthal in his "Triumph of Mass Idols" illustrates how the heroes created by the media become "heroes of consumption," positioning the spectator or viewer so that no link is made between the hero and the nation's history. Examining the content of biographies about celebrities, Loewenthal shows that for the spectator, or in this case the reader, "the real battlefield of history recedes from view or becomes a stock backdrop while society disintegrates into an amorphous crowd of consumers. Greer Garson and Mahatma Gandhi meet on common ground: the one likes potatoes and stew and never tires of breakfast of porridge and haddock; the other's evening meal is simple—a few dates, a little rice, goat's milk" (216). Yet neither Benjamin nor Loewenthal wants to forsake an art that is accessible to the public and subject to its criticism. While Benjamin calls for the promotion of a revolutionary criticism and response from the public, Loewenthal, it seems, would like to disentangle, via public criticism and response, the malevolent forces in the media which inhibit democracy, so that once again the public might see the link between hero, or art object, and history. While both presume a public that might have access to art and hence the means to criticize its authority, neither considers that the public might be culturally diverse and that the dominant culture might systematically obscure its oppressive relationship to another culture by minimizing the latter's existence and real difference.

Context is displaced when art is produced for its "exhibition value," and while this displacement enables the general public to criticize and respond, the object produced by a marginalized culture loses its connection to the culture from which it came along with its differences and its history. You can go to a movie and understand what the movie represents because you are familiar with the world of the movie. Viewing a Pomo basket in a museum is like viewing a movie frame depicting a close-up of water; it could be water anywhere, or nowhere.

Cult objects—baskets, bigheads, pipes, cocoon rattles, clappers, and whistles—did not have the same kind of relationship with members of Pomo society as did cult objects—crucifixes, madonnas—with members of Western European society. From the stories I have heard, and from what little I have read, baskets, like other objects of Pomo society, were integrated deeply into every aspect of a culture composed of many secret societies in which individuals possessed powers that other people could not discern. There were of course known doctors and chiefs or headmen and headwomen, but anyone, man or woman, might possess formidable power, generating not fear but, in my estimation, respect. These secret powers could be turned on anyone, no matter what their status, to inflict disease or death, either committing a fresh injustice or avenging an old one. Many baskets, most notably the "sun baskets," were used in these secret societies. But talk about a pristine or pre-contact Pomo culture has ultimately the same effect as the museum exhibition: a renunciation of the present, and hence, of history. We immediately forget *how* we are looking.

As I mentioned at the beginning of this book, the Pomo still exist in large numbers on over a dozen reservations, locally known as rancherias, and in many of the towns and cities in Lake, Mendocino, and Sonoma counties. The old songs are still sung, dances danced, and stories told. And, as mentioned, a shrinking number of basket weavers weave, and Mabel McKay still speaks. To say that museums are worthless—that Pomo art should not be displayed or discussed—would deny the Pomo existed or exist at all and ultimately support a kind of relativism that would promote continued intolerance given the fact that Pomo people— indeed all Indian people—are already relegated to the margins of society and are victims of a battle that continues to destroy what is left of them and what they might tell others, not only of their culture but simultaneously of the others' culture. What we need is a way to connect with what we don't know, or are missing, and might learn as a result, a way we might find in the context of viewing and discussing the Pomo basket.

If the institution that exhibits and disseminates knowledge about Pomo basketry suffers from and promotes a blinding distance from the subject of the sort I have been describing, internal divisions within the institution only aggravate the problem. I am talking specifically about the university, where specialized discourse—discourse about itself— becomes departmentalized. Edward W. Said, in "Opponents, Audiences, Constituencies and Community," laments the "narrowly based university environment . . . with the self-policing, self-purifying communities" (155). He says the context of university activity is maintained "by an unquestioned ethic of objectivity and realism, based essentially on an epistemology of separation and difference. Thus each field is separate from others because the subject matter is separate. Each separation corresponds immediately to a separation in function, institution, history and purpose. Each discourse 'represents' the field, which in turn is supported by its own constituency and the specialized audience to which it appeals" (155). The proliferation of "professionalism" within the academy promotes this specialization: nowhere else is survival so dependent upon specialized knowledge.

Said suggests that "instead of noninterference [between disciplines] and specialization, there must be *interference,* crossing of borders and obstacles, a determined attempt to generalize exactly at those points where generalizations seem impossible to make" (157). In this manner he suggests we "open the culture to experiences of the Other which have remained 'outside' (and have been represented or framed in a context of confrontational hostility) the norms manufactured by 'insiders'" (158). Perhaps this way we can "have the recovery of a history hitherto either misrepresented or rendered invisible" (158). And Said reminds us: "Stereotypes of the Other have always been connected to political actualities of one sort or another, just as the truth of lived communal (or personal) experience has often been totally sublimated in official narratives, institutions, and ideologies" (158).

I used to drive Mabel to a place along Dry Creek in the northern reaches of the Healdsburg Valley. We'd park the car, cross cattle-guards, and hike with trowels and buckets to the sandy banks of the creek. We'd settle near the water, on the northern side of the creek as I recall. That was when I was sixteen. For me, the fun was driving Mabel's car. Mabel would pray, sometimes sing a song before we started digging. On the way home she always told stories about the "ancient times" and about her life and people and places she had known. Again for the sheer thrill of driving Mabel's car, I drove Mabel up to Stewart's Point to visit Essie Parrish at the Kashaya Reservation. And again I'd hear the old stories as the two women talked. Once Mrs. Parrish, sensing my meager interest, turned and said, "There is much to this that we are talking about, you know." Always polite, I said "Yes," though my attention was elsewhere. There was a man I knew of, a spook man as they are called, who would be on his front porch one minute and just minutes later, while passing the Old Courthouse Square miles away, you'd find him on the park bench. Much of what Mabel had to say, alone or with Essie, just struck me as did this man—weird. Ironically, it wasn't until I was at UCLA as an undergraduate and Carlos Castaneda published his books, *A Separate Reality* and the like, that I found people actually curious about these things, and they were not Indian people!

It wasn't until I saw Mabel answering questions about her baskets before a large non-Indian audience that I realized something of the importance of what she had to say. Watching the audience and listening to their questions, I realized not so much what they were missing— which was obvious to me—but how much I had missed and how earnest Mabel had been over the years in her attempts to tell me something. I felt at once ashamed and anxious to defend her, yet no one could take better care of Mabel than Mabel. Since then Dry Creek has been dammed; the place where Mabel and I dug roots is hundreds of feet under the waters of what is now called Lake Sonoma. Mrs. Parrish passed away and the traditional Kashaya roundhouse has been closed. People come by and take pictures; a few summers ago an anthropologist from Germany came looking for the famous Essie Parrish and was given directions to her grave in the Kashaya cemetery. It was not just these places and people I lost but something about them that speaks far beyond what little I could understand, something that might have better prepared me for the loss. The loss creates an urgency, and perhaps that is part of what motivates Mabel.

She still speaks. When she was a young woman, barely in her teens, the Spirit said to her: "You will be a great doctor someday. You will travel and talk in the schools." Perplexed, Mabel responded: "How can I go in the schools and talk when I never even went to the school?" We, as an audience, have the answer in the way Mabel presents herself. When we cannot understand everything she says in responding to our questions about basketry, Dreams, or even about herself, if there are black holes of uncertainty, borders and obstacles that seem impossible to cross, we must not only continue to question and to talk to one another—art historian, linguist, and anthropologist alike—but remember our own limitations and accept difference for what it is, an indication of the distance we have yet to travel by means of a sublime sensitivity to the Other and to the history, "hitherto either misrepresented or revealed invisible," that accounts for the world from which Mabel speaks. And her baskets—all Pomo baskets—cannot be any less perplexing than her talk.

The context of presentation will always signify a certain kind of relationship and, not unusually, the history of that relationship. Where Walter Benjamin saw the emancipatory potential in what film and other forms of reproducible art might accomplish (when "aura" has been diminished), we might look at exactly what these forms of presentation cannot accomplish. The museum must tell a story of its relation for the Pomo basket, and extend that story to the viewer.

Ultimately it is important to know what our relationship to the baskets signifies. In "Reader-Response and the Aesthetic Experience of Otherness," Gabriele Schwab cites Gregory Bateson, who says that "general interaction patterns show that all forms of culture contact that tend to rigidify boundaries in order to maintain an unchanged internal coherence lead to an increase of external conflict and hostility ultimately destructive for all agents involved" (134).[1] Though Mabel has sold many baskets, none has been produced without the Dream. People may order a basket, even pay for it, but she will not move until the direction is given. Certainly many of those old-timers who first started selling their baskets for a source of income dreamed designs and messages too, and these designs and the inherent messages were presented to the collectors and traders. Certainly these Pomo women—like all Pomo—knew what their relationship to the dominant society signified to the Pomo and, for that matter, the world at large. Mabel once pointed to a basket under glass in a museum and told a long and horrifying story. "My grandmother knew that basket," she began. "It is not something to look at."

One basket that Mabel wove and presented to Essie Parrish in 1959 has a particular message. Robert Oswalt recorded Mrs. Parrish's response to the basket while he was studying and recording the Kashaya Pomo language. In a trance, where Oswalt footnotes in his translation that "the intonation is markedly different from that of ordinary speech" (331), Mrs. Parrish spoke:

> Our Father, the good power
> The power of good words
> The good power hand. She made this basket.
>
> Our Father. This holy basket, just renewed, has spoken to me: Some day, some year, some week, a terrible pestilence will arrive in this land. At this time this basket will be wiping sweat off itself [will be working hard]. Some poison disease will arrive—it is said. That is why I was told to have this sacred basket renewed. That is why I was told to have this basket prepared ahead of time.
>
> This sacred basket is something—something of great power. When I received this basket I felt the power increase. And then, when I was given the sacred basket rules, I was given the rules [for use of] pitch. That [pitch] is medicine for the inside of this sacred basket.

1. Schwab takes this material from Bateson's "Culture Contact and Schismogenesis," in *Steps to an Ecology of Mind*. She notes further that Bateson suggests "a dynamic balance [between two or more cultures] requires a reorganization of boundaries and a new creation of inner coherence based on change. Defensive attempts at self-preservation tend to become, in the long run, self-destructive, whereas the open and transformative strategies might, up to a certain limit, be the self-preserving ones. In non-destructive culture contact, self-preservation presupposes self-transformation, or, more generally, the recognition of otherness/Other induces a self-transforming interaction" (134).

I was given pitch for coating it—from four places—redwood pitch, fir
pitch, Bishop pine pitch, sugar pine pitch. Thus I was told.

When a dangerous illness arrives, at that time these things might happen.
For that reason, for that reason, this night you have learned what this is that I
am doing—what this is that I am doing.

(Oswalt 330–33)

When I went away to college Mabel gave me a "prayer basket," a
miniature basket so small I need a magnifying glass to see its designs.
"For your travels, where you go among the crowds, what you do, who
you are," she said that evening as she pinned the tiny basket to my shirt.
She told me how to feed the basket with water once a month, and she
told me how to pray, what songs to sing.

Her baskets are living. They live with her. They live with their holders.
Since her bout with arthritis, Mabel has not been able to weave as much.
She said: "My baskets haven't forgotten me though." Mabel's baskets
and so many Pomo baskets I have known have stories, songs, and
genealogies. They have helped us on our travels and told us who we are
as a people. They have healed the sick and forecast momentous events.
The weaver's hands move, and the basket takes form so that the story
can be known. And the baskets keep talking.

A few years ago I drove Mabel up to the annual Strawberry Festival
on the Kashaya Pomo Reservation. Since Essie Parrish's death Mabel
officiates this spring ceremony. Even while Mabel is not a Kashaya
Pomo, she is highly respected by Essie's family who consider Mabel their
ceremonial leader. Essie once said to her people: "She [Mabel] is picked
from above. I was told [by spirit]. She is now my sister, your auntie.
Remember this. Through our ceremonies you will know . . . you will
know." As I was driving Mabel to Kashaya for the festival that spring
day, I had my mind on my school work. I was a graduate student at
Stanford. Mabel said: "You think about your basket. This ceremony
feeds it, keeps it going."

Often at these annual ceremonies I feel awkward. I am introduced to
people who are related to me as if I am supposed to know them. I forget
how I am related or not related to everyone there. And there I stand with
my fair skin and blue eyes. Mabel gathers us around the food—seaweed,
acorn mush, stews, salads, cakes, pies, and strawberries everywhere, on
pies, in bowls, on skewers. She tells us where to stand. She tells us to take
hold of our costumes—our baskets, ceremonial handkerchiefs, tribal
crosses—and she prays and sings. After, we eat and eat, talk and talk.

This spring I left the dinner while people were still talking and eating and took a walk to the old roundhouse. I saw the shake roof had been ripped apart by the winds. A padlock chain held the door closed. I turned to where the brush house, or outside dance house, was every summer. Nothing now but junked cars, mounds of dirt, rusted mattress springs. I remembered seeing Mabel and Essie dancing together one summer. As the singers sang Essie's dream songs, she and Mabel danced, their hands locked together above their heads, their long ceremonial dresses twirling in the firelight. From the top of a car parked outside the brush house, I could see over the redwood brush fence. I wondered what the two women were doing.

I was about fourteen then. I didn't know who my father was, my genealogy. I was just hanging out, a bombed-out kid, in trouble a lot. That spring night, at the Strawberry Festival, my youth seemed so far away. I took hold of the basket pinned to my shirt and headed back to the dinner.

CHAPTER FOUR

Telling Dreams and Keeping Secrets

The Bole Maru as
American Indian Religious Resistance

"Do we tell them our stories?" I asked.

Seated at Auntie Violet Chappell's table with many of my aunties and uncles, I wondered whether our trip to Stanford University was a good idea after all. It was now three in the morning. We had prayed and sung ceremonial songs for the trip, and after the prayer ceremony, around midnight, we had sat down to eat. We were still talking. In order to arrive at Stanford by ten in the morning we would have to leave the reservation at six, in just three hours.

A former professor of mine had asked if I could get some members of my family to speak before a large audience about the popular and widely distributed ethnographic documentary film *The Sucking Doctor.* I said yes enthusiastically, even before consulting my family. The film covers the second night of a Kashaya Pomo healing ceremony in the Kashaya Roundhouse. Essie Parrish, who is Auntie Violet's mother, sucks a pain out of her patient's body. The audience hears many of her doctoring songs and witnesses her dancing and her work to locate and extract the disease. Mabel McKay claimed Essie's death was related to her making of this film, not to the making itself perhaps but to the showing of our ceremonies to people unfamiliar with our rules. "She had to sacrifice," Mabel said. "I seen it in my Dream."

Anita Silva, the outspoken Kashaya politician, looked up from her coffee. "The question isn't, do we tell them? It's, what do we say?"

"Oh," Violet said from her place at the head of the table. "There's just so much to this." Her voice was shaky, uneven.

"It's hard for her," said Anita.

"That's what I mean," I interjected; "we don't have to go. So much is at stake."

Violet set her coffee on the table and picked up an unlit cigarette. "They're going to show the film and I have to see Mom in front of all *those* people. Oh . . ."

Her anxiety increased my own. This was my family after all. Many of them are related to my grandmother. We share and practice the same religious beliefs. For weeks, even after they had agreed to come forth publicly for the first time since the film was made nearly thirty years ago, I worried that I might be setting them up to be compromised. Again, I felt that old tug between my university life and my life as an Indian.

"We don't have to do it," I said again.

"Look," Violet said, exhaling a cloud of smoke and dropping a match into her ashtray. "It's true what you said, Greg, how you approached us about this matter. It's time for us to stand up, speak out. It's something I've been thinking about for a long time. It's prophecy. It's prophecy, who we are in the history of things. It's Mom's Dream we're thinking about right here. That's why we prayed first. For inspiration. For truth and protection in what we do according to Mom."

Auntie Violet cleared bowls and glasses as if to make room for what she had to say next. She set her cigarette in the ashtray. "OK, what happened? When Mom made that film she knew she was getting tricked. Those people from the universities told her it would be hers, just for her. Her family. So why did she do it? Because in her Dream she seen what was coming. She knew phonies would come out of the woodwork, Indian and white. After her death they would come around saying they are Dreaming her. But it's the devil they're seeing. So she did that film— something never done before—for truth, for protection. We who know the rules can heal ourselves with that."

Violet paused and took a puff from her cigarette. "OK, Mom knew moonsick women would hear those doctoring songs. She knew people would see things they shouldn't see. She knew what would happen. She knew it would come to this right here tonight. But she left us a tradition, something to keep thinking and talking about in our lives, something to carry through all time. But it's up to us to do it. And this is the next step. You see, we're sitting here talking about it, about prophecy, about the teachings. We're knowing who we are."

"Yes, Auntie," I said, "and that's what's bothering me. How do we tell that to others? I mean . . ."

Anita leaned forward. "It goes back to what I said. What do we say? But I'm not worried. It'll come. I know."

"I'm not worried either," Violet said. "Not anymore. I guess that's what I was getting to. We know who we are. We know what to do. We'll know . . ."

"But . . ."

"But nothing," Anita snapped, getting up from the table. "Have faith. You're letting the white come out in you. Hah! I just say."

In *The Sucking Doctor* Essie Parrish is wearing her white dress. The three helpers who sing with her wear white dresses also. The dresses are sacred, unique to Essie Parrish's doctoring ceremonies, something given to her in her Dream. The practice of sucking to extract disease is ancient among the various central California Indian tribes. Among the Pomo tribes, sucking doctors traditionally have been considered the most valuable and powerful healers. While Essie Parrish was a sucking doctor, she was also, as I have noted, the Bole Maru, or Dream Dance, leader, directing all Kashaya Pomo religious activity from the dictates of her Dream. She directed the dances and singing and designed all the costumes, such as the white dresses, for given ceremonies. The film thus not only documents a healing ceremony among the Kashaya Pomo but also captures a feature of the Kashaya Bole Maru religion.

The Bole Maru, or Bole Hesi as it is called among the southwestern Wintun immediately east of the Pomo, is not ancient. Rather it is a revivalistic religion, a religious, and ultimately political, response to European and Euro-American domination and ideology.[1] Like the Plains Ghost Dance religion, the Bole Maru was instigated in some degree by the doctrine of Wovoka, the Paiute prophet, who prophesied cataclysmic destruction of the earth and of all the invaders and a return to the pre-contact Indian way of life.[2] In the winter of 1871–1872 Richard Taylor, a Long Valley Cache Creek Pomo medicine man, called all the Pomo, Wappo, Coast, and Lake Miwok tribes, as well as some tribes of Wintun and others from the central California region, to the eastern shores of Clear Lake in Lake County, where his followers had constructed seven semi-subterranean earth lodges to protect the faithful against the flood that Taylor claimed would cleanse the world of white people.[3] Over a

1. Readers might be interested in A. F. C. Wallace's "revitalization" model and his *Death and Rebirth of the Seneca*. Wallace provides a description and analysis of American Indian revitalization.

2. For an interesting discussion of the Plains Ghost Dance religion, see James Mooney's *The Ghost Dance Religion and the Sioux Outbreak of 1890*.

3. Cora DuBois notes: "The Bole Maru probably originated with the Hill Patwin prophet, Lame Bill, who also supported the Earth Lodge cult" (497). Mabel McKay told me the Bole Maru, or Dream Dance, started with her grandmother's brother, Richard

thousand people gathered in the seven earth lodges. Of course they were disappointed when Taylor's Dream proved untrue. But what they carried home with them, what they had heard during their stay in the lodges, was the spirit of revitalization. Each Pomo tribe subsequently produced their own prophets, or Dreamers, who carried on and developed the Bole Maru religion in specific ways, with specific dances and rituals.

While the influence of these Bole Maru Dreamers was different from tribe to tribe, and while each tribe had its own Dreamer and individual dances, songs, and costumes associated with that Dreamer, certain features new to Pomo religion and social organization emerged throughout Pomo territory. Where once there had been many private or secret cults within a tribe, now an entire tribe was united under one cult, the Bole Maru. The Dreamers stressed the afterlife and preached the Protestant work ethic and Puritan principles of cleanliness and abstinence. They forbade gambling and drinking. They insisted that women keep their bodies covered at all times, particularly during ceremonial activities, in Victorian-style, high-necked long dresses that covered the legs and upper arms. The Dreamers were predominantly women, and while they were not called chiefs, they assumed the role of tribal leaders, organizing their respective tribe's social and political activities around the doctrine of their Dreams.

Cora DuBois, an anthropologist who studied the Bole Maru in the 1930s, saw the movement as a significant revivalistic effort. Yet she seems to imply that in the long run it generally opened the door to further Christianization and the decline of Indian religion and ideology. In 1939 she wrote: "At the moment it represents one of the terminal points in a progressively Christianized ideology, for which the Ghost Dance and its subsequent cults were the transitional factors" (499). Remember that by the winter of 1871–1872, massacres, disease, and slave raiding had significantly reduced Pomo tribes to well below their pre-contact population numbers. They had lost ninety-nine percent of the land they once called home and lived by permission on the land of local ranchers, to whom they provided a source of cheap labor (Bean and Theodoratus 299). Christian groups moved into Pomo territories, Catholics and Prot-

---

Taylor. "There's no such thing as Hill Patwin," she said. "It's just more white man names for us." *Patwin* is a southwestern Wintun word for "relations." Mabel has always claimed that she is Long Valley Cache Creek Pomo (another white term) as was her great uncle Richard Taylor. (Again, the Long Valley Cache Creek Pomo central village was called Lolsel, "wild tobacco." "I am people from Lolsel," Mabel says, " 'wild tobacco' people." Mabel's mother, Daisy Hansen, was from Lolsel. Her father, Yanta Boone, was a Pomo from Potter Valley.)

estants, and agreed to protect and help those Indians who converted. Given these conditions and the general domination and oppression of the Pomo up to the present, it is no wonder that DuBois, like the settlers and missionaries before her, saw the Pomo Indians integrating Christian religion and Victorian ideology into their culture at the expense of their own identities and beliefs as Indians.[4] Clearly, the Pomo could not afford to show how a blending of different religious and cultural ideals laid the foundation for a fierce Indian resistance that exists in many places to this day.[5]

The Pomo Indians donned Victorian clothing and lived seemingly Christian lives, but, as I indicated in the beginning of this book, their Bole Maru leaders inculcated an impassioned Indian nationalism in the homes and roundhouses. Everything associated with the white world was deemed taboo; interactions with whites except for necessary work-related situations were forbidden. Intermarriage with the foreigners was prohibited. Some tribes practiced the infanticide of mixed-blood children. It was taught that the invaders had no place in the afterlife and that unnecessary association with them could cost a person the reward of everlasting life. Seen thus from an Indian nationalist perspective, the assimilation of Victorian ideology looks very different. The ban on drinking, gambling, and adultery not only assured the continuance of individual tribes but also of given family lines within the same tribes. And while the Bole Maru united each tribe around one particular cult, it influenced the revival of other ancient cults and secret societies. Families associated with certain secret cults again had sons and daughters who could learn and carry on special traditions. So while the Bole Maru was emergent in terms of its doctrine and social and religious structure, it simultaneously enhanced the resurgence and fortification of many pre-contact structures integral to Pomo life and ideology. In sum, it seems

4. It is likely also that DuBois, like many anthropologists and others studying other cultures during that period, tended to see and describe what was present, before her eyes, rather than consider, in addition to what was present, that which was covert, invisible, or unspoken.

5. To what degree Pomo people were conscious of the historical process and intentionally applied a specific strategy of resistance—disguising the tactical, political nature of the "blending" in a conspiratorial way—is unclear and perhaps not a relevant concern. The anthropologist Tim Buckley said to me, "I think that such tactics and processes are very rarely so conscious or intentional or conspiratorial; I think something more intuitive, unconscious, cultural (and therefore somehow even grander) goes on in these specific kinds of cases." The Pomo were conscious that whites would not approve of or in any way be happy with the Bole Maru, the Indians' doctrine of revitalization and resistance to white cultural domination.

more likely from this perspective that the Pomo adopted what was useful in Victorian ideology and biblical religion.

Of course, an understanding of the dynamics of any resistance movement and its success or lack of success depends upon who is doing the study, what the context and circumstances are, and which methods are being employed. Any perspective has its limitations. Representatives from the dominant culture exploring the resistance of a subjugated people are likely to see little more than what those people choose or can afford to show them. In turn, a subjugated people may not see the ways their resistance may further their alienation from the dominant culture and so weaken their resistance to it and even hasten their demise as a result. And it must also be remembered that the method and the narrative format of any such study or account of the Bole Maru, written or not, will compromise the experience of the movement in given ways. The possibility of open cross-cultural communication productive for both cultures usually will be strained, even in safer, postcolonial, and more comfortably pluralistic contexts, by the history of domination and subjugation and the persistent patterns of intercultural communication associated with that history.

The Pomo are generally private, adverse to open exchange with persons outside their respective tribal communities. The Bole Maru with its emphasis on local, individual Dreamers reinforced the stringent localism of the pre-contact cultures. Secrecy as an aspect of pre-contact culture became an asset for the resistance. As Essie Parrish once said of a university professor who wanted to interview her: "I watched. I listened. I let him show who he was. The white people, they're not like us. They show fast."

And this brings me back to the issues that concern me now, just as they did that night before our trip to Stanford to discuss *The Sucking Doctor*. In creating narratives for others about our histories and religions, in what ways are we not only compromising those histories and religions but at the same time compromising our identities, which are largely dependent upon these, as well as our resistance to the colonizer and dominant culture? How might my particular discussion of the Bole Maru from an insider's perspective be appropriated by outsiders for their purposes, political or otherwise? My writing or even speaking about the Bole Maru requires that I use certain narrative forms, alone or together, that are accessible and intelligible to those who are not Kashaya Pomo. The ways I hear about and experience the Bole Maru religion are generally not similar to my narrative form of presentation and explanation here, which is, at least in the middle part of this chapter, "hypothetical-deductive" (Rosaldo 1989, 132).[6] I present a subject, say the Bole Maru, and deductively prove or disprove given hypotheses regarding it, and the reader's sense and understanding of the Bole Maru is based largely on this narrative model. The model affords little sense of my Kashaya Pomo Bole Maru religious experience, of the songs I sing, and the stories I am told. Is the fact that for non-Kashaya readers I must distort and reinvent my Bole Maru experiences assurance that they are safe? Will significant content leak out and be appropriated regardless? What can possibly be achieved here for both the reader and me?

Again, while I am related to many of the Kashaya people, my religious affiliation with them is through Mabel McKay. I did not come to Kashaya religious doctrine as a child on the Kashaya reservation growing up with the particular teachings of the Kashaya Dreamer. Rather, I came as an outsider, or an insider coming back from the outside, with an outside Dreamer who had teachings similar to and compatible with those of Essie Parrish. All the more reason for me to be concerned with anything that might jeopardize my position, such as compromising Kashaya family members and revealing private information. In addition, there was my lengthy relationship with universities as a student and now as a professor. I must mediate not only between different purposes regarding the study of American Indian culture and texts but at the same time between different modes of discourse about those different purposes.

Renato Rosaldo (1989) observes that social analysts—and, I would add, literary critics, since they are often one and the same these days—can "often belong to multiple, overlapping communities" (194). He says "the social analyst's multiple identities at once underscore the potential for uniting an analytical with an ethical project and render obsolete the view of the utterly detached observer who looks down from on high" (194). The position of having multiple identities at once as a result of belonging to multiple, overlapping communities may underscore the potential for new and inventive projects, but a borderlands position often is not an easy or comfortable one to be in, nor does it guarantee a project or report agreeable and intelligible to all of the communities

6. Renato Rosaldo uses the term *hypothetical-deductive* when paraphrasing philosopher W. B. Gallie. The passage reads: "According to Gallie, alternatives to textbook versions of explanation have been suppressed by the dominant Anglo-American philosophical tradition, which at one time did, and in many quarters still does, claim that the only valid form of explanation is the hypothetical-deductive model" (132). See Rosaldo's (1989) discussion of narrative history and analysis.

involved. I must think about the many communities where I live and work, and I must remember my allegiance to my Indian community.[7]

So far I have only mentioned features of the Bole Maru that are generally known or that if known are of no particular threat to my people. I have spoken of the movement in the past tense. I have not disclosed, for example, how Kashaya Pomo values are retained or how the retention constitutes resistance. A discussion of orality and oral tradition does not necessarily open the cultural territory of the oral tradition for the purpose of finding answers to issues of resistance any more than a discussion of secrets necessarily reveals their contents and significance. Obviously, we no longer don Victorian clothing; times have changed. An important feature of the Bole Maru tradition is the stipulation that dances, songs, and costumes brought about by the Dreamer must cease to be used with her death. Prayer songs and costumes given by the Dreamer to particular individuals for protection and health may continue to be used after the Dreamer's death only if she has given explicit permission. In some cases certain songs or dances may be passed down to a successor. But everything else associated with the Dreamer stops with her death. New or revived ceremonies must come only with a new Dreamer recognized by the entire tribe. This practice not only reinforces the unique characteristics and manifestations of the Bole Maru in individual Pomo communities but also allows for a continuous reinvention of the tradition in those communities, always adapting the tradition and Indian identity to changing historical circumstances.

Specifically, what I have not talked about in any detail is the present state of the Bole Maru at Kashaya. At this point, you might know that

7. Again, as I have suggested early on in this book, there is not a necessary or unavoidable conflict between the academy and the Indian community. I am not suggesting that academic discourse must be abandoned as a method of discussing my community or any other community. Rather, I am suggesting and I hope demonstrating that academic discourse, with its various argumentative and narrative styles, be interrogated by and integrated with other forms of discourse, perhaps to broaden what we (academics) mean by academic discourse or to collapse the rather arbitrary dichotomy between academic and nonacademic, nonpersonal and personal discourse. I am an academic and discourse that is academic is part of my experience. To deny my academic background would be as dangerous and unprofitable for both Kashaya Pomo and non-Kashaya Pomo (particularly non-Kashaya academics) as it would be to deny my personal life and experience in my Indian community. Both groups would lose an opportunity and a means to talk about each other to one another. Both groups would lose an opportunity to inform and be informed by the other. When I mention my allegiance to my Indian community, I am speaking about information regarding particular ceremonials or whatever my elders and others have instructed me not to write about or discuss outside the home. There is much I can talk about in order to raise issues regarding intercultural communication and understanding between Kashaya Pomo and non-Kashaya Pomo.

Essie Parrish has died and that we have been without a Dreamer to lead dances and so forth for over ten years. You know we sing, pray, and tell stories. But how do the songs work to maintain Bole Maru ideology? What do the stories suggest? How is the Bole Maru doctrine and practice being used and how is it changing? We do not refer and, according to Violet Chappell, we have never referred to that tradition as Bole Maru. "Those are white men's words," Violet says. DuBois says Bole Maru "is a compound term consisting respectively of the Patwin and Pomo words for the cult" (497), but what Pomo was she referring to? Pomo and Patwin are also "white men's words," terms ethnographers used to categorize us by language families they invented with linguists to order and make sense of the cultural diversity they encountered among native peoples in the area.[8] We are Pomo, Kashaya Pomo, or whatever Pomo because we must be for the purposes of the Bureau of Indian Affairs (BIA) and other U.S. government agencies. It is something we must don like the Victorian clothes of old. However, the Kashaya Pomo are and have been since time immemorial *wina·má·bakĕ ya,* "people who belong to the land."

Enough already.

Many Kashaya people might not agree with what I have said; and those immersed in other religions might not care.[9] It means something to my family and it means something to you, the reader, since you are reading this. Wanting to know this or that for whatever reasons is nothing new for many people coming to Indian territory.[10] But now we, and I mean the family of Kashaya Pomo who share and practice the Bole

8. Mabel McKay claims the word Pomo translates to "red earth" among the Potter Valley tribe of central Pomo. Linguists suggest the various Pomo languages belong to the Hokan family which also includes the languages of tribes such as the Chumash of southern California and the Karok of northern California.

9. Again, as I noted at the beginning of this book, there are families on the Kashaya Reservation who are Mormon. There are also Pentecostal families.

10. I am thinking of the current interest in American Indian art and religion. The New Age Movement with its appropriation of American Indian religion is a good example of how citizens of a dominant society take what they find—what they came into Indian territory wanting to know—for their own purposes. Here the interests, or need to know, may not directly affect the political well-being of a particular Indian community, but the interests nonetheless ultimately result in recreations of Indian life and ideology that may, through the creation of stereotypes and so forth, be damaging in the long run. Pictures of Indians as religious ideologues in portraits such as Carlos Castaneda's Don Juan decontextualize religion from culture and history. *The Sucking Doctor* viewed without any knowledge of the Kashaya Bole Maru has the same effect. Abdul R. JanMohamed and David Lloyd observe: "The pathos of hegemony is frequently matched by its interested celebration of differences, but of differences in the aesthetized form of recreations. Detached from the site of their production, minority cultural forms become palatable: a form of practical struggle like *capoeira* becomes recuperable as breakdance" (11).

Maru doctrine, are coming forth. As Auntie Violet said, "It's time for us to stand up, speak out . . . it's who we are in the history of things."

When we left the reservation that morning for Stanford University it was still dark. None of us had slept; we were wide awake, still talking. Driving down the mountain I noticed a pink eastern sky. Red sky in the morning, sailors take warning, I thought to myself.

Anita and Violet rode with me; Vivien, Violet's sister, and her family and three of Anita's children followed in separate cars. In Santa Rosa and Rohnert Park we stopped to pick up more relatives. Seven cars pulled into Stanford, and I think my former professor was quite surprised. He stood in the middle of the parking lot where he was waiting for us, watching one car after another pass alongside of him.

I introduced him to Auntie Anita and Auntie Violet, and then the congregation of about thirty people followed him to a large lecture hall. The hall was full of students and faculty who wanted to hear what Essie Parrish's family had to say about *The Sucking Doctor*. The three of us—Anita, Violet, and myself—took our seats at a table at the front of the room. The others found seats in the back of the room or stood along the walls.

The professor introduced Violet and Anita as the daughters of Essie Parrish, the legendary Pomo medicine woman and tribal leader. "The same one you saw in the film," he said, "and they are here to talk about that and whatever else they might want to say." He then took a seat in the audience.

Anita is actually Essie Parrish's niece.

I stood up immediately and introduced the entire family, explaining how everyone was related to everyone else. As I sat down, Anita quipped for all to hear, "Whites ain't so good with genealogies."

Nervous laughter from the audience. Then silence.

Finally, Anita turned to Violet. "Do you want me to start?"

Violet nodded.

"OK," Auntie Anita said facing the crowd, "what do you want to know?"

The audience seemed stunned, confused. They were motionless in their seats, looking at my aunties in their dark stretch pants and brightly colored blouses. The crowd expected a lecture of some kind; they expected to be talked to. I had seen Mabel McKay turn the tables on audiences in this manner. With Mabel people often became confused, disoriented. With Anita the audience was likely to be intimidated as well as confused and disoriented. She is a large woman, forthright, with a powerful voice. "I am a rock," she says. "I know who I am and nobody's going to take that away from me."

The second hand on the clock on the wall circled twice. I saw the professor biting his nails.

"OK," Anita boomed. "These things you want us to talk about—all the things in our lives—are sacred. Do you know what that means, what sacred is?"

A moment passed and then a young man close to the front of the room raised his hand. "I want to go back to the first question," he said. He was nervously picking at his beard.

"My pleasure, sir," said Anita with a teasing chuckle.

"Can you tell us something about the film we saw . . . Well, we saw two films, the one with your mother making acorn mush and the ceremony one. Can you say something about the ceremony film?"

Anita and Violet glanced at one another.

Anita looked back to the student. "Why do you want to know?"

The student blushed, then came back with, "We have to write about it."

"Hah! How the hell you going to write about something you don't know anything about? Me, I'm sixty years old and I couldn't write about that film. It's too, too . . . What's the word I want? Complicated, that's it. There's so much to Auntie's teachings. It's full of meaning . . ."

Violet jumped up and turned to the blackboard. "Look," she said. She picked up a piece of chalk and drew several horizontal lines. "OK, the film about the acorn mush, where Mom demonstrates making that mush, that's down here, this bottom line. Say lesson one. The doctoring film is way up here on top. Like she said, 'It's complicated.' All this, all of it is complicated. You can't just figure out this up here and not know the rest."

Violet sat down.

"That's a dumb assignment you got," Anita said to the student. "Maybe I won't get asked back here, but I just had to say that. Maybe I'm not too gracious."

"Look," said Violet, "I'm trying to think in your terms. All of this is like a book to us, Mom's teachings, her stories. We're still reading it. We won't be finished until we die. You want to finish the book, say what it is, and go on. Am I saying anything to you? We read to understand, ask questions."

With trepidation I shot a glance at the professor. He was red-faced, sunk low in his seat, seemingly choked in his tweed coat and tie.

Violet acknowledged another student, a woman in a long black over-coat with bobbed, magenta-colored hair.

"Is this . . . if you believe can you be healed? Is that how it works?"

Anita leaned forward, pointing at the woman. "You was going to say 'is it all in our minds,' wasn't you? That's OK. Don't be ashamed. Be honest. In enough time we'd find out about each one of you. And that's what I'm looking for right now—where you people are at." Anita sat back and adjusted her glasses. "Thank you, I know something about you, young lady."

I thought of the woman's question and remembered Mabel McKay's response: "Whether you believe it or not it's true." I wanted Anita to answer the woman, to say what Mabel had said, but no such luck.

Anita patted her permed black hair. "See, I got a set of antennas up here. I'm zeroing in." She broke into raucous laughter. "Oops, I didn't mean to scare you."

I worried people might take Anita literally; you know, think of her antennas as spiritual apparatuses of some kind. Again, I wanted her to clarify matters. But what would she say? Her antennas, as she calls them, *are* spiritual apparatuses, a part of her.

A woman wearing several buttons on her leather jacket stood up in the back of the room. "Well, that's what I've been bothered about all quarter. What you said Violet, I mean Mrs. Chappell. We read all this American Indian literature, the folklore and everything, and I don't know what I'm reading. I don't know anything about the Indians. I was hoping to know something after today. Like where to start."

"You just said it," Anita said. "You don't know anything. That's where to start. Excuse me, Violet, but I just had to pick up on this one."

The woman wrung her hands. "But then how can we know about Indians or this film? I wanted to learn something."

"Sorry, Violet, I got to open my mouth again. Listen," Anita said looking back to the woman, "do you know who you are? Why are you interested? Ask yourself that. I think you are asking yourself right now. My antennas again."

Violet straightened in her chair. "Get to know us, mingle. Watch. Something will pop out that will say something to you."

Violet and Anita continued to answer questions. Violet spoke of her mother's life and of her experiences as the daughter of a renowned Indian doctor and tribal leader. "Oh, I used to watch Mom. She'd pick prunes in the hot sun all day, or at the cannery standing on the line maybe ten, maybe twelve hours. Then all of us. She had fifteen kids.

Then off she'd go somewheres, two hundred miles maybe to doctor the sick. How does she do it? Then I'd think what everybody said: Mom is a special person." Anita spoke of her work with the Sonoma County Indian Health Board. She talked about her work educating medical doctors regarding the ways Indians perceive their bodies and illnesses. "You know, they don't always listen," she said.

The conversation always seemed to come back to issues of listening and knowing or not knowing. Now I wouldn't even glance at the professor. I knew he didn't get what he wanted.

That night, after dinner, the professor, now in Levi's and tennis shoes, showed *The Sucking Doctor* in a student dorm. For my family, viewing this film constitutes participation in a ceremony. As always certain rules apply. We didn't say much; we waited. This could be the most difficult part of the trip.

A small crowd turned up, mostly Indian students and interested faculty. The woman wearing the button-covered jacket was there also. She was sitting in front of me and I kept trying to read the buttons on her shoulders and back. "WOMEN ARE PEOPLE TOO." "TAKE BACK THE NIGHT AND KEEP IT." "EARTH FIRST."

During the film, Auntie Violet dabbed her eyes with a handkerchief. She took deep breaths, easy for anyone to hear, as if trying to compose herself. Afterwards, Anita asked for questions. "What did you see?" she asked.

People said various things. I remember my dissertation advisor, Mary Pratt, said: "I felt her power was endless. I've never felt anything like this."

Such a candid response from Mary impressed me. I don't remember much else about what happened just then. I was thinking that things turned out OK after all. Violet was able to start talking and she was answering questions with Anita. My professor friend appeared engaged and relaxed.

I started thinking.

I had brilliant answers to my questions about this trip. The Bole Maru had become in this instance at Stanford an interrogative text. It was a historic move; from a secret cult to one that facilitated cross-cultural discourse about itself and other cultures and doctrines, the Bole Maru had again been reinvented, modified in a given historical context. "The next step," as Auntie Violet had said the night before. The Bole Maru was providing all of us a way to talk, to survive together, to understand. The dialogue it prompted exposed our differences and similarities, the bridges we had to cross in reading and knowing one another. What was the price? Our time and energy. Little else. I started thinking of the paper I would write about this experience, of course never imagining at the moment how my interpretation and presentation of the trip might be biased by my own perspective.

Then I looked up and saw the room was empty. The woman with the leather jacket was turned around in her seat, talking to Violet. "Something did pop out," she was saying. "I was thinking of my own mother. She died a year ago."

I looked away, embarrassed. Their exchange was none of my business. I was an intruder. Then I stopped thinking. I was hearing what Auntie Violet had said when she first spoke after the film, what I figured the woman had heard, and it told everything.

"This is my mother you're talking about, and we loved her dearly."

PART THREE

Hearing the Old Ones Talk: The Literate Experience

CHAPTER FIVE

Reading Narrated American Indian Lives

Elizabeth Colson's Autobiographies of Three Pomo Women

One cold winter night some twenty-five years ago I listened to Great-Grandma Nettie tell the following story about her life:

"Come that man what his name. That one, that old man come. Come there that time. Put hands on table, like that [gesturing with her hands turned down]. Give meat, first thing. That way know if poison man. Come to poison or what. Don't know. Watch. Listen.

"Just girl that time. Ten, maybe twelve. But that man stranger man. Come looking for mother. Says that, come looking for mother. Saying that. Where mother? Says that. Not here. No mother here. Come in anyway, that man. Come in like that.

"Me just girl that time. Ten years. Ten. Sitting alone. No mother. But start looking for meat. Only thing dry meat—*bishe*. Need live meat old rule way. Need live meat for poison people. But put dry meat out. Put there. Put like that.

"Don't talk Indian, that man. Talk only Spanish. Look like Spanish, too. Light skin, that man. Still, half-Indian know something. Like old man Sensi. Done like that. Done old lady Mary other side creek like that. Done basket putting like that. He done like that, they say.

"Don't touch meat, that man. Nothing. Talking Spanish. Talking, talking, talking . . . Ten that time, 'bout that age. Only girl. Only know sí. Mean yes. Yes. I say sí [laughing]. Say that, that's all. Say sí. Say like that. Say sí.

"Then happen man eat meat. Then happen never go again. Sitting

there all day, that man. Sitting there hands on table, like that [gesturing
with her hands turned down]. Hands like that, same. Maybe rape, do me
like that. I start working roots. Start working basket roots, watching that
man. Work, watching that man. Put food out sometime, acorn.

"Nighttime mother come up. Come up road there. Later time mother
say good thing keeping busy. Good watching that man. Fool that man.
Fool that way. Trust no stranger people. No stranger people. Old man
Sensi. Done old lady like that, they say.

"Don't know what. Not poison me. What. Don't know. Don't know.
Mother don't say. Just talking to that man. Just talking. Talking like that.
Talking, talking, talking, talking . . ."

At the time Great-Grandma Nettie, as she was known to half our
neighborhood, must have been ninety years old. She was small and
wizened, with a shock of straight white hair. Yet Nettie was formidable.
She commanded attention. You saw when she flicked her wrist, pointed
with her extended chin and great downturned mouth. She sat leaning
forward in an overstuffed chair opposite the television, her gnarled
hands clutching the ends of the armrests, as if at any moment she would
spring to her feet and set things straight.

That particular night Old Auntie Eleanor was visiting Great-Grandma
Nettie.[1] Eleanor was a big, boisterous woman who lived down the road.
She was younger than Nettie, but not by much. She walked over a mile to
visit and reminisce with Nettie. Sometimes they argued about this or that.
They gossiped. They always conversed with one another in Indian, in
their central Pomo language, and talked, whether or not anyone was
listening, no matter how loud the television was. And that's what caught
my attention: Great-Grandma Nettie switched to English. And when she
saw that I was listening, she cast a suspicious glance. I felt self-conscious,
confused. Was she saying something *for* me or *about* me? Was I an *insider*
or an *outsider?*

Unlike most of the children in the room just then, I was not a direct descendant of Nettie's, not one of her grandchildren or great-
grandchildren. And I was a mixed blood. I was living back and forth in
Indian and white families. Nettie was telling a story from her life, but
with her suspicious glances and all that talk in English about strangers,

1. "Nettie" and "Eleanor" are not the women's real names. Neither woman is living
now, and knowing the Pomo custom for privacy I feel it appropriate to use fictitious names.
At the time of the event I am describing both women were living in Santa Rosa, in the
southern Pomo territory, which is approximately sixty miles south of Ukiah, the town in
the central Pomo region close to where both women were born and raised.

she called to mind my own life, that uncomfortable borderlands existence that I was reminded of at times like this.

I became Indian. I ignored her. Silence, the Indian's best weapon, an
aunt of mine once said. Be an Indian, cut yourself off with silence any
way you can. Don't talk. Don't give yourself away. I knew certain
Kashaya words, phrases. The Kashaya Pomo, or southwestern Pomo,
language is different from but similar to the central Pomo language
Great-Grandma Nettie and Old Auntie Eleanor spoke. When Nettie
finished her story, or at a given point in the story, she switched back to
her Indian language. I was still listening, even with my eyes fixed on the
televison. She repeated the word *bishun,* or a word that sounded like
bishun, which means "stranger" in Kashaya. Then she said something
like *chu 'um qat 'to mul,* "Don't forget this!" And now, looking back, I
imagine she said something that meant the same as this: *mi qe bake 'eh
mau ama diche mu,* "This story is for you."

Great-Grandma Nettie's story haunts me. Throw it out the back door
and find it looking through the front room window. I see it in a glance,
the way someone is looking at me. I hear it in people's voices, in the
words they use to talk to me. They don't say the exact words, but I hear
the words all the same. Insider. Outsider. Indian. White.

I found this story again as I read and thought about Elizabeth Colson's *Autobiographies of Three Pomo Women.* Though Colson changed
the three Pomo narrators' names as well as the place-names of the area in
which they lived, it is clear that the narrators, called Sophie Martinez,
Ellen Wood, and Jane Adams, were central Pomo.[2] And, like Nettie and
Eleanor, who were central Pomo, the narrators were born during the
latter part of the nineteenth century. They probably spoke a central
Pomo language identical or similar to Nettie and Eleanor's. Each of the
three Pomo women came from a different central Pomo group and spoke
a different central Pomo dialect (Colson 1). Nettie and Eleanor probably
spoke one of these dialects. They probably would have been able to
understand to some extent whatever language any one of these three
Pomo narrators spoke. They shared the same history as the three Pomo

2. It is impossible to know exactly which groups of Pomo in this region the three Pomo
narrators come from since Colson changed names and place-names "in order to afford as
much protection to all concerned as is possible" (14). It is only known that Colson worked
somewhere in the central Pomo region, probably around Ukiah. Colson notes that "[she]
sincerely hope[s] the material will cause no embarrassment to [the narrators], or to any
other Pomo" (14). It is not clear if Colson was responding to the general Pomo concern for
privacy, or if she was aware of this concern. She does not say.

narrators. They talked about some of the same things: people's names and how Indians name people; the poisoners and the medicine men and women and their stupendous deeds; the slave raids and the "raping time," first with the Spanish and then with the Mexicans and the American squatters who followed the Spanish as invaders of Pomo territory.

> My mother called me *tidai*. She would say that to me. She called me *mata* too. *Tidai* is just language. *Mata* means "woman," but not that way. In some different way, I think.
>
> Sophie Martinez (Colson 40)

> I was sick. I had lain in bed about five months. . . . Everybody doctored me that time. . . . That's why we have no beads. We paid those five people. They were all singing doctors.
>
> Sophie Martinez (Colson 78)

> Those days when first Mexicans came up here, they just grab the girls and take them in bushes. Have the pistol in one hand and do what they want and then let them go. My old aunt say they take her once. They put them in a house. One night she pried a board away and got away.
>
> Ellen Wood (Colson 112–113)

> Once I was sick for a long time. Something was wrong with my legs—somebody had poisoned me. They had taken my shoes and put them in a poison place.
>
> Ellen Wood (Colson 169)

> When I was a little girl, I used to go around with my mother digging basket roots. It wasn't so hard that time. We sneak around the river. But now [white landowners] won't let you. They make you get out of their place.
>
> Jane Adams (Colson 202)

So I thought of Great-Grandma Nettie and Old Auntie Eleanor as I read. But when I gave the text a chance, when I looked at what I was reading, I found much that was different from what I remember hearing, especially in terms of language and narrative format and what was said or not said about certain things. I remember Nettie's English as different from that of the three Pomo narrators. Nettie repeated herself often. She seldom used pronouns and frequently began sentences with a verb which she repeated in successive sentences. Nettie rarely talked to strangers, especially about strangers. "Don't talk much with outside people," Nettie and Eleanor admonished. "Careful what you tell." When the professors visited each summer, Nettie became silent. Eleanor gave short, flat answers and told stories no one in the house had ever heard. My memory of Nettie's silence and Eleanor's short answers reminded me that the three Pomo narrators were talking to Colson. Isn't it likely that the three Pomo narrators edited their stories in certain ways for Colson?

The anthropologist Elizabeth Colson not only went into the central Pomo community and collected the autobiographies, which has something to do with what was said, but she also edited and wrote them, which has something to do with their language and narrative format.

As I thought about the three Pomo narrators and Colson, I remembered hearing the old ones talking that winter night. I thought of Great-Grandma Nettie's story and her suspicious glances. I felt uncomfortable again. My impulse as a critic was to say what was truly Pomo, so that I could show what Colson missed, how ignorant she was as an outsider to Pomo culture. But who am I to speak for and define the central Pomo or any Pomo? To what extent would I be creating an Indian just as Colson had, albeit an Indian different from Colson's? Who am I as a spokesperson for either the Pomo or Colson? Who am I as a Pomo Indian? Who am I as a critic? I am caught in the borderlands again. Nettie's story once more. *Autobiographies of Three Pomo Women* is also a story for me. The text says to me: *mi qe bake 'eh mau ama diche mu.*

In this chapter I want to read *Autobiographies of Three Pomo Women* (hereafter referred to as *Autobiographies*) so that I may begin to understand it as a cross-cultural project. But, at the same time, I must begin to understand it as a story for me, not only as a story that positions me in certain ways but also as a story that can inform me about that position. In light of the constitutive characteristics of narrated American Indian autobiography and of critical work surrounding the genre, I will etch out a way to read the text so that I can see the text as well as myself as reader, so that I might inform the text and allow the text to inform me. Then I will come back to and further the discussion of myself and the text that I have started here. Of course even in my discussion of the genre and an approach to it, I will be talking about myself and the text, specifically in terms of the questions this relationship provokes. While much of this discussion is narrow in focus, principally because it concerns one reader and one text, I hope that it raises questions and offers suggestions about reading narrated American Indian autobiography in general, and so might contribute to larger discussions of reading cross-cultural texts in various cultural contexts.

READING STORIES, READING STRANGERS: READING *AUTOBIOGRAPHIES OF THREE POMO WOMEN*

Naturally not all American Indian autobiographies are narrated. Here I am discussing narrated autobiographies, and distinguishing them from those that are written. With narrated autobiographies, a recorder-editor records and transcribes what was given orally by the Indian subject.[3] Written autobiographies, on the other hand, are written by the Indian subjects themselves with or without the assistance of editors.[4] Arnold Krupat, who refers to narrated Indian autobiographies as Indian autobiographies, as opposed to autobiographies (written) by Indians, notes: "The principle constituting the [narrated] Indian autobiography as a genre [is] that of *original bicultural composition*" (31). This principle not only provides the key to the narrated autobiography's discursive type but "provides as well the key to its discursive function, its purposive dimension as an act of power and will. [It is the] ground on which two cultures meet . . . the textual equivalent of the frontier" (Krupat 31). Yet seldom is the story of that meeting apparent or revealed in the text. While there is a wide spectrum of editorial strategies for dealing with point of view in narrated Indian autobiography, the oldest and most common is what David Brumble calls the *Absent Editor* strategy, where the editor edits and presents the Indian's narrative "in such a way as to create the fiction that the narrative is all the Indian's own . . . that the Indians speak to us without mediation (Brumble 1988, 75–76).[5]

3. R. D. Theisz refers to narrated Indian autobiographies as *bi-autobiographies,* distinguishing them from their two bordering relatives, biography and autobiography (66). While Theisz' term is useful in that it serves to remind the reader that at least two people were responsible for the production of the autobiographical text, Theisz' term might just as easily be used for written autobiographies where an editor helped write or edit, perhaps in significant ways, what the Indian had written. In this chapter I discuss only narrated autobiographies where one party (Indian) speaks and another party (non-Indian) writes. Eighty-three percent of the more than six hundred published American Indian texts that are autobiographical are narrated; of these forty percent were collected and edited by anthropologists, the other forty percent were collected and edited by non-Indians from many other walks of life (Brumble 1988, 72).

4. Contemporary and well-known written American Indian autobiographies include *The Names* and *The Way To Rainy Mountain* by N. Scott Momaday, *Storyteller* by Leslie Silko, and *Interior Landscapes* by Gerald Vizenor. Before these contemporary Indian writers, Sarah Winnemucca Hopkins (*Life Among the Piutes: Their Wrongs and Claims,* 1883) and others wrote autobiographies that were more extensive than the eighteenth and early nineteenth century apparently unmediated accounts of conversion to Christianity by Indians such as Samson Occom, William and Mary Apes, and George Copway.

5. It is well known, for example, that John G. Neihardt, editor of *Black Elk Speaks,* the best-known narrated American Indian autobiography, not only rearranged Black Elk's narratives in certain ways but added to them. The passage on the last page of the text about the death of a people's dream and Black Elk's conception of himself as "a pitiful old man who had done nothing" (230), which lends the book its tragic sense, is not Black Elk's but Neihardt's. Neihardt wrote a preface about how he met Black Elk and so forth, yet he allows the reader to believe that the actual autobiography is only Black Elk's.

At the other end of the spectrum of editorial strategies for dealing with point of view in narrated autobiography is the editor who self-consciously inserts himself or herself into the entire text. See, for example, Vincent Crapanzano's *The Fifth World of Enoch Maloney: Portrait of a Navaho* and *The Fifth World of Forster Bennett: Portrait of a Navaho.* Extremely self-conscious editors often seem to wallow in self-reflexivity, forgetting the

The notion of autobiography as fiction, or interpretation, is nothing new. The autobiography, whether narrated or written, is not the life but an account or story of the life. A narrated American Indian autobiography then is in actuality an account of an account, a story of a story; the name of the self is hardly the Indian's own (Eakin 214). As Vincent Crapanzano (1977) observes, "[the life history] is, as it were, doubly edited, during the encounter itself [between recorder-editor and narrator] and during the literary reencounter" (4). In the encounter between non-Indian recorder-editor and Indian narrator, it is important to remember that given the specific social contingencies of the exchange, the Indian may be editing and shaping his or her oral narrative in certain ways, just as Old Auntie Eleanor gave the professors short, flat answers and told stories no one in the household had ever heard. Then, after the Indian has presented an oral narrative, the recorder-editor translates and shapes it in certain ways. The language and format of the original narrative are often altered significantly as they are translated into English or into a more "standard" English and shaped to meet the requirements of linear chronology, human motivation, and so forth imposed by the autobiographical genre. Yet, as mentioned, the extent to which the Indian's narrative is altered in these ways by the recorder-editor is often unclear and is not discussed at length, or at all, by the recorder-editor. In addition, it is difficult for the recorder-editor to know the ways the Indian narrator may have edited the narrative for the recorder-editor.

In *Autobiographies* Elizabeth Colson provides introductory material about her collecting and editing the Pomo womens' autobiographies. She also offers "a considered sketch" (2), or brief ethnography, of Pomo culture as well as her analysis of the autobiographies. She notes in her introductory material that for each of the three Pomo narrators she provides a long autobiographical account and a brief autobiographical account.[6] She says that her method was first to collect this latter brief account from the women and then to ask questions to get them to enlarge on certain points, to identify persons mentioned, and to present

---

voice and presence of the Indian narrator. Brumble argues, and I would agree, that Crapanzano's texts mentioned here are not autobiographies, not of the Indians anyway. "Crapanzano's heroic extremes of subjectivity" result in a book about Crapanzano, his thoughts and ideas, and not so much about the Indian (Brumble 1988, 88–93).

6. Colson refers in her "Table of Contents" to the longer accounts as *life histories* and to the brief accounts as *autobiographies*. Here I see life history and autobiography as the same since, in varying degrees, both are bicultural texts and collaborative endeavors. Note Vincent Crapanzano's discussion of life histories as "doubly edited" texts in "The Life History in Anthropological Field Work," *Anthropology and Humanism Quarterly*, no. 2 (1977): 3–7.

material in chronological order (Colson 4). She then combined each one's brief initial account with the responses to these questions to produce the longer autobiography. She says the verbatim record of the brief autobiography can be found in an appendix after each long autobiography "since for some purposes it is essential to know just what was regarded as important by the narrator, or at least what she was willing to tell of her life given the time and circumstances" (2). Colson talks not only about the questions she asked and about how she combined them with the brief autobiographical narratives but also about the changes she made in the narrators' English (the interviews were conducted in English). But everything Colson says in her introductory material about her collecting and editing the narratives is from her point of view. What of her biases that she may not have been fully aware of? What of the ways her presuppositions about language and narrative format influenced her decisions regarding her editing of the narratives? How much could she have known about each Pomo woman's community and her position in it? What of the Pomo women's point of view about what Colson says? Or their point of view about the collaboration in general? Or about the written text? All that can be known from Colson's introductory material regarding these last three questions is that the Pomo women did not take part in the literary reencounter, that is, in the editing of what they had already said for Colson. They were not consulted in any way. Colson made the decisions about editing the spoken text on her own.

It is not enough then just to study Colson's introductory material if I want to understand how *Autobiographies* was made, how both Colson and the three Pomo women participated in its production.[7] Except for including in the longer autobiographical accounts the questions she asked the narrators, Colson does not place herself in the texts of the narrators and functions as Absent Editor. She does not say in her introductory material how the questions she asked may have influenced the women's responses.[8] Granted, her introductory material regarding her collecting and editing of the narratives is abundant, more extensive than

7. R. D. Theisz suggests that readers study recorder-editors' introductions to determine the manner of collaboration and so forth regarding the production of narrated American Indian autobiographies (65–80), but the questions I have raised in this chapter regarding Colson and the production of *Autobiographies* make it clear that studying recorder-editors' introductions is not enough.

8. Colson does say the narrators "seemed to have no objection to having what they told written down as they spoke" (6–7) and that sometimes "the informant indicated that a touchy spot had been hit" (7). But she does not say what was or was not "touchy." She does mention that "common questions dealt with the identification of persons mentioned in the account since these were rarely named or indeed identified further than 'that man' or 'that woman,' for the Pomo avoid the names of both living and dead." But apparently the narrators identified the persons when asked to.

that of many other recorder-editors. But fundamental questions about what each collaborator contributed to or omitted from the text remain. How do I deal with those fundamental questions, specifically those I raised about Colson and her biases? About the Indian women's biases and how the Indian women may have edited their spoken narratives for Colson? I have come back to my original questions then. How do I begin to understand *Autobiographies* as a collaborative endeavor? And what of my own biases, my position as a reader? If I can inform the text in given ways, how might the text in turn inform me?

It is clear at this point that my approach to *Autobiographies* must consider the cultural and historical background of both Colson and the Pomo narrators. Then I might be able to gain a sense not only of what each collaborator contributed to the text and of the nature of the relationship between the collaborators but also of myself as a reader. If I overlook or do not consider seriously one of the collaborator's roles in the production of the text, I am blinded to what that collaborator may have contributed to the composite text and hence to what makes for a fuller understanding of the relationship between collaborators. But, just as important, I may be blinded to the ways I am reading, to my presence and the nature of my relationship with culturally diverse perspectives. When I consider both Colson and the Pomo women, I am reminded of my often uncomfortable position in the cultures of both Colson and the Pomo women and of the ways those cultures intersect in time and place. Those cultures intersect in *Autobiographies*. By using what I know from research and experience, I can *speculate* on what each collaborator brought to their meeting that resulted in the text at hand. Thus I can gain a broader picture of the relationship between Colson and the narrators and of what constituted the relationship and the making of the text. What constituted the relationship, say patterns of avoidance or projection in the case of one or both parties, illuminates and is located in the history of Pomo and white interrelations. Since I am located in this same history and am positioned as a cultural subject by it, I can now begin to see more clearly how these particular interrelations affect me and in turn how I might affect them. Reciprocity characterizes the approach; I inform a text which informs me.

I emphasized the word *speculate* for definite reasons. The objective here is not to frame *Autobiographies*, not to tell the story of the text's making or of Colson or the Pomo women. Since in the text there are at least two parties present, in addition to a reader, there is no one story, nor can there ever be. And, again, as a reader I cannot assume knowledge and authority to speak for others and their relationships. Rather, the

objective is to open a dialogue with the text such that I can continue to
inform and be informed by the text. Then my dialogue, my representation of my relationship with the text, can inform and be informed by
other readers with different stories who read the text. In this way, the
history, and what constitutes the history, of interrelations between the
Pomo and white communities is continually opened and explored. The
text can be opened and explored in terms of other histories or a larger
history of which the text may be a part. So much depends on the readers
and what they bring to the text and to my reading of the text and on what
the text and my reading can suggest to them.

The danger, and likely consequence, of assuming knowledge and
power in my encounter with *Autobiographies,* specifically in the ways I
might define Colson or the Pomo narrators, is that in losing sight of my
presence as a reader I will not see how my critical work is tied historically
and politically to a real world. Scholars of narrated American Indian
autobiography sometimes position themselves in their encounters with
the texts in such a way that they do not seem to see the limits of their
work or its consequences in a historical and political realm. They may
define the autobiographical works as bicultural and composite, but they
do not consider each of the collaborator's histories and cultures on the
respective collaborator's terms, at least not in a way that might enable
the scholars to think about the nature of their work as scholars and its
consequences.

Arnold Krupat, for example, argues for a historic approach in his
principal study of the genre, *For Those Who Come After.* He examines
the relation of various narrated autobiographies to a historical period, to
the discursive categories of history, science, and art (literature), and to
Western modes of emplotment (xii) in order to answer questions regarding the text's production. But the historical period Krupat discusses in
detail is, in point of view, distinctly Euro-American. He observes that
recorder-editor S. M. Barrett, influenced by the objectivism of turn-of-
the-century American social science and salvage anthropology, presents
Geronimo, in *Geronimo's Story of His Life,* in a way that Geronimo is
"denied the context of heroism [and] of individuality as well; for he is no
different from 'any captive,' any 'prisoner of war,' no world-historical
figure, but just another 'vanishing type' " (63). But what about Geronimo and Apache history, culture, and language? What about the ways
Geronimo may have accommodated or resisted such a presentation of
his life? Krupat does not see or discuss how he also has denied Geronimo
context, in this case as a collaborator in the making of a composite text.

David H. Brumble in *American Indian Autobiography* may account for the Indian's part in the production of a particular narrated auto-biography, but he invents "an Indian" as a way to make sense of this individual. He identifies anything nonrecognizable or unfamiliar in a narrated American Indian autobiography, such as the presentation of seemingly disconnected deeds or actions, as authentic, as Indian as opposed to Euro-American. From this identification he deduces a tribal (Indian, nonliterate, unacculturated, ahistorical) sense of self distinguishable from an individual (Euro-American, literate, cultured, historical) sense of self. Brumble concludes that Gregorio's sense of self in *Gregorio, The Hand Trembler* "was essentially tribal": "[For Red Crow, like Gregorio] we search in vain for any examination of his self, any self-definition, any sense that he might have been other than he was. . . . We are allowed to see clearly just how a preliterate, unacculturated, tribal man conceives of his life and what it means to tell the story of a life" (101–11). The reality of the situation is that the self which is identifiable as Indian, and has come to signify Indian in the text, is Indian in contact with non-Indian. As Brumble points out, Gregorio listened while Alexander and Dorothea Leighton interviewed other Navajos in his neighborhood before he told them his story in 1940 (111). Gregorio probably ordered and presented an account of his life in a way he thought appropriate given the circumstances; he probably talked about things he figured the Leightons wanted to hear and that he had heard other Indians discussing with the Leightons. Seemingly disconnected deeds or actions are likely to indicate Gregorio's unease with the genre and circumstances rather than his inability to examine and define his self. Of course Brumble was looking for the ways Gregorio, as he is presented textually, fit Brumble's definition of "Indian," and he did not consider the ways Gregorio and the situation of the text's making may have qualified that definition.

In *American Indian Women: Telling Their Lives,* Gretchen Bataille and Kathleen Sands examine "several autobiographies in terms of what they tell us about the reality of American Indian women's lives" (viii). They propose a "close examination of individual texts . . . to discern the thematic patterns [of tradition and culture contact, acculturation, and return to tradition]" (24). But Bataille and Sands seem to forget that these themes or thematic patterns not only may have been invented by them for the texts and understood in terms of their particular interests (and their lives as non-Indian women), but also may emerge in the written documents as a result of the particular interests of the recorder-editors. Bataille and Sands never question how their themes may or may not be relevant from the point of view of the Indian women narrators.[9]

Just as Brumble invents an "Indian self," so Bataille and Sands use themes and interests to frame or make sense of the Indian. The Indian has no voice of his or her own; the Indian is not considered in terms of his or her history, culture, and language. Krupat, Brumble, Bataille and Sands have all thus essentially positioned themselves so that questions of Indian history, culture, and language cannot inform their work. If Krupat, for example, in his encounter with *Geronimo's Story of His Life,* had in fact considered Apache history, culture, and language, particularly as presented by Apache Indians orally or otherwise, he might have seen himself as present and gained a broader understanding of the text. He would have had to ask, or at least he would have had the opportunity to ask, questions that might have reminded him of his presence and bias. Can Apache stories, songs, and so forth be read or heard and thus understood in terms of Euro-American-specific expectations of language and narrative? If not, why not? What is gained or lost when they are? What from Krupat's perspective or an Apache perspective hinders Krupat's understanding of Geronimo? What might help Krupat understand? How might answers to these questions promote a better understanding of Barrett, or of that history, culture, and language in *Geronimo's Story of His Life* which may have seemed more familiar to Krupat? If Krupat knew more about himself as a reader and more about Geronimo, he might have been able to ask more questions about his reading of Barrett and so to see Barrett in new ways. Likewise, the Indian narrator's background might have helped Brumble and Bataille and Sands open a broader understanding of themselves and the texts they read. They might have seen the limits and consequences of their inventions and themes in their attempts to understand the Indian narrators. In any event, what all these scholars do not seem to see is that while purportedly defending Indians and enlightening others about them, they replicate in practice that which characterizes not only certain non-Indian editors' manner of dealing with Indians but also that of an entire European and Euro-American populace of which these editors and scholars are a part. The Indians are absent or they are strategically removed from the territory, made safe, intelligible on the colonizer's terms.

9. Not all of the Indian women's autobiographies that Bataille and Sands discuss are narrated. Bataille and Sands provide lengthy discussions of Maria Campbell's *Halfbreed* and other autobiographies written by Indian women. Here my comments pertain only to their discussions of narrated autobiographies.

The questions and issues raised in terms of these scholars' work should not be thought of as simply insider/outsider problems. It is important to note that, regardless of the reader's cultural and historical affiliations, he or she is not a perfect lens into the life and circumstances of either the non-Indian recorder-editor or the Indian narrator. A non-Indian scholar using a historical approach, for example, to understand a non-Indian recorder-editor's historical and cultural influences, may be unfamiliar with or unaware of the recorder-editor's community, place, and time and of how these affect what has been recorded and how the recorded material has been edited. S. M. Barrett worked at a time before Krupat was born. Differing subjectivities are at play within any tradition. An Indian, either as a scholar working in the university or as a nonuniversity tribal scholar working as a consultant for a non-Indian's scholarly enterprise, is not an objective purveyor of the so-called truths of his or her culture. This is certainly the case among the Pomo, where what constitutes, among other things, authentic cultural and religious practices can vary in definition from group to group and even from family to family within a group. And what an Indian knows from his or her tribe may not apply to other tribes. In terms of their histories, cultures, and languages Indian people are different, sometimes radically different, from tribe to tribe.

In any narrated American Indian autobiography there are at least two parties present. And, just as in my own reading of *Autobiographies,* readers cannot assume knowledge and power to know and represent others and their relationship to a text. If a reader is knowledgeable about a given historical period or a particular collaborator's culture, questions still remain regarding what constitutes the reader's knowing. Specifically, how does the reader understand and use his or her own knowledge to frame or make sense of elements in a text? For the presence of both a non-Indian and a Pomo Indian in the single text provokes those questions. Who am I as a reader? Indian? Non-Indian? Scholar? How do I position myself and what are the consequences of that positioning? For many non-Indian readers questions might arise as a result of their encounters with the Indian narrator's culture and language. Whatever it is, wherever the tensions are felt, is a place to start, a place for readers to open dialogue with both the non-Indian recorder-editor and the Indian narrator in a text. It is a place to see the questions that arise from the tension, and ultimately a place where the reader can begin to explore the questions and possible answers. The dialogue that starts in one place opens the text and the readers' stories of their relationships with the text, stories that, in turn, inform other readers' stories, continually opening and exploring the *original bicultural composition* at hand.

So much of what we do as readers of texts is unconscious. We aren't aware of all the cultural and personal influences that determine how we read; we aren't aware of our self-boundaries and how we work to tighten or widen them in our encounters with texts. In the approach I have described the reader can begin to unravel what may be unspoken and unconscious in the making of a bicultural text as well as what may be unspoken and unconscious in the reader's reading, in this case of a text put together by two culturally diverse individuals. Readers can understand their encounter with the text as an instance of culture contact, where, as Gabriele Schwab notes, "[the reading] would not only consider our individual acts of reading as a form of culture contact, but also the processes by which we are socialized into our own reading habits. It could stress the social powers that control our reading inducing us to reduce the text's otherness as much as it could stress the subversive powers of the text that reside in its otherness" (112).[10] As Schwab suggests, the task is not to assimilate the text or any element of it to ourselves nor to assimilate ourselves to the text. It is not to reduce difference to sameness nor to exoticize or fetishize it. Rather, the task is to become aware of our tendencies to do any of these things. Maintaining a dialogue that works to validate and respect the subjectivities of text and reader is a way to accomplish the task (Schwab 107–36). In terms of narrated American Indian autobiography, beginning and maintaining that kind of dialogue makes for a way to begin to understand the interrelations between cultures within a text and, hence, between the reader and those interrelations within a text of which the reader has become a part.

It seems that I have been in the middle of Pomo and white interrelations for as long as I can remember. As I have said, my life is made visible in a glance, the way someone is looking at me, and in the sound of a voice. It is made visible with stories, too.

Insider. Outsider. Indian. White.

Of course in many cases I am self-conscious, projecting my own

10. Here Schwab uses the term *culture contact* in the widest sense possible. She cites Gregory Bateson, who said: "I suggest that we should consider under the head of 'culture contact' not only those cases in which the contact occurs between two communities with different cultures . . . but also . . . in cases within a single community. . . . I would even extend the idea of 'contact' so widely as to include those processes whereby a child is molded and trained to fit the culture into which he was born" (64).

insecurity. Great-Grandma Nettie's story about the stranger who came
to her home may not have had anything to do with me. My insecurity
and fear might have shaped the way I heard her voice and understood her
glances that night. Certainly Colson and the three Pomo women did not
have me in mind in their meeting together during the summers of 1939,
1940, and 1941. But *Autobiographies,* like Great-Grandma Nettie's
story, provokes the same insecurities, the same tension. It is the glance,
the sound of a voice again. It is the face looking through the front room
window. I want to fit in. I want to belong. I don't want to be told I am a
stranger.

When I was fourteen, a mixed-blood Indian named Robert taught me
to box. Actually, it was Robert and another guy named Manuel, who
was Portuguese. Robert was part Portuguese. People whispered that both
of them were really black. They were a few years older than me and the
roughest guys in town. They said I had what it took to be a good fighter.
"Hate in your eyes, brother," they said. "You got hate in your eyes." By
the time I was sixteen I beat the hell out of people every chance I could,
mostly white people. In the city park I beat the hell out of a white boy just
because I didn't like the way he was looking at me. Not many Indians I
knew liked and trusted whites. I was a good Indian then. Any Indian
could see I was.

Rejection. Distrust. Anger. Hatred.

These things seem to characterize so much of the history of Pomo and
white interrelations. Again, think of the Spanish invasion, the missions.
Think of the slave raiding. Think of the land theft. On and on. Think of
the Indian resistance, the Bole Maru. The infanticide of mixed-blood
children by certain Pomo tribes continued even as the same tribes attended Christian churches and listened to the sermons of Catholic and
Protestant clergy who provided the Indians food and shelter. The Indians
feigned Christianity, and the clergy and surrounding white community
thought they finally had converted and civilized the Indians. The Indians
attended separate "Indian" churches; they remained Indians, separate
from and not equal to the whites, but understandable, or seemingly
understandable, on the whites' terms.

Old patterns of domination, subjugation, and exclusion by whites
continue, albeit in different and sometimes more subtle configurations.
And the Indians continue to react. My father was heralded by his high
school as one of its most valuable and cherished athletes. Yet when he
went to date the town fathers' daughters, the wealthy white girls, he was
told at the door, "Sorry chief, we aren't hiring any gardeners. Get lost."

My father got five of those white girls pregnant. My mother was one of them.

My father became a professional boxer. In the Navy, where he started boxing, he was undefeated. His friends say he knocked down Floyd Patterson. When my father fought, he went crazy, his friends say. You could see it coming in his eyes. The same as when he drank.

My father married three times. Three white women. Two of them told me he beat them. He died of a massive heart attack at fifty-two, after years of chronic alcoholism.

A cousin told me that my father's mother, my grandmother, used to tell my father to "stay away from those white girls. You'll get in trouble and they'll have your ass strung up on a pole. They're like that."

My mother died ten days after she had me. She was sixteen. My father was twenty-one at the time and married to his first wife. My mother and father had been seeing one another for three years, since she was thirteen and he was eighteen. She never breathed a word, never said who the father of her baby was. She could have had his ass strung up on a pole.

"Don't marry no white woman," my cousin says to me. "Look, it was your father's downfall." Every time my cousin sees me she admonishes, "Them whites are no good. White women are whores."

Rejection. Distrust. Anger. Hatred.

This history is not just mine. It is not just my story. It informs *Autobiographies*. It informs the world in which Elizabeth Colson found herself the moment she stepped out of her car, or off the train, on that summer day in 1939. It was there, in Mendocino County, and she became a part of it. *Autobiographies* can say something about this history. It can tell a story.

From the three Pomo women and from other sources, Colson learned that "the Pomo had a generalized hatred of whites and that they resent Pomo treatment at the hands of whites and feel them the source of much of their discomfort" (222). But what Colson could have known about this history, and how well she could have understood what she learned, depended on who she was at the time of her meeting with the three Pomo narrators. Here Colson's abundant commentary—her introductory material, overview of Pomo culture and history, analysis of the autobiographies—is useful, for in it she reveals, often inadvertently, much about herself at the time she stepped into that world of the three Pomo women. Yet, as mentioned a while back, as I begin to consider the text here, specifically in terms of what Colson reveals about herself and her background and her editing of the narratives, I must at the same time consider the narrators as Pomo speakers and thinkers. And, again, only in that way can a broader picture of the relationship between Colson and the Pomo narrators and of the making of their collaborative text be discerned. Only in that way can *Autobiographies* illuminate its history, my history, and tell a story.

It is important to remember that Colson was an anthropologist in a given time and place, which of course had much to do with how she thought and positioned herself in the Pomo community and, subsequently, with what she did or did not see about herself and the Pomo women. As Colson notes in her introductory material, the autobiographies "were gathered during the summers of 1939, 1940, and 1941, when [Colson] was a member of the Social Science Field Laboratory under the direction of B. W. and E. G. Aginsky" (2). Specifically, she was interested in issues of acculturation and wanted to gain "insight into the life of Pomo women of a particular generation" (1). She worked at a time when the field of anthropology had become increasingly enmeshed with neighboring sciences, particularly psychology. Still, this newer anthropology, like its Boasian forerunner, maintained the split between fact and interpretation. When Colson writes that "this paper is the presentation and analysis of the life histories of the three Pomo women" (1), she is apparently assuming that what is presented as actual life history, whether in a given narrator's long or brief account (remember, Colson provides a long as well as a brief autobiographical account for each narrator), is different from the analysis of the life history, in that the accounts are presented to the reader as artifacts independent of Colson's interpretation, that is, of her editing of the narratives. She is likely assuming that her editing of the presentations has not affected them as "pure products" (Clifford 1988), as mirrors that reflect the Pomo women's lived lives.

What Colson notes about her transcriptions of the Pomo women's narratives makes questionable the extent she presents facts or pure products. She says: "An attempt has been made to make the English more grammatical and at the same time to preserve some of the terms of speech which give the flavor of the original. Connectives have been placed where no connectives existed; identities have been made a little more secure by such devices as substituting the appropriate gender of pronouns; and occasionally whole sentences have been inverted and knocked into a more 'English' shape" (9). As Colson observes, the three Pomo women "speak habitually and think in this language" (1), and while the interviews were conducted in English, the Pomo English that Colson edited undoubtedly has features typical of, or associated with, the mother language. To see what Colson might have edited here, or to see what was at stake in terms of a "pure product," it is important to explore, if only briefly, features of the mother language that may have influenced the shape of the narrators' English.

In *Kashaya Texts* Robert Oswalt notes that Kashaya Pomo, which, again, is grammatically similar to the women narrators' central Pomo, "has no articles and, although it does have a pronoun for 'he,' 'she,' and 'they,' such reference is customarily accomplished by verbal suffixes indicating the relative timing of the actions of the two verbs and whether there is a switch or combination of agent between the verbs. |ba|, for example, signifies that the verb to which it is attached is subordinated in an adverbial way to the main verb in time, and that both have the same agent" (18). It is no wonder then that English speakers who "speak Pomo habitually and think in this language" would have trouble with connectives and articles, and Colson's adding connectives or appropriate genders of pronouns would not necessarily affect the meaning or sense of the text as the narrators presented it.

But what might have happened when Colson "inverted and knocked whole sentences into a more 'English' shape"? Again Oswalt notes "a common feature of Kashaya Pomo narrative style . . . is the verb repeated in successive sentences with only one small new piece of information: He ran off. Having run off, he ran along. He ran like that. He arrived running" (19). In his translation Oswalt presents the pronoun "he" not only as the subject of the sentences but also as the salient feature of the sentences and indeed of the entire passage. Yet Oswalt infers—and is correct—in his study of Kashaya grammar that the salient feature of the language is the verb. *Action*, and not *subject*, is thematized in Kashaya Pomo. The subject of a Kashaya sentence, whether a pronoun or not, is characteristically suffixed to, and subordinate to, the verb. The verb |*mensi*| ("to do so") often begins the second sentence (i.e., of a narrative) and serves only as a carrier for the suffix (Oswalt 19), thus further stressing the action. Note the same passage Oswalt refers to in a more literal translation:[11]

---

11. I am grateful to my aunt, Violet Chappell, for her help with the literal translation. Here I am assuming, quite arbitrarily, that Pomo—or any traditionally non-written oral language—can be textualized as such. As Paul J. Hopper remarks, "Discourse with languages outside the Western tradition can only be fitted with great difficulty and obvious artificiality into Western-style written sentences" (19). Even this "more literal translation" was difficult.

mobe		*mensiba*		*mobe*		*menmobe*	
run off		having run off he		run off		like that run off	

mensiba		*bele*		*mo*
having run off he		come		here

While Pomo English speakers of the generation Colson interviewed—
those Pomo born during the latter part of the nineteenth century—
cannot replicate Pomo syntax in English, they often attempt, intentionally or otherwise, to thematize action when speaking English. You
might hear something like: Run off, way off, he did. Running like that.
Running till he come here. Kathy O'Connor, a linguist who studied
central and north central Pomo languages, notes that here too the verb is
the salient feature of the language as it is in Kashaya Pomo. Again, the
languages are similar grammatically and sound somewhat alike. (The
Kashaya are the southwestern tribe of Pomo located approximately sixty
miles west and south of the central Pomo tribes.) O'Connor suggests,
however, that the central and north central Pomo speakers do not seem
to use the verb |*mensi*| ("to do so") as often as the Kashaya Pomo. Still,
we can look back at Great-Grandma Nettie's central Pomo English as I
remember it and see again how she repeated verbs in successive sentences
and worked to thematize action, at least in terms of the topical features
of her English. This must have had much to do with her dominant central
Pomo language. Now examine the following passage from an autobiography of one of the central Pomo narrators Colson talked with. The
narrator, Sophie Martinez, was from the same generation and general
locale as Nettie.

> Those boys made that thing. They were singing, singing, singing; and they
> were making some kind of feather basket with red feathers. They put it on the
> top of their heads and they put a fish tail on it. Just like a fish they made it.
> Then they put marks on something on it, and they put it in the water. It was
> finished. They sang as they put in the water. It floated around there, and they
> called it back again.
>
> (51)

The copious use of verbs is apparent. But imagine a text where the verb,
or action, is thematized:

> Singing, singing, singing, making thing, them boys. Singing and same time
> putting red feathers on. Singing and putting red feathers. Making thing with
> fish tail on, them boys. They putting mark on later time. Putting mark, like
> that. Then singing more and putting in water. Putting fish tail thing in water.

Putting so floating around there. Then calling back, them boys. Calling back
later time. Calling back like that.

Of course the passage quoted from *Autobiographies* may be quite
close to the way it was presented by Sophie Martinez. Perhaps Martinez
and the other Pomo narrators spoke a more "standard" English than
Great-Grandma Nettie. Perhaps they altered their English for Colson in
a way they thought suitable for her, more in line with Colson's English.
Unfortunately, there is no way of knowing. For, as Colson claims, she
"no longer [has] any of the field notes used in preparing the accounts" (i).
Yet Colson does say that "occasionally whole sentences have been inverted and knocked into a more 'English' shape." It is clear here that she
edited the narrators' English, but it is not clear how often or to what
extent. What does Colson mean by "occasionally"? Again, there is no
way of knowing since there is no record of the narratives as they were
presented by the narrators. But in light of my cursory study of Pomo
linguistics and my experience with Pomo elders from the same generation as these Pomo narrators, it seems that when Colson "inverted" and
"knocked" she is likely to have masked the narrators' efforts to stress
action in a subject-oriented language. Or, if the narrators were not
stressing action but adjusting their Pomo English for Colson, then what
Colson was likely to have edited was the narrators' slips, or lapses, into
their Pomo English. Even if the narrators regularly used an English close
to what we find in Colson's transcription, Colson probably edited slips,
or lapses, that revealed a Pomo English. Undoubtedly, there is more here
to talk about than the thematization of action or subject; undoubtedly, I
have ignored many other factors regarding the narrators' grammar and
Colson's transcription of it that may have affected the presentations as
we see them. Suffice it to say that Colson's editing altered, perhaps in
significant ways, the text's purity as a product of "Pomo women of a
particular generation."

It is important to note here that linguistic features thematized in a
language do not necessarily represent how the speaker thinks, or conceives, of his or her world. As Chester C. Christian, Jr. observes, "It is
futile to create a science either of culture or of language through the use
of language characteristics of any given culture" (149). Further, he cites
in a footnote M. Edgarton, Jr. whose work he suggests "implies not only
the limitations of language as an instrument of science, but also the
persistence of culture and the relation of language to culture" (155).
Violet Chappell, a fluent speaker of Kashaya Pomo, says: "Yeah, us

people of the [Kashaya] language think different, like our language is different [from English]. But it's more to it than just that." To suggest that linguistic features alone reveal how the narrators truly conceive of their world is to ignore the complex relation of language to culture and history and, consequently, important cultural issues related to the collaborative endeavor in question. To begin to understand the complex relation of language to culture and history, it is imperative that scholars and other readers have an accurate sense of the speaker's language.[12] If Colson or her readers take the Pomo narrators' textualized narratives as virtually pure presentations, or representations of those presentations, unaffected by Colson's editing, an understanding of that relation of language to culture and history is lacking. It seems ironic, given Colson's interest in issues of acculturation, that she doesn't consider seriously the relation of the women's Pomo English to their Pomo language and culture and history. If she had, might her readers have found a different text, a different English used by the Pomo women?

Colson has not just edited the narrators' grammar, but also certain features of their narrative formats, which again raises questions regarding the "factual" state of the presentations. Colson mentions in her introductory material that "in presenting the data, [she] has attempted to arrange them in chronological order, which has meant in general the sacrifice of the sequence of thought of the informant. The accounts given in the interviews have been cut and chopped to fit into the procrustean bed of chronological sequence. Also where several accounts of the same event are available, these have been combined and worked into one running description" (9). Older Pomo narrators, like speakers from many other traditionally oral cultures, move back and forth in time and place to use the past to comment on the present and vice versa. When Mabel McKay tells me stories she moves in and out of given time frames. She might be talking about a man she knows and then in the next moment begin talking about her great-grandmother and then shift back to the man. For Mabel there is probably a clear connection between these time frames and the players in them, a connection I often do not readily discern and that only becomes intelligible to me in subsequent

12. I am not implying here that it is always possible to have an exact transcription of a speaker's narrative. An exact transcription might not only be impossible given the limits of syntax, punctuation, and so forth, but might prove unreadable to many audiences. Rather, by an "accurate sense" I mean an idea about what might have been lost or gained in the transcription and editing of the speaker's spoken words. In a very short space I have attempted here to provide an "accurate sense" of features of Pomo and types of Pomo English.

conversations and personal reflections or not at all. Speakers from traditionally oral cultures are not the only ones who repeat stories and details or disrupt "the procrustean bed of chronological sequence." Imagine editing Faulkner's *Go Down, Moses, The Sound and the Fury,* or *Absalom, Absalom!* to fit into this bed and how such editing would affect meaning as Faulkner understood and intended it.

A Pomo narrator's mere mention of a place or name can work to set the scene or to thematize action in a story. The narrator might, for example, mention a taboo mountain which will color events in a narrative in given ways for a Pomo listener familiar with the lore associated with the particular mountain.[13] The narrator will often repeat things— the name of a place or person, certain anecdotes—to underscore a theme or idea. The name of the taboo mountain, or an anecdote associated with it, might be repeated over and over again by the narrator to achieve a certain effect or response from the listener. Or the narrator may repeat the name or anecdote simply because it is integral in some way to the story as the narrator understands and remembers it for himself or herself. I remember that Great-Grandma Nettie kept repeating her age when she told the story that winter night in Santa Rosa. She might have been reminding herself and Old Auntie Eleanor of how young she was at the time and how she nonetheless knew to behave in given ways around strangers. Or she may have had other reasons for repeating her age. She may have had many reasons. I don't know. But to edit out, or to "combine and work into one running description," Nettie's repetitions of her age or anything else is to overlook and make unavailable for readers these possibilities in Nettie's narrative.

In rereading my version of Sophie Martinez's passage, I note that I mention "red feathers" twice. In Colson's edited presentation of this narration, Martinez, as I also note, mentions "red feathers" only once. For many Pomo the color red is associated with human blood, with evil, and is, hence, taboo. Red feathers—the red feathers of a woodpecker's

13. Again, Renato Rosaldo illustrated with Ilongot storytelling how "people whose biographies significantly overlap can communicate rich understandings in telegraphic form. People who share a complex knowledge about their worlds can assume a common background and speak through allusion" (107). As noted in Chapter 1, Keith Basso observes that among the Western Apache "geographical features have served for centuries as mnemonic pegs on which to hang the moral teachings of their history" (44) and that "narrative events are 'spatially anchored' at points on the land, and the evocative pictures presented by the Western Apache place-names become indispensable resources for the storyteller's craft" (32). This familiarity with place is not unusual for a community that has shared over millennia the same landscape and various stories associated with the landscape, and often accounts for the paucity of description and human motivation typically found in the literature from such a community.

topknot—are used in "sun baskets," baskets made for the purpose of poisoning people. Perhaps as a Pomo scholar I inadvertently repeated "red feathers" because of my own associations with them and the color red. Interestingly enough this passage was excerpted from a story about how a lake became taboo. Might Martinez also have repeated "red feathers" more than once? Again, there is no way of knowing.

Colson says, "since condensing many accounts into one leaves the reader with no indication as to the common motives or particular interests of the informant, the recurrence of themes or an eagerness to repeat a given event will be indicated in a footnote or dealt with in the final analysis" (9). Naturally, it is impossible for Colson, who spent only three summers in the central Pomo community, to fully comprehend the significance for the narrators of certain places, names, or anecdotes that are repeated, unless perhaps Colson asked about the repetitions. But the reader cannot tell from anything Colson says in her introductory material and analysis or from the questions she poses (and inserts) in the narratives whether she asked about the repetitions.[14] All that can be known is that Colson made the decisions as to what constituted a "common theme" or a "recurrence of theme," and, as with the issues of grammar, Colson's biases are likely to have influenced her decisions.

Colson does mention that she is "fully aware of the disadvantage involved in thus extensively editing life history materials, especially in the drastic revisions necessary to humor the historical bias of our own culture" (9). And she concludes that she has "attempted to compromise somewhere halfway between the popularized life history and the truly scientific account" (10). If this is an admission regarding the extent the presentations are in fact interpretations and that she is present in the autobiographical accounts as an editor, then it is eclipsed by her additional material, particularly her brief ethnography of Pomo culture "both past and present" (2), without which, in Colson's words, "the life histories lose much of their point" (2). This overview frames the narratives in given ways and works to maintain that split between fact and interpretation, as if the ethnography were a key that unlocks the raw presentations. Readers are provided an ethnography written by Colson that describes

14. Colson does mention repetitions in her footnotes, but does not indicate whether she asked specific questions regarding the meaning of the repetitions for the narrators. She merely compares details and attempts to draw her own conclusions about the significance of the repetitions. She writes, for example: "SM repeated this incident several times, and was always interested in speaking of it. Twice this account was substantially the way it is here. Once it was an abbreviated version which differed only in the omission of certain details . . ." (88).

pre-contact and post-contact Pomo against which her readers can measure or place the women's "unedited" lives and see the extent to which the women are acculturated. The underlying assumption is that the ethnography is objective, a clear record of Pomo lifeways, just as the women's narratives are clear records of their lived lives. Both are presented as if Colson is fundamentally absent.

Colson's mention of her editing of the narratives' format may refer to her work on the longer autobiographical accounts, since she notes that the brief autobiographical accounts she provides for each narrator are "verbatim" (2), as opposed to the longer ones where she asked the narrator questions to have them enlarge on certain points and where she presented the material in chronological order. But given the issues of grammar discussed above, one wonders how verbatim even the brief autobiographical accounts are. Sophie Martinez, for whom "speaking in English was probably an effort" (Colson 6), uses the same English in both her long and brief narratives. Despite David H. Brumble's observation that "no interpreters were used" (*An Annotated Bibliography* 11), Colson notes that "on one occasion [Sophie Martinez] asked [her granddaughter] to act as an interpreter" (Colson 6). Colson continues: "The greatest amount of editing has been done on the account of Mrs. Martinez. That of Mrs. Wood and that of Mrs. Adams stand substantially in the language in which they were given" (9). Interestingly enough, the English of Wood and Adams, in both their long and their brief accounts, is largely indistinguishable from that of Martinez.[15] Is this mere coincidence? Did Colson shape Martinez's English to look like that of Wood and Adams?

It is important to note that Colson influenced the direction of the "spontaneous" (5), brief autobiographical accounts, even if it was merely to suggest that Sophie Martinez "start when she could first remember and tell as much as she could remember about her life" (4). With Ellen Wood, Colson asked specific questions (i.e., "What did children about that age do when you were young?") in several interviews before asking for a life history (4). Colson says, "The spontaneous, unquestioned, life history had already been obtained [by another fieldworker] from Mrs. Adams" (5). It is not clear then how spontaneous or unquestioned Mrs. Adams's

15. Martinez's English appears slightly more polished in terms of subject-verb agreement and so forth, which must be due to the great amount of editing Colson did of Martinez's accounts. This makes Martinez's unedited speech patterns all the more curious as a "pure text," since she was, of the three narrators, the least comfortable with English, according to Colson. Again, there is no way to see Martinez's unedited speech since Colson "no longer [has] any of the field notes used in preparing the accounts."

account is since Colson either did not know or does not mention whether the fieldworker asked any questions of Mrs. Adams or gave her any suggestions regarding what to talk about. But given the suggestion Colson gave Martinez and the questions Colson asked Wood, how can the autobiographical accounts of Martinez and Wood be considered "spontaneous, unquestioned"?

Thus far I have talked only about language and narrative format, specifically about the ways Colson's editing may have affected the texts as mirrors in which Colson and her readers can see reflected the Pomo women's lives. It might be assumed that if Colson had left the women's narratives alone, if she had transcribed them exactly as they were spoken (if that were even possible), we might in fact have "pure products." But, as Vincent Crapanzano pointed out, the spoken text is not only edited by the recorder-editor in the literary reencounter with the recorded text, but it is also edited by the narrator as she is speaking for the recorder-editor. Just as Colson edited what she recorded, so the three Pomo women are likely to have edited *what* they told Colson. Perhaps Sophie Martinez did not repeat "red feathers" on purpose because she was talking to Colson. The point is that Colson's presence in the Pomo community surely positioned the narrators as speakers (and Colson as a recorder-editor) in certain ways. Even though an autobiographical account seemed spontaneous to Colson, it was nevertheless most probably being edited by the Pomo narrator in telling it to Colson.

Although Colson learned from the three Pomo women and from other sources that "the Pomo had a generalized hatred of whites and that they resent Pomo treatment at the hands of whites and feel them the source of much of their discomfort" (222), she claims her relationship with these women was good because she and other members of the Field Laboratory treated them "as equals" (8) and because she was "someone who was fairly neutral and who made no attempt to judge them" (8). The question remains whether these Pomo women treated Colson as an equal, or as one of them, that is, a nonwhite insider. Given Colson's appearance and her education, her obvious membership in the dominant white culture, and given the Pomo Indians' "generalized hatred of whites," it is unlikely that the three narrators saw Colson as one of them. And it must be remembered that these particular narrators grew up at a time when the revivalistic Bole Maru movement which preached Indian nationalism and isolationism was at its peak among the Pomo. Speaking or interacting unnecessarily with non-Indians was viewed by the Bole Maru advocates as sinful, as compromising the movement's resistance to white cultural and religious domination. To speak with a white person was to speak with the devil. As an Indian, you exercised extreme caution. You never said any more to a white person than you had to.

The Pomo I know are generally very private, not given to open exchange with outsiders, particularly about personal and religious matters. From what I have been told by my Pomo elders, this reserve was characteristic even before contact with the European invaders. People from one village were cautious and respectful of those from another village, even a village just across the creek or at the other end of the same valley. Furthermore, telling stories and long tales during the summer months—when Colson did all her interviewing—was considered taboo. Many elders still follow this ancient rule, insisting that they will speak of stories and such things only in winter. "[The ground] got to be clear of snakes, crawling lizards," Old Auntie Eleanor used to say. Mabel McKay said: "If you think about them things [tales and stories] during summer, you going to step on lizard, snake, or something. Not watching where you are going. Don't talk about to nobody then." So by approaching these women during the summer months, Colson may have invaded their privacy and asked them to break taboo. Colson notes how Sophie Martinez "would suddenly switch [topics of conversation] to a description of basket types or of food before [Colson] had realized that someone was approaching" (6). She received "some material regarding the women by other informants" (9), largely about topics the women did not discuss, such as one woman's involvement in a religious cult (99). In changing the topic of conversation and in omitting information about their lives, it is clear the narrators edited their material for Colson.

The fact still remains that the Pomo women were willing to talk to Colson and to tell her stories. Certainly money had much to do with the women's willingness to speak. Colson relates that "almost every informant at some point argued that [twenty-five cents an hour] was insufficient and that they had been advised by other Pomo not to work unless they were paid more" (7). These Pomo women interacted with Colson at a time when virtually every Pomo community had had over thirty years of experience with ethnographers and others who were interested in various aspects of Pomo culture and willing to pay for information and material goods. Ethnographer S. A. Barrett had worked with the northern, central, and eastern groups of Pomo as early as 1906. Pomo women had been selling and trading their baskets to whites since the 1870s. Clearly, the Pomo saw in these interested whites the opportunity to make money, which they usually desperately needed. From what Colson notes about the narrators' mention of money, it seems these three Pomo women too saw the opportunity to make money, in this case by working with Colson.

Of course money does not guarantee unedited information. I have watched Pomo informants, as they have been called, make an art of editing what they tell "them scientists." One Pomo woman calls it "giving-them-a-piece work." She says: "I give them pieces of this and that. I tell them a few things. Even things we shouldn't talk about [to non-Indians]. They never get the whole picture, not with just pieces of this and that. Besides, they make up what they want anyway. They tell their own stories about whatever I tell them." Another Pomo elder refers to her experience with anthropologists as "money-storytelling-time." Speakers will often compare notes about their stories for anthropologists, and these discussions are full of raucous laughter. The so-called informants I know come from a long tradition of "giving-them-a-piece work" and "money-storytelling-time." At the time the three Pomo narrators worked with Colson, this tradition was probably already over thirty years old and had been in existence for as long as Pomo speakers had been talking to anthropologists and other whites interested in learning about Pomo culture.

This is not to suggest that the three Pomo women were lying to Colson or that they were editing their accounts in the manner of these Pomo speakers just described. Sophie Martinez, Ellen Wood, and Jane Adams talked to Colson about some of the same things I remember hearing Great-Grandma Nettie and Old Auntie Eleanor talk about, but Nettie and Eleanor were more guarded about some of these same things. When the professors visited each summer and asked about "charms" and "poisoning," Old Auntie Eleanor told stories no one in the house had ever heard. She certainly did not talk to the professors about these things in terms of people she knew or in reference to members of her own family, whereas the three Pomo narrators did talk about these things and often in terms of people they knew or in reference to their own families. Sophie Martinez, for example, related the following about a snake charm:

> My father's wife tried to get a baby that time. Some of them who want a baby would catch a bull snake. They catch it alive and put it around the woman's waist. I couldn't stand that bull snake around my body, but I saw them do that. She was crying and afraid of the bull snake. My grandfather did that [to her father's wife].
>
> (Colson 43)

Colson notes Martinez also mentions "ten deaths in her immediate family which she ascribes to poisoning" (223).

Given what these narrators did say, the question arises again regarding what motivated these women to work with Colson. Surely there may have been factors besides monetary payment. Perhaps the Pomo women saw in a recorded and written record of their lives the opportunity to clear up community rumors about them, to set the record straight about their lives and their families. Maybe in talking about the deaths of her family members Martinez saw the opportunity to convey her grief or view of what happened to others. In talking about her Dreams Ellen Wood might have been using her conversation with Colson to convey to others her power as a Pomo Dreamer. Perhaps these narrators wanted to show other Indians in their community that in talking to Colson and earning money they could talk about certain "private" matters without giving away valuable tribal information. Perhaps they had their individual versions of "giving-them-a-piece work." Any combination of these possibilities and others I have not thought of or mentioned may have motivated the narrators to work with Colson.

Today a number of Pomo elders want to record life histories, songs, and tribal stories. Often they want a written record for the younger generations. They take pride in working with anthropologists, since in many ways the anthropologists' presence in their homes signals to others the elders' knowledge of tribal history and culture. I doubt, however, that the three Pomo narrators worked with Colson to pass down tribal information or to demonstrate to others how knowledgeable they were about their history or culture. They grew up at a time when talking about these things to outsiders was taboo, and apparently these narrators were still guarded about many subjects they discussed with Colson, particularly in front of other Indians. I have heard a rumor more than once about Colson having been forced by the narrators to change names and place-names because the narrators did not like what Colson had written. A Pomo elder told me: "One of them ladies [narrators] said to that white lady she was going to have her done in. Killed. Poison Indian way. Fix her for writing them things. She say to that white lady 'you better change my name, not say where this place is.' " Did one of the narrators talk about certain things and then change her mind about having them printed? Was she bending under community pressure? Was it a way for her to get paid and still be safe or unaccountable for anything she should not have talked about?

We can only conjecture at this point about what motivated the Pomo women to work with Colson, about how the women edited their life stories for Colson, and about the kind of English they spoke. More should be said, particularly from a Pomo perspective, about the intersecting cultures and histories of Colson and the Pomo women and the contingencies of exchange as they have affected the production of the autobiographical narratives. More stories should be told, not to figure out the story or truth of the collaborators' relationship and the making of their composite text but to further explore linguistic and cultural factors as they may have affected the collaborators' work. More should be said from a Pomo woman's perspective about the relations between white women and Indian women in the central Pomo region. White women in one town in the central Pomo region passed an ordinance near the turn of the century forbidding the hiring of Indian women as domestics. This ordinance came after the Pomo women had been working in the same white households for nearly two decades and it expressed the white women's concern about the half-breed children of the domestic help. This story is told among Indian women today, and from what my cousin said to me about white women and my father, it seems that some Pomo women still do not particularly care for white women. However, the ways in which I can understand my cousin's remark and her anger are limited, since what I can know and understand culturally and historically about the relations between Indian women and white women is shaped in gender-specific ways. Pomo women and white women and women who are both Pomo and white and women who are neither Pomo nor white can tell stories and open the text in ways I cannot, in ways that are relevant to them and that inform my own story of and relationship with the text.

My discussion of Colson and the Pomo women serves only to suggest possible factors and scenarios that may have been at work as Colson and the Pomo women made *Autobiographies*. It shows what may have constituted fundamental differences in language and culture between Colson and the Pomo narrators that may have affected how they understood their own and each other's lives and how they were able to communicate. Of course the history of interrelations between these cultures that is associated with these differences also affects interaction between members of the respective cultures. In short, it is clear that Colson's presence as a recorder in the Pomo women's community and her work as an editor of the women's spoken texts have affected the content, language, and shape of the women's texts that are presented in *Autobiographies* and consequently the pictures readers get of the Pomo women's lives. These pictures do not simply mirror the women's lives as the narrators see and understand them. They are not pictures the women might have drawn in other situations and for other listeners. Rather the pictures here are composite ones, which again is the case for any narrated American Indian autobiography.

Anthropology, like other social sciences at Colson's time, stipulated that the social scientist could and should be objective, that the social scientist's presence, including culture-specific biases, could and should be put aside, transcended during the "scientific" undertaking. It becomes understandable, then, why Colson positioned herself as absent from her work, and why, as a result, she did not see how her presence affected the presentation. If she did not see herself as present in the Pomo women's community, as someone sharing a history and associated with the Pomo women, how could she have seriously considered the ways the women might have been editing their accounts for her? If she did not see herself as present in her literary reencounter with the women's recorded texts, as someone influenced by certain linguistic and narrative biases, how could she have seen the ways her editing may have been significantly altering the spoken texts? How could she have begun to understand the Pomo women (and herself) other than she did?

In her "Analysis of the Life Histories" she treats the autobiographical accounts as raw data. Her tone is detached, authoritative, conclusive. She writes, for example, "When one turns to in-group relationships the picture is entirely changed [from the Pomo's relationship with outsiders]. There is evidence from the life histories that aggressive feelings find an outlet in three forms: physical violence, poisoning, and gossip" (223). Another example: "This last fact [of Catholics underwriting Pomo subsistence] may account for the relatively little concern evinced in the life histories for subsistence" (225). This last observation appears ironic, given Colson's earlier testimony that "almost every informant at some point argued that [twenty-five cents an hour] was insufficient and that they had been advised by other Pomo not to work unless they were paid more." It seems that even while the narrators in their accounts may show little concern for subsistence, they certainly did in fact care about issues of money and subsistence. Colson seems to be forgetting throughout her "Analysis" that she is looking only at the accounts that she received from the narrators and then edited. She overlooks much of what she actually experienced with the women narrators, such as their concern for money.

In any event, had Colson been more aware of her role and influence in the collaboration, she might have seen the Indians differently. She might have come to different conclusions about the Pomo women and their lives. Despite the fact that these three Indian women lived in the midst of cultural flux and that they had many marriages, raised and lost several children, and moved from place to place, Colson concludes: "Pomo life, as portrayed in these three life histories, emerges as a fairly simple one from the point of view of its participants, for they live through much of the same events with little variation in happenings to distinguish their lives" (233). Colson's interest in the lives of these three Pomo women was in large part scientific. For, and to some extent with, the Pomo women she created a language that was flat and simple, a language which might lead one to think that "Pomo life, as portrayed in these life histories, emerges as a fairly simple one from the point of view of its participants." Here, it seems, the text begs its interpretation.

The story I have drawn of Colson and the making of *Autobiographies* is not unusual or surprising. Krupat pointed out that earlier in the century the objectivism of American social science influenced S. M. Barrett in the making of *Geronimo's Story of His Life*. This objectivism not only influenced a host of recorder-editors working on Indian life histories, but also many others, most of whom were social scientists working with American Indians and other indigenous peoples. The detached observer mode was standard. Lately, some social scientists and various social critics have seen objectivism as a myth and pointed to its limits and dangers (Clifford 1983, 1988; Marcus and Fischer 1986; Rosaldo 1989). They have pointed to the limits of what "objective" observers can see and know about themselves and those they observe, and they have pointed out that under the guise of objectivism these observers often assume authority to make sense of and represent others (i.e., Clifford 1983), an attitude often affiliated with hegemony and empire, particularly in members of a dominant group in their inter-actions with subordinate groups (i.e., Rosaldo 1989). These scholars are not suggesting that critical activity is impossible, but they seem to be saying that critical activity is tied always to the subjectivity of observers and the relationships they establish with what they are observing or reading.

By positioning herself as an objective observer in relation to the women, Colson does not appear to notice the history she shared with them nor the ways her scholarly endeavors may have replicated and reinforced historical patterns of Pomo and white interrelations. It ap-pears that to some degree Colson made the narratives sensible or intelli-gible to herself so that she could analyze them in her own terms; and, in making the decisions about editing the accounts without consulting the narrators, Colson's encounter with the women repeats historical patterns of Pomo and white interrelations. Pomo country is again cleaned up, made intelligible on white people's terms. Open, proactive intercultural communication collapses. Colson, like the nineteenth-century Catholic and Protestant clergy who provided the Pomo people "Indian" churches, could not see or imagine how the Indians were anything but what they seemed to her as an "impartial" observer. Just as the clergy did not see the Pomo in terms of their participation in the revivalistic Bole Maru cult, so Colson did not see what various aspects of Pomo language, culture, and history may have revealed about them (and her), nor could she appreciate how her behavior reinforced certain Pomo attitudes about whites, especially those interested in learning about Indians. The Pomo elder who told me one of the narrators threatened to kill Colson said: "See, that's how them whites are. No respect. Do things, write anything they want. So don't tell them about us in the school. Don't trust them. They're like that white lady [Colson]. I tell all [Indian] young people about that."

I believe Colson was sincere when she said she was "someone who was fairly neutral and who made no attempt to judge [the women]" (8). I believe she treated the women "as equals" to the best of her ability and did not regard the Pomo Indians in the racist manner of the general local white community at the time. The discussion thus far is not meant simply to criticize Colson and place responsibility for problems regarding Pomo and white interrelations on her shoulders. Colson could not have fully understood the nature and consequences of her work, and indeed no one can see all of the ways he or she is not "fairly neutral." The story of Colson and the Pomo women and their making of *Autobiographies* teaches not only about the possible limits and dangers of objectivism, but also about the necessity for collaborators in any cross-cultural project to see themselves as present, as persons working in a given place at a given time, if they are to begin to understand the nature and consequences of their work.

Social scientists who discuss the limits and dangers of objectivism stress the necessity for participants in a cross-cultural endeavor to see themselves as present, often speaking of subjective knowledge and self-reflexivity and of polyvocality, both in one's encounter with others and in one's representation of the encounter. But all of this must also hold for the practice of reading texts, especially those where readers must negotiate differing cultural perspectives. Again, in narrated American Indian autobiographies readers must negotiate not only what in the texts may be different or upsetting in terms of their own lives but also what in the texts may create differences or tension between the parties that made the texts. Of course I am not the first to suggest readers think about, or historicize, their positions as readers and critics. David Bleich (1986) and Edward W. Said (1989) have certainly sounded the trumpet. But these critics, like others in various fields of study, present their arguments in conventional argumentative narratives, the forms of which usually hide not only a record of the critic's interaction with the text but also the critic's autobiography, a necessary component of the reading practice the critics are calling for.[16] Hence the politics of reading (Boyarin 1991) are not seen.

In this chapter I hope to have documented in some degree my inter-action with *Autobiographies*. Any story or lesson, any reading, if you will, that I gather from the text has to do with that interaction. Other readers can see, at least in terms of what I have revealed, what constitutes my reading; they have in hand both my reading of the text, which opens and extends its story in certain ways, and my encounter with it, which shows my influences and biases as a reader. They can see, to some extent, how my reading of *Autobiographies* is my own. Other readers can engage with what this document contains and point out my limits and possibilities, failures and successes, and replications and inventions in terms of this text and its history as well as other texts and other histories. The making of *Autobiographies* cannot be described by just one story based on one reader's interaction with the text since the text itself

16. In his essay "Intersubjective Reading," David Bleich, for example, notes: "In very few instances does the critic actually study his or her own readings, much less the readings of others, while the great majority of discussions give all the attention to the texts" (402). Bleich goes on to discuss the work, or ideas, of others (i.e., Gadamer, Barthes). The language, tone, and narrative format of the essay is typical of contemporary academic prose, specifically that of literary criticism and theory. Bleich is analytical and detached. Nowhere does he discuss his reading or historicize his position as the writer of this essay. He concludes the essay by commending that work which "lead[s] toward a rationality of multiple voices and common interests, toward readings 'responsible for the meaning of each other's inner lives'" (420). Can he commend his own work?

I am not suggesting, nor do I think the scholars I have cited here—Clifford, Marcus and Fischer, Rosaldo, Bleich, Said—are suggesting, that the critic's subjectivism as it may be presented by him or her in a paper is alone the answer, or that it automatically establishes honesty or authenticity. After all, critics as writers can tell any kind of "personal" story they want, truthful or not. Rather, I am suggesting the critic's history can help open the stories of the critic's relationshp with a text, which contributes to the reader's reading. Again, in my work I am attempting to open a dialogue with the text I am reading such that my history and critical activity inform and are informed by the text, and my representation of that dialogue as a critical chapter is offered to other readers who can continue the dialogue in writing or other ways.

provides the opportunity for many stories, readings, and a great deal of critical exchange; however, one story can start the talk, touch other stories, teach the reader. My one story is brief and, as I noted, not so unusual in certain ways, but from it I see much of my history and understand, finally, how *Autobiographies* is a story for me.

HEARING THE OLD ONES TALK

For a long time I wanted to dismiss Colson. I wanted to show her as ignorant, arrogant, typically "white." I wanted to run her out of the territory.

I wanted my anger.

As an Indian that's what I know best. But that isn't exactly my case. My anger is also that of a mixed blood caught in the middle.

Early on I learned to take sides. I chose the Indian side. Or I was quiet, never letting anyone know my predicament. I passed as white. Always, I denied. I took a stand within myself. I took a stand against myself.

In the academy we are trained to take a stand and defend it, and perhaps I have done well and become a professor because of all that early training. In the academy scholars now want "an Indian point of view." And Indians want and need to talk, to tell their stories. But what constitutes "an Indian point of view"? By what and whose definition is a point of view "Indian"? How might an Indian's story in turn define "Indian"? What of an Indian's story that is not "Indian"?

I felt I had to take sides. As a scholar I had to be "Indian," a Pomo Indian who knows and discusses what is "Pomo," which in turn can help make sense of *Autobiographies* from a "Pomo point of view." I could say what was "Pomo" and what was "Colson." I kept looking at *Autobiographies* from an "Indian point of view." I kept thinking of how "Indians" really are. I wanted to utilize a so-called Indian perspective, one that is, say, anti-white, and that shows outside scholars always to be the enemy, who is always wrong about us. I didn't want to be reminded of my situation in two worlds. I didn't want personal experience to get in the way of my "Indian analysis and discussion" of the text. It would cloud a pure, authoritative reading from an "Indian" perspective. It would cloud a distanced academic stance that was now Indian. Indian and objective.

More denial. Rejection. Frustration and anger.

So I wanted to take my anger out on Colson. I could do it objectively, truthfully.

Objectivity, or that which inheres in any supposed practice of it, namely the user's separation from his or her self and from whatever it is that is being viewed or studied, kept my anger alive. It also kept me blinded. By taking an "Indian stance," by keeping myself separate from both my larger personal experience and the text, I continued old patterns. My "Indian" objective truth based on my so-called Indian perspective versus Colson's objective truth as a non-Indian scientist. Either truth precludes our seeing the larger picture of the forces which position us as knowers of ourselves and others. Either truth precludes our seeing the limits and consequences of the truth we paint. In the case of Colson and the three Pomo women and myself, we become a part of an old and vicious cycle. One says what the other is. The other gets defensive and says what the one is. No one sees what we do to ourselves and one another. No one sees beyond themselves. Personal and cultural boundaries are rigidified. We don't see how our worlds are interrelated. We don't see our very real situations in both worlds. There is nowhere to see, no way to talk to one another. Oppressive situations are internalized by individuals in given ways and played out again by the same individuals in given ways. It is the operation of a vicious cycle, a mean history.

Denial. Rejection. Frustration and anger.

Luckily, I kept hearing Great-Grandma Nettie. She wouldn't stay down. She and Old Auntie Eleanor were, after all, the only central Pomo I knew from the same generation as the three Pomo women. When I looked to Nettie and Eleanor for answers about what was "Pomo," they shot back those suspicious glances. Who was I? Was I Indian? Was I a stranger? They didn't allow me to represent or define them for others. They reminded me of my story. And if I am reminded by them of my story, then I am taught by what I discerned in *Autobiographies* why I should not forget my story. And that's how *Autobiographies* is a story for me. It shows me the dangers of being absent, of attempting to separate myself from what I do, from my own life situation as a scholar, an Indian, and a human being in time and place. It shows me not only the importance of my stories but also the importance of talking about them openly and honestly, so that I might, in whatever I do or read, see them anew. It brought me back to the old ones, to their stories, and to hearing the old ones talking, so I can see how something they say might be for me.

I am that man, that one at the table. With light skin. I am a quarter-breed man. But like half-breed man, I know something too. I know Indian poison. White poison, too. I know many ways to poison.

The old medicine people say a good medicine person must know about the poisons. Only that way can the medicine doctor know what to do to counteract them. What herbs to use. What songs to sing. The doctor has to know those poisons so well that the doctor could use them against other people. But a good doctor doesn't do that. That's not the purpose of learning about the poisons. Good medicine people know better.

What I have to say can work like good doctoring songs, good medicine.

Listen to my story.

So when I sit before you talking, talking, talking, talking, you know who I am. Listen because I carry our history, yours and mine, ours. Some of it, anyway. Whoever you are.

Talk back. Tell stories. Put food out, meat. I will eat it. I'm not here to harm. I'm talking, telling stories. Watch. Listen.

Then you'll know I'm no stranger.[17]

17. I want to thank those who have helped me along the way in writing this essay and otherwise, particularly Mary Sarris, Andrea Lerner, and three Pomo women—Mabel McKay, Violet Chappell, and Anita Silva.

CHAPTER SIX

Reading Louise Erdrich

Love Medicine *as Home Medicine*

"Your grandmother didn't want to be Indian," my Auntie Violet re-marked as she put down the photograph of my grandmother I had given her. She leaned forward in her chair, as if for a closer inspection, one last look at the picture, then sat back with resolve. "Nope," she said, "that lady wanted to be white. She didn't want to be Indian. I'm sorry to tell."

I shuffled through the assorted black and white photographs I kept in a plastic K-Mart shopping bag. They were pictures I had taken from my grandmother's family album. I handed Auntie Violet another picture, hopeful that she would change her mind, discern something similar, something good, Indian. We were all related, after all. We shared the same history: the invasions by the Spanish and Russians, the Mexi-cans, and the Americans. We shared the same blood: my father's great-grandfather Tom Smith, my grandmother's grandfather, was married at one time to Auntie Violet's great-grandmother, the Kashaya Pomo matri-arch Rosie Jarvis. My grandmother grew up among her grandmother's people, the Coast Miwok who lived south of the Russian River in Sonoma and Marin counties, and she had lived in San Francisco and Los Angeles. Violet and many of my other relatives identified as Kashaya Pomo grew up on the Kashaya Reservation in Kashaya Pomo territory north of the Russian River. I wanted desperately to know everything I could about my grandmother whom I had never known. Grandpa Hi-lario, her husband, didn't know that much about her Indian back-ground, only where she was from. "Take what pictures you want," he said as I looked through her album. "Maybe those ladies up there [at Kashaya] can tell you something."

Violet held the picture close to her face, scrutinizing. She adjusted her glasses, then carefully placed the photograph in the neat line of photos she was making before her on the kitchen table. She reached for her cigarettes. "Nope," she said. "You see, Greg, those Indians down there, those south people, they lost it a long time ago. Those ones around there. Shoot, they don't have no one speaking their language now. They speak more Spanish, Mexican. A few of them, they didn't even want to be Indian. They're mixed, light-skinned.

Violet stopped talking to light her cigarette. She pushed the pack of cigarettes to Auntie Vivien who sat directly across from me. Violet was at the head of the table. It was late, around one in the morning. We often visited, talked about people and places until sunup. Now I was sharing the pictures and what I learned from my grandfather during my recent visit with him. In the quiet of the room, in those spaces between our words, I heard loud music coming from a neighbor's house. The heavy bass sounded through Auntie Violet's trailer home walls. I looked down at her clean white-and-orange-flowered oilcloth. Up here on the reservation, on top of a mountain in the middle of nowhere, at least forty long, winding miles from Healdsburg, the nearest town, and all this noise.

"Drinking, fighting each other," Vivien said, as if reading my thoughts. Vivien was quiet, to the point.

"No," Violet said, exhaling a cloud of smoke, "a few of them people down there, they would ignore us if they seen us in town. Those Bodega ones, especially. Act too good, act white, them people. Like that guy, what's his name. YOUR cousin, Greg. Now he wants to be Indian. But, oh, his mother. Stuck up. Used to be she see us Indians and laugh at us. And what's she got? Who is she?"

Auntie Violet didn't say all that she could have just then. I knew the stories, the gossip that one group armed themselves with against the other. Indians, I thought to myself. "Indians, you know how we are," my Miwok cousin once said.

I opened the plastic bag, then closed it. What I was sensitive to, what made me uncomfortable, was Auntie Violet's dismissive tone. I knew she loved me; she and Uncle Paul were like parents to me. But wasn't my grandmother a part of me also? Wasn't there some common ground that could be talked about?

"But my grandmother didn't like white people," I protested. "Look, she married a Filipino. In those days a Filipino was considered low as an Indian. And Grandpa Hilario is dark."

"Well, she might not liked whites, but she must not liked herself, too. She didn't want to claim all of what she was. Those people, well, besides they had no Indian upbringing really. No language. I know those people. Laugh at us, but others are laughing at them. To whites they're nothing either."

Violet shifted in her chair, tugged at the ends of her white cotton blouse. "Viv," she said, "remember what's his name's mother, how she act when she seen us downtown that time? I felt like saying . . . I just wouldn't lower myself to THAT level."

Just then a woman screamed from the house across the way. There was a loud crash, a spilling of things, as if a table had been overturned, and the music stopped.

"Oh," Violet sighed, blowing smoke. "How embarrassing. Gives Indians a bad name."

I looked down at the oilcloth and the Tupperware bowls of leftovers from dinner. Beans, fried chicken, salad, a plate of cold tortillas. Auntie Violet's pink poodle salt-and-pepper shakers. I looked at her row of my grandmother's photographs. My grandmother, Evelyn Hilario, looking up to Auntie Violet in at least a half-dozen different ways. All of us, I thought, fighting each other. I reached into the plastic shopping bag for another photograph, one where my grandmother might look more "Indian."

Families bickering. Families arguing amongst themselves, drawing lines, maintaining old boundaries. Who is in. Who is not. Gossip. Jealousy. Drinking. Love. The ties that bind. The very human need to belong, to be worthy and valued. Families. Who is Indian. Who is not. Families bound by history and blood. This is the stuff, the fabric of my Indian community. It is what I found in Louise Erdrich's Chippewa community as I read *Love Medicine*.

In the first chapter of the novel Albertine Johnson comes home to her reservation after hearing the news of her Aunt June's death. Albertine is one of Erdrich's seven narrators whose interrelated stories readers follow throughout the novel. The death of June Kashpaw becomes the occasion around which the narrators tell their stories, stories that chronicle in a variety of ways life on and around the North Dakota Chippewa reservation. As Albertine comes home, readers witness with her the general

reservation setting and the interpersonal dynamics of her family. When I
found Albertine caught in the middle of her mother and aunt's bickering
about who was white and who was Indian, I immediately thought of the
time I came home and spent the night showing Auntie Violet picture
after picture of my grandmother. So much seemed familiar.

> "That white girl," Mama went on, "she's built like a truckdriver. She
> won't keep King long. Lucky you're slim, Albertine."
> "*Jeez,* Zelda!" Aurelia came in from the next room. "Why can't you just
> leave it be. So she's white. What about the Swede? How do you think
> Albertine feels hearing you talk like this when her Dad was white?"
> "I feel fine," I said. "I never knew him."
> I understood what Aurelia meant though—I was light, clearly a breed.
> "My girl's an *Indian,*" Zelda emphasized. "I raised her an Indian, and
> that's what she is."
> "Never said no different." Aurelia grinned, not the least put out, hitting me
> with her elbow. "She's lots better looking than most Kashpaws."
>
> (*LM* 23)

The bickering about who and what is or is not Indian is not the only
phenomenon about Albertine's Chippewa reservation and family that
made me think of home. There is the drinking and associated violence.
And the bickering, gossiping, and drinking Albertine introduces readers
to in the first chapter continue throughout the novel. The general scene
readers walk into with Albertine does not change particularly, even
though, as some critics (McKenzie 1986; Gleason 1987) suggest, certain
characters seem to triumph over it. Images and sounds, bits and pieces of
conversations, people and places from home and from the novel came
together and mixed in my mind. Albertine in a bar, "sitting before [her]
third or fourth Jellybean, which is anisette, grain alcohol, a lit match,
and a small wet explosion in the brain" (*LM* 155). My cousin Elna
seated in the neon light of an Indian bar on lower Fourth Street in Santa
Rosa. Marie Lazarre Kashpaw responding to the gossip about her: "I
just laugh, don't let them get a wedge in. Then I turn the tables on them,
because they don't know how many goods I have collected in town"
(*LM* 70). My Auntie Marguerita: "Ah, let them hags talk. Who are they?
Just women who kept the streets of lower Fourth warm." "My girl's an
Indian." "Your grandmother didn't want to be an Indian." Albertine
jumping on June's drunken son King and biting a hole in his ear to keep
him from drowning his wife in the kitchen sink and the fighting that
follows and the cherished fresh-baked pies getting smashed: "Torn open.
Black juice bleeding through the crusts" (*LM* 38). The loud crash, a
spilling of things, as if a table had been overturned.

Drinking, fighting each other.

I began asking questions, if at first only to sort things out. Are these two communities, one in northern California and one in North Dakota, really that similar?[1] Are these conditions and scenes the same for all American Indians? Is this situation the common ground, finally, on which over three hundred different nations and cultures meet? Is there more to see and know about this situation than Erdrich has painted? Where does all of this come from, this bickering, this age-old family rivalry and pain?

This last question brought me back to the feuding families in *Love Medicine:* the Kashpaws, the Lazarres, the Lamartines, and the Morrisseys. They reflected in their quarrels and pain my own relatives and the families on the Kashaya reservation feuding with other Kashaya families and with Coast Miwok families from the southern territories.

I thought again of the history of the Kashaya and the Miwok families. The Coast Miwoks in the southern territories suffered cultural and political domination early on. The Spanish missionized the Coast Miwoks and broke apart most of the tribes early in the nineteenth century. The northern Indians, the Kashaya Pomo who were colonized by the Russians, were not affected in the same ways. The Kashaya were virtually enslaved by the Russians, but they were not converted to Christianity, nor were they broken apart as a tribe. The Miwoks learned Spanish and changed their ways earlier and faster than the Kashaya Pomo to the north. They had to. No wonder the Coast Miwok people "don't have no one speaking their language now."[2] No wonder my grandmother wasn't Indian in ways Auntie Violet is. Still, what the Coast Miwok and Kashaya Pomo people have in common, albeit in somewhat different forms and situations, is that history of cultural and political domination by European and Euro-American invaders. Today so much of our pain, whether we are Kashaya or Miwok or both, seems associated with that history, not just in our general material poverty but also in the ways we have internalized the domination. Low self-esteem. A

1. For purposes of clarification and simplicity I am referring to both the Coast Miwok community and the Kashaya Pomo community as my one Indian community. As noted at the start of this book, Coast Miwok and Kashaya Pomo people share a long history of trade, intermarriage, and cultural exchange.

2. Mrs. Juanita Carrio, a Coast Miwok elder who passed away in 1991, did possess a large Coast Miwok (Nicasias dialect) vocabulary, but she did not consider herself a fluent speaker. No one living knows as much of any Coast Miwok language as Mrs. Carrio did. People may know a few words or phrases. Sarah Smith Ballard (1881–1978), a Bodega Miwok, was the last fluent speaker of a Coast Miwok language. Her Bodega Miwok dictionary was published by the University of California Press in 1970.

sense of powerlessness. Alienation from both past and present, the Indian world and the white world, and from the ways the two worlds commingle. We often judge ourselves in terms of the dominator's values ("laughing at 'Indians'") or create countervalues with which to judge ourselves ("they act white"; "they're mixed, light-skinned"). We internalize the oppression we have felt and, all too often, become oppressor-like to ourselves.

So one answer, at least, to my question regarding the origins and perpetuation of family bickering and pain at home is internalized oppression. I began seeing signs of internalized oppression as I remembered again people and events at home on the Kashaya Pomo reservation and in the town of Santa Rosa. Our quarrelling, name-calling, self-abuse. And when I looked back at *Love Medicine*, I found the same signs reflected from my community. And couldn't this be the case? Just as Erdrich's Indian community reflected in ways my Indian community, might not my community with its history reflect that of Erdrich's in her novel? After all, the Chippewa Indians, on whose stories Erdrich's fiction is based, suffered European and Euro-American domination also.

But to answer my question about whether the concept of internalized oppression as I see it pertaining to my community can be applied to Erdrich's fictional Chippewa community, I must turn back to my first questions. Are the two respective Indian communities really that similar? Is life on and around the Kashaya Pomo reservation the same as life on and around Erdrich's fictional Chippewa reservation? Are the conditions and scenes I have noted about both my community and Erdrich's in *Love Medicine* the same for all American Indian communities? I think of Auntie Violet arranging photographs of my grandmother and seeing in the photographs what she wanted to see, what she knew to be true, and of how I might be doing the same thing with respect to *Love Medicine*. How might I be perpetuating biases, limiting communication and understanding, rather than undoing biases and opening communication and understanding? My community and that in Erdrich's text do not exist side by side, nor do they necessarily reflect one another in the manner I describe, independently of me. As a reader, and ultimately as the writer of this book, I position the mirror so that certain reflections occur. I am the reader of both my community and the written text. How am I reading? Am I merely projecting my experience and ideas from my community onto the text? Am I thus framing or closing the text in ways that silence how it might inform me? What about the cross-cultural issues between Kashaya Pomo culture and Chippewa culture? What do I know of Chippewa life? Again, are these two different communities really so similar that I can make generalizations suitable for both?

Current discussion regarding reading cross-cultural literatures centers on these same questions. How do we read and make sense of literatures produced by authors who represent in their work and are members of cultures different from our own? If, say, we compare and contrast themes or character motivation, how are we comparing and contrasting? What of our biases as readers? What of the ways we hold the mirror between a canonical text such as *Hamlet* and a text such as Leslie Silko's *Ceremony?* Can we read these different texts in the same ways? In this chapter I want to continue relating how my reading of *Love Medicine* helped me to recognize and think about (and ultimately talk about) what Erdrich's character Albertine Johnson felt as the "wet blanket of sadness coming down over us all" (*LM* 29). To relate the story of my reading, I must also discuss my own reading, asking how I read or how anyone reads American Indian literatures written by American Indians. Remember, as many of my questions suggest, my being Indian does not necessarily privilege me as a reader of any and all American Indian texts. My discussions and stories, then, while concerned with my reading of *Love Medicine,* contribute to current discussions regarding reading of American Indian literatures in particular and cross-cultural literatures in general.

What makes written literatures cross-cultural depends as much on their content and production as on their being read by a particular reader or community of readers. Many Americans from marginal cultures with specific languages and mores write in a particular variety of English or integrate their culture-specific language with an English that makes their written works accessible in some measure to a large English-speaking readership. These writers mediate not only different languages and narrative forms, but, in the process, the cultural experiences they are representing, which become the content of their work. Their work represents a dialogue between themselves and different cultural norms and forms and also, within their text, between, say, characters or points of view. This cross-cultural interaction represented by the texts is extended to readers, many of whom are unfamiliar with the writers' particular cultural experiences and who must, in turn, mediate between what they encounter in the texts and what they know from their specific cultural experiences. As David Bleich observes regarding literature in general, the texts are both *representations* of interaction and the *occasion for* interaction (418). Of course this general truth can become more pronounced and obvious in situations where literatures that represent cross-cultural experiences in their content and production are read by readers unfamiliar with the experiences.[3] And here the questions surface regarding how readers respond to what they encounter in texts. In their practices of reading and interpretation do they reflect on their making sense of the texts? Do they account for their interaction with what constitutes the content and making of the written texts? In their practices of reading are they limiting or opening intercultural communication and understanding, undoing biases or maintaining and creating them anew?

Scholars who study American Indian oral literatures have become increasingly aware of the fact that the *oral* texts they *read* have been shaped and altered not only by those people (for the most part non-Indian) who have collected, translated, and transcribed them but also by the Indians who have told them to these people. As noted, Arnold Krupat defines narrated Indian autobiographies, where a recorder-editor records and transcribes what was given orally by the Indian subject, as *original bicultural compositions* (31). His definition holds for many, perhaps most, of the American Indian oral texts—songs, stories, prayers—read and studied. Scholars such as Dennis Tedlock and Barre Toelken account for and question their encounters with both the Indian speakers from whom they collect texts and the texts themselves, which they transcribe and attempt to understand.[4] At its best their work provides a record of the various dialogues they have with the Indians and the Indians' texts. Readers have an account of how these scholars collected the Indian material and how their transcriptions and analysis continue the life of the material in given cross-cultural ways.

Such is rarely the case for Indian literatures written in English by Indians, or for what I am calling in this essay American Indian written literatures.[5] Most critics neither question nor account for the ways they

3. This general truth can become more pronounced and obvious also when readers are familiar with the culture or cultural experiences being represented and have difficulty with the representation or the ways in which the writer has presented the cultural experiences. Some contemporary Kiowa readers, for example, might have trouble with N. Scott Momaday's prose and narrative format in *The Way to Rainy Mountain*. How would certain Chippewa readers see their experiences as represented in Erdrich's rich, figurative, largely standard English?

4. Toelken lists Tacheeni Scott, an Indian speaker and collaborator, as co-author of *their* work together on certain texts.

5. Certainly non-Indian fiction writers, most notably James Fenimore Cooper, have written about Indians in their fiction. For purposes of clarity here I would refer to their work about Indians as non-Indian literature about Indians. Without a doubt, their work is cross-cultural; after all, they mediate and represent what they find in people from cultures different from their own—American Indians.

make sense of what they encounter as readers of these written literatures. Some critics do consider the ways certain Indian writers mediate, or make use of, their respective cultural backgrounds or specific themes considered to be generally "Indian." But these critics do not seriously consider or reflect upon how they are making sense of and putting together the writers' cultural backgrounds and the writers' texts. They attempt to account for the interaction represented in the texts, but not for their own interaction. They might, for example, attempt in their various approaches to locate and account for an "Indian" presence or "Indian" themes in a text, but they do not consider how they discovered or created what they define as Indian. Citing Michael Glowinski's observation about so much contemporary literary criticism, Bleich notes that critics provide "a *history* of the literature, while rejecting [their] own historicity" (402). The result is that they do not see how their practices of reading and interpretation are limiting or opening intercultural communication and understanding. They don't see themselves and their work as an integral and continuing part of the cross-cultural exchange. Their practices are characterized by one-sided communication: they inform the texts, but the texts do not inform them and their critical agendas, or at least not in ways they make apparent.

Lester A. Standiford, in his essay "Worlds Made of Dawn: Characteristic Image and Incident in Native American Imaginative Literature," notes that "it is important that we seek a greater understanding of [Native American imaginative written] literature" (169) and that to gain a greater understanding we must not enforce "old assumptions on those new aspects of a literature that draws from sources outside the Anglo-American heritage" (170). Standiford's strategy for approaching and, subsequently, for helping other readers gain a greater understanding of these cross-cultural texts is to use a generalization gleaned from his studies about Indians and their literatures to find and hence account for that in the texts which is "Indian." Standiford writes:

> I will be speaking of contemporary Indian American poetry and fiction according to this archetypal concept of the poet as shaman who "speaks for wild animals, the spirits of plants, the spirits of mountains, of watersheds" (Snyder, p. 3). If you must have a worldly function of the poet, base it on this example from Snyder's remarks: "The elaborate, yearly, cyclical production of grand ritual dramas in the societies of Pueblo Indians . . . can be seen as a process by which the whole society consults the non-human powers and allows some individuals to step totally out of their human roles to put on the mask, costume, and mind of Bison, Bear, Squash, Corn, or Pleiades; to re-enter the human circle in that form and by song, mime, and dance, convey

a greeting from that other realm. Thus a speech on the floor of congress from a whale" (p. 3). . . . Poetry that speaks with the voice of the whale resounds with the true power of Indian American imaginative literature.

(171)[6]

Standiford typically moves thus from a generalization about Indians to a citation from an Indian or authoritative non-Indian to support and make legitimate his use of generalization to identify and understand things Indian in the text(s). He then further generalizes or restates the previous generalization, eventually returning to the written Indian text(s). See the pattern again within the following paragraph:

> Here [in Durango Mendoza's short story "Summer Water and Shirley"] the key to understanding is the Native American concept of the great and inherent power of the *word*. Because the boy [in Mendoza's story] can force his will out through his thoughts and into words, he succeeds in his task. This sense of the power of the word derives from the thousands of years of the Native American oral literary tradition. From its labyrinthine and tenuous history the word arrives in the present with inestimable force. As Scott Momaday points out in his essay "The Man Made of Words," the oral form exists always just one generation from extinction and is all the more precious on that account. And this sense of care engendered for the songs and stories and their words naturally leads to an appreciation of the power of the word itself.
> (183)

Using a similar strategy, Paula Gunn Allen, renowned Laguna Pueblo/ Sioux literary critic and poet, summarizes (interprets) what she saw in Cache Creek Pomo Dreamer and basket-weaver Mabel McKay and in Kashaya Pomo Dreamer and prophet Essie Parrish and then makes generalizations based on what she saw to further develop and support what she calls a "tribal-feminist" or "feminist-tribal" (222) approach to Indian women's written literatures. Allen says that "the teachings of [Mabel McKay and Essie Parrish] provide clear information about the ancient ritual power of Indian women" (204). She summarizes what she heard Mrs. McKay say during a basket-weaving demonstration as follows:

> Mrs. McCabe [*sic*] spoke about the meaning of having a tradition, about how a woman becomes a basketmaker among her people—a process that is guided

6. Standiford in this instance cites Gary Snyder, a romantic non-Indian poet who generalizes about Indians to support his ideas about ecology and so forth. Here, then, Standiford is basing his generalization about Indians on another's generalizations about Indians. How might individual Indian voices from a particular tribe talk back to or inform these generalizations across tribal cultures and histories? How might the generalizations be qualified in the context of a specific culture and history?

entirely by a spirit-teacher when the woman is of the proper age. It is not transmitted to her through human agency. For Mrs. McCabe, having a tradition means having a spirit-teacher or guide. That is the only way she used the term "tradition" and the only context in which she understood it. Pomo baskets hold psychic power, spirit power; so a basketweaver weaves a basket for a person at the direction of her spirit guide.

(204)

Allen then summarizes what she heard from Mrs. Parrish on a "field trip with [Allen's] students to the Kashia[7] Pomo reservation" (203) and what she heard and saw in the documentary films on Mrs. Parrish and Kashaya religious activities:

In one of [the films], *Dream Dances of the Kashia Pomo*, [Essie Parrish] and others dance and display the dance costumes that are made under her direction, appliquéd with certain dream-charged designs that hold the power she brings from the spirit world. She tells about the role of the Dreamer, who is the mother of the people not because she gives physical birth (though Essie Parrish has done that) but because she gives them life through the power of dreaming—that is, she en-livens them. Actually, the power of giving physical birth is a consequence of the power of giving nonmaterial or, you might say, 'astral' birth. . . .

The Dreamer, then, is the center of psychic/spiritual unity of the people. . . . In another film, *Pomo Shaman*, Mrs. Parrish demonstrates a healing ritual, in which she uses water and water power, captured and focused through her motions, words, and use of material water, to heal a patient. She demonstrates the means of healing, and in the short narrative segments, she repeats in English some of the ritual. It is about creation and creating and signifies the basic understanding the tribal people generally have about how sickness comes about and how its effects can be assuaged, relieved, and perhaps even removed.

(204–6)

Allen relates other observations she has about Indian women and shamanism from a few other tribes (e.g., Kiowa) and proclaims finally:

One of the primary functions of the shaman is her effect on tribal understandings of "women's roles," which in large part are traditional in Mrs. McCabe's [sic] sense of the word. It is the shaman's connection to the spirit world that Indian women writers reflect most strongly in our poetry and fiction.

(208)

It seems that in Allen's strategy to develop and support a tribal-feminist or feminist-tribal approach to American Indian women's writ-

7. "Kashia" is a variant spelling of Kashaya. "Kashia" is used in many of the ethnographies and older government records.

ten literatures—an approach that can both locate an Indian (woman) presence in the texts and critique patriarchal tendencies to suppress Indian women's power and subjectivity—she replicates in practice what she sets out to criticize. Allen does not question how she reads each of the Pomo women's words and performances she translates and discusses in her scholarship. She does not examine the women's particular histories and cultures to inform her ideas regarding what she saw and heard. She says these women provide "clear information about the ancient ritual power of Indian women," but in actuality the Dreaming and other related "ancient" or "traditional" activities associated with Mabel McKay and Essie Parrish that Allen cites to substantiate her claims are tied to the nineteenth-century Bole Maru (Dream Dance) cult, a revivalistic movement discussed in Chapter 4. Though many, if not most, of the more recent Dreamers have been women, the first Bole Maru Dreamer, Richard Taylor, and many of the earlier Dreamers were men. The Kashaya have had four Dreamers in this order: Jack Humbolt, Big José, Annie Jarvis, Essie Parrish. My grandmother's grandfather, Tom Smith, who was half Coast Miwok and half Kashaya Pomo, was one of the most influential Dreamers and doctors throughout the Coast Miwok and southern Pomo territories. How does what Essie Parrish demonstrates in her healing show "the basic understanding the tribal peoples generally have about how sickness comes about"? Which tribal peoples? Where? When? Neither Mabel McKay nor Essie Parrish is allowed to talk back to or inform Allen's conclusions about them. Neither woman has an individual voice represented in the text. Allen provides no direct quotations. Like Standiford, Allen has shaped what she heard and saw to inform the Indian presence in the texts she reads.

How then can Allen's readers take seriously any account she might give of the interaction represented in Indian women's written literatures or of her interaction with the Indian women's texts she reads? While Allen opens important and necessary discussions about American Indian women and their written literatures which make a significant contribution to American Indian and feminist scholarship, she, perhaps inadvertently, closes discussions with those women and the texts she sets out to illumine.[8]

8. At various times in her work, Allen sets out to show how people from various communities read the same Indian text differently. In her essay "Kochinnenako in Academe: Three Approaches to Interpreting a Keres Indian Tale" (in *The Sacred Hoop*), Allen presents "A Keres Interpretation" (232) and "A Feminist-Tribal Interpretation" (237). Yet

William Gleason, in his essay " 'Her Laugh an Ace': The Function of Humor in Louise Erdrich's *Love Medicine*," works to avoid the tendency to generalize across tribal cultures and histories that is associated with the work of Standiford and Allen. Gleason looks at the ways Trickster, which Gleason refers to as a "pan-Indian character" (60), is presented and functions in Chippewa stories and legends. But then Gleason takes what he has gleaned from his studies of Trickster in Chippewa culture and lore and, without reflecting on how he understood what he studied or on how he uses it in *his* reading of *Love Medicine*, he frames what he finds in the novel.[9] He says of Erdrich's character Gerry Nanapush:

> Gerry *is* Trickster, literally. Alan R. Velie records that "the Chippewa Trickster is called Wenebojo, Manabozho, or Nanabush, depending on how authors recorded the Anishinabe word." This Trickster (as is true for most tribes) is able to alter his shape as he wishes. . . . The first time we meet the adult Gerry he performs a miraculous escape: though spotted by Officer Lovchik in the confines of a "cramped and littered bar . . . Gerry was over the backside of the booth and out the door before Lovchik got close enough to make a positive identification."
>
> (61)

Later, in another scene from the novel, Gleason finds that:

> By . . . teaming with Lipsha to defeat King in a quick card game ("five-card punk," Gerry says), Gerry unwittingly re-enacts a classic Chippewa Trickster

each point of view or perspective appears a generalization created by Allen. She writes, for example: "A Keres is of course aware that balance and harmony are two primary assumptions of Keres society and will not approach the narrative wondering whether the handsome Miochin will win the hand of the unhappy wife and triumph over the enemy, thereby heroically saving the people from disaster" (234). Is this the case for *all* Keres individuals? Another example: "A feminist who is conscious of tribal thought and practice will know that the real story of Sh-ah-cock and Miochin underscores the central role that woman plays in the orderly life of the people" (239). And, again, I ask: A feminist who is aware of *which* tribal thought? What tribe? What feminist? In creating and presenting multiple points of view, how might Allen, as creator/writer of these points of view, have diminished the complexity and power of those points of view? Who is Allen as mediator and presenter of the different points of view?

9. Earlier in his essay Gleason refers to scholars such as Freud in his discussion of the function of humor in general. Can Freud's model of the function of humor be applied to all American Indian cultures? To Chippewa culture? If so, how and under what particular circumstances? How is Gleason reading both Freud and the Chippewa Indian culture to make sense of what he encounters in *Love Medicine?*

In this essay I have not discussed critical approaches that are comparative, where critics examine, say, written literatures by different Indian writers in relation to one another or to Western canonical works (e.g., *The Odyssey, Absalom, Absalom!*). Clearly, and perhaps even more obviously, the questions and concerns I have raised throughout this essay would apply to comparative approaches.

story. For, according to legend, Manabozho/Nanabush journeys until he meets his principal enemy, "the great gambler," whom he defeats, saving his own life and the spirit of the woodland tribes from "the land of darkness."

(62)

Here the strategy and the end result are the same as in Standiford and Allen: nail down the Indian in order to nail down the text. The Indian is fixed, readable in certain ways, so that when we find him or her in a written text we have a way to fix and understand the Indian and hence the text.

I am not suggesting that whatever these critics—Standiford, Allen, Gleason—might be saying is necessarily untrue, but that whatever truth they advance about Indians or Indian written literatures is contingent upon their purposes and biases as readers and their particular relationship with the worlds of what they read or otherwise learn about Indians and with the worlds of the written texts they study. And here I am not suggesting that critical activity is impossible and that critics and other readers cannot inform the Indian worldviews and Indian written texts they encounter. What I am suggesting is that the various Indian worldviews (and whatever else comprises the Indian written texts) as well as the texts themselves also can inform the critics and their critical enterprises, and that genuine critical activity—where both the critics' histories and assumptions as well as those of the texts are challenged and opened—cannot occur unless critics can both inform and be informed by that which they encounter. At some level or at some point in the encounter and interaction between critic and text, there is a dialogue of sorts, even if it is merely the critic responding (dialoguing) by saying, "this is what you are saying to me and I won't hear anything else," that is, responding in a way that prohibits the text from talking back to and informing the critic about what the text said. But the critics I have cited, and most other literary critics for that matter, do not record their dialogue or even the nature of the dialogue they may have had with what they are reading. Instead, they report the outcome, what *they* thought and concluded.

Of course, by looking at the essays of Standiford, Allen, and Gleason, much of what characterizes their work as critics becomes apparent. As I have noted, these critics tend to generalize, to "circumscribe and totalise" (Murray 117) the Others' cultures and worldviews in order to "circumscribe and totalise" the Others' written texts. Each uses, most plainly in their encounters with the Indians' cultures and worldviews, what Johannes Fabian has called the "ethnographic present tense." As David Murray observes:

> The effect of this is to create a textual space, in which a culture is shown operating, which is *not* the same historically bound present as the one in which the reader and the writer live, a product of grammar (the present tense) rather than history (the present). Accompanying this ethnographic present tense is a generalising of individual utterances, so that they illustrate an argument, or fulfill a pattern, rather than function in the context of any dialogue.
>
> (141)

When Standiford, quoting Snyder, describes "this archetypical concept of the poet as shaman 'who speaks for . . .' " or when he states "this sense of the power of the word derives from the thousands of years of the Native American oral literary tradition," he is creating this space Murray describes. Note how Allen describes the work and art of Mabel McKay and Essie Parrish, and how she proclaims "one of the primary functions of the shaman is her effect on tribal understandings of 'women's roles,' which in large part are traditional in Mrs. McCabe's [*sic*] sense of the word." Gleason quotes Velie: " 'The Chippewa Trickster is called. . . . This Trickster (as is true for most tribes) is able to . . .' " Again, these critics overlook their own historicity; they remove themselves from the present of the occasions of their interaction with whatever they encounter and create in their reports a world from which they attempt to separate themselves and purport to understand and describe plain as day. The communication is one-sided and represented textually so that it stays that way. What would happen if Standiford were to question an Indian shaman or storyteller from a particular tribe? How might the content of the Indian's responses and the Indian's language and history inform Standiford's "archetypical concept of the poet as shaman"? How might the Indian's responses, language, and history illuminate the gaps in Standiford's conclusions, his generalizations about Indians? In what ways is the Indian more or less than the poet/shaman who communes with nature? And wouldn't answers to these questions, or at least a consideration of these questions, at least afford Standiford the opportunity to see himself present as a biased thinker tending to shape in certain ways what he hears or reads? Wouldn't he then have the opportunity to see and question how his critical activity opens or closes intercultural communication or how it maintains and creates biases about American Indians? If Mabel McKay and Essie Parrish could talk back to Allen, if Allen could know more of their personal lives and particular cultures and histories, wouldn't she have, or have the opportunity to have, a broader understanding of two women as well as of herself and her critical practices? Might she not see herself as present, as an Indian woman silencing in certain ways those women she wishes to defend and give voice to? How might other elements of Chippewa culture, and the ways Erdrich might understand them, inform both an understanding of the Chippewa Trickster and the character of Gerry Nanapush? Couldn't these other elements inform William Gleason and his approach?

At this point one might ask why readers of American Indian written literatures seem to be generally less reflexive in their work than contemporary readers of American Indian oral literatures such as Tedlock and Toelken. Perhaps because the former are written in English and intended for a reading audience, readers feel that they have the texts carte blanche, that the cross-cultural elements that comprise these texts are somehow transparent (Murray 117), or can be made so, because the writers have provided the readers a medium (English) for looking at them.[10] Perhaps those who study oral literatures—folklorists, anthropologists—are more aware of the current discussions in their respective disciplines regarding translation, representation, and interpretation of the Others and their works of art and literature. Perhaps readers of written literatures cannot escape the tenets of New Criticism and text positivism. I am not sure. But given what constitutes Indian oral literatures and Indian written literatures—songs, stories, as-told-to autobiographies—readers must consider the worlds of both the Indian speaker and the recorder-editor who has mediated the speaker's spoken words for the reader. With Indian written literatures the Indian writer is both Indian speaker and cross-cultural mediator, and readers must consider the Indian writer's specific culture and experience and how the writer has mediated that culture and experience for the reader. In both situations—with oral literatures and with written literatures—readers must interact with the worlds of the texts which are cross-cultural, comprised of many elements foreign to the worlds of the readers.

The task is to read American Indian written literatures in a way that

---

10. As Murray points out, "the ideal of transparency here is also an ideal of totality—a totality of understanding, in which we can seal off the work of art, and see it whole, or we can circumscribe and totalise the other culture in which it operates" (117). He suggests that even while Tedlock is reflexive and dialogical in his work, Tedlock works with, or toward, an ideal of totality, of obtaining a full and complete knowledge of the Other (117).

establishes a dialogue between readers and the texts that works to explore their respective worlds and to expose the intermingling of the multiple voices within and between readers and what they read. The objective here is not to have complete knowledge of the text or the self as reader, not to obtain or tell the complete story of one or the other or both, but to establish and report as clearly as possible that dialogue where the particular reader or groups of readers inform and are informed by the text(s). The report, or written criticism, then, would be a kind of story, a representation of a dialogue that is extended to critics and other readers who in turn inform and are informed by the report. Thus in the best circumstances reading and criticism of American Indian written literatures become the occasion for a continuous opening of culturally diverse worlds in contact with one another.

Of course any report, or piece of criticism, represents a dialogue of sorts that the critic has had with the text he or she has read, even if the dialogue is presented as mere conclusions, and that report is extended to critics and other readers who will dialogue with it. But at each step of the way—reading, criticism, response to criticism—the critics as readers, as I suggested above, remove themselves from the encounter, from the present of the occasion of their interaction with what they encounter, so that by the time they write their reports they may not see or think about how they have interacted and are interacting, how their response may be, for example, "This is what you are saying to me and I won't hear anything else." The Other, the text or whatever else has been encountered, is that which can remind the critics of their presence, of their own differences and culture-specific boundaries. If readers don't hear the texts, if they don't notice and explore those instances where the texts do not make sense to them, where the texts might question, qualify, and subvert the readers' agendas, the readers systematically forsake the opportunity not only to gain a broader understanding of themselves, of their own historicity, but also of the text. Criticism that reveals the questions and problems of reading, evoked by the experience of reading itself, can help illuminate for the critic and for others what has made for cross-cultural understanding or misunderstanding.

More often than not it is something strange and unfamiliar that can make us aware of our boundaries. For many non-Indian readers of American Indian written literatures it may be elements of a particular Indian culture represented in the text that stop them and ask them to think and rethink how they read and make sense of the Others. The same perhaps could be said for Indians reading other Indians' written literatures.

In my own case, as I continued to read and think about *Love Medicine,* I found myself coming back to the concept of internalized oppression. Erdrich's fictional Chippewa characters manifested the symptoms of this disease just as plainly as many people I knew and was thinking about from home. Marie Lazarre Kashpaw, Albertine Johnson's grandmother and one of the most notable characters in the novel, continually wants acceptance in terms of others' definitions. She believes others' ideas about her and sees no value in who or what she has been, where she comes from, her heritage. Nector Kashpaw, in looking back at his first encounter with Marie who would become his wife, says of her: "Marie Lazarre is the youngest daughter of a family of horse-thieving drunks. . . . She is just a skinny white girl from a family so low you cannot even think they are in the same class as Kashpaws" (*LM* 58–59). To a large extent Marie accepts this view of herself. She says early in the novel that "the only Lazarre I had any use for was Lucille [Marie's sister]" (*LM* 65). And when she overcomes the fear of losing her husband, Nector Kashpaw, to Lulu Lamartine, she says, "I could leave off my fear of ever being a Lazarre" (*LM* 128).

Marie not only internalizes others' ideas about her, but attempts to beat those others on their own terms in order to gain self-worth in their eyes. As a young girl Marie was determined to go "up there [to the convent] to pray as good as they [the black robe women] could" (*LM* 40). She saw the convent "on top of the highest hill. . . . Gleaming white. So white the sun glanced off in dazzling display to set forms whirling behind your eyelids. The face of God you could hardly look at" (*LM* 41). Of course she realizes in retrospect that she was under an illusion, and, in a hilarious and ironic manner, she does beat the nuns at their own game, getting them to worship her, "gain[ing] the altar of a saint" (*LM* 53). As a young married woman, Marie reveals her plan: "I decided I was going to make [Nector] into something big on this reservation. I didn't know what, not yet; I only knew when he got there they would not whisper 'dirty Lazarre' when I walked down from church. They would wish they were the woman I was. Marie Kashpaw" (*LM* 66). Marie succeeds: Nector becomes tribal chairman. Then Marie goes to visit Sister Leopolda at the convent, not to see Leopolda but, as Marie says, "to let her see me. . . . For by now I was solid class. Nector was tribal chairman. My children were well behaved, and they were educated too. . . . I pulled out the good wool dress I would wear up the hill . . . It was a good dress, manufactured, of a classic material. It was the kind of solid dress no Lazarre ever wore" (*LM* 113). Marie battles with Leopolda and sees, finally, the limits of her endeavors to win Leopolda's approval. Marie learns something about love and forgiveness, which she shows when Nector comes home from Lulu Lamartine. Yet as much as learning this lesson may constitute a personal triumph for Marie, it does not seem to help her come to terms with herself as a Lazarre, with the self-hatred associated with her background, which appears to influence so much of her behavior.

Marie says, "I don't have that much Indian blood" (*LM* 40), which, incidentally, is one reason she felt she could "pray as good as [the nuns] could" (*LM* 40). Indeed, Marie is light-skinned, a mixed blood so fair that Nector in his first encounter with her calls her a "skinny white girl" (*LM* 40) as an insult. At the time, face to face with another Indian, Marie would have taken Nector's comment as an insult, but Marie knows that among her Indian people white physical attributes are valued. She says: "I could have had any damn man on the reservation at that time. I looked good. And I looked white" (*LM* 45). She knows how to insult Nector by hissing at him, "Lemme go, you damn Indian. . . . You stink to hell" (*LM* 59). These characters at times both judge themselves and others in terms of the oppressor's values (e.g., white physical attributes), which they have internalized, and hate the oppressor and any sign (e.g., "skinny white girl") of the oppressor in their own ranks. Racism and hatred are at once directed outward and inward. These characters can't win for losing. Again in the scene cited at the start of this chapter, where Albertine Johnson is caught in the middle of her mother and aunt's bickering, her mother implies that King's wife and white people in general are undesirable. Her Aunt Aurelia says that Albertine is "lots better looking than most Kashpaws," implying that because Albertine is a mixed blood, "light, clearly a breed," she is better looking and more attractive than the full-blood Kashpaw side of the family.

These characters' gossip and verbal abuse of others simultaneously work to belittle the other and to elevate the self. They take inventories of others' looks (e.g., light or dark skin) and maintain arsenals of information that can be used against others at any time. Marie Lazarre Kashpaw, responding to the gossip about her, says: "I just laugh, don't let them get a wedge in. Then I turn the tables on them, because they don't know how many goods I have collected in town." Of course, when it's wrong to be Indian and wrong to be white, when these people can judge one another in terms of the oppressors' values and in terms of their own counter-values, they don't have to look far to find faults in themselves and others. When Albertine Johnson thinks of her family and life on and around the reservation, she thinks of the phrase "Patient Abuse," a title from her nursing textbook. She says: "There are two ways you could think of that title. One was obvious to a nursing student, and the other was obvious to a Kashpaw" (*LM* 7).

As I also noted earlier, this patient abuse can be physical as well as verbal. Albertine has been home only a few hours when she finds June's son King, who is drunk, beating up his white wife and attempting to drown her in the kitchen sink. King constantly tells stories about his duty in Vietnam; he bills himself as a war hero in an attempt to remedy his low self-esteem, to garner for himself attention and significance (again on others' terms). As his wife points out, the truth is that King "never got off the West Coast" (*LM* 239). It seems that when his storytelling does not gain for him the attention he needs from others, or when it is questioned, he resorts to violence to feel power and self-worth. Feeling both guilty about his oftentimes violent past with June and hopeless about his life in general, Gordie Kashpaw drinks himself into oblivion: "Everything worked against him. He could not remember when this had started to happen. Probably from the first always and ever afterward, things had worked against him. . . . He saw clearly that the setup of life was rigged and he was trapped" (*LM* 179). While driving drunk, Gordie hits a deer and then, assuming it is dead, that he has killed it, he puts it in his back seat. The deer, still alive, raises its head, and Gordie clobbers it with a tire iron and believes he has killed June. In his drunken stupor he has acted out his self-fulfilling prophecy: he has killed June, he is guilty, nothing works out right for him, and he deserves to be punished. He finds his way to the convent, and outside a nun's window he says, "I come to take confession. I need to confess it. . . . Bless me father for I have sinned" (*LM* 184).

Internalized oppression cuts a wide swath. The oppression that occurred during the colonial period has been internalized by the oppressed in ways that the oppressed in postcolonial periods can become agents of their own oppression and destruction. Ironically and inadvertently we work to complete what the oppressor began. At times certain characters sense the depth and breadth of this internalized oppression as a deep, unconscious fear. Albertine says of King: "He's scared underneath" (*LM* 35). Lipsha Morrissey, King's half brother and June's other son, asks what King is afraid of, but Albertine can only say she "really didn't know" (*LM* 36). Albertine can't spell out what causes King's fear or, for that matter, that "wet blanket of sadness coming down over us all." She does not have a way to talk about it. Lipsha wonders "if Higher Power

turned its back, if we got to yell, or if we just don't speak its language. . . .
How else could I explain what all I had seen in my short life—King
smashing his fist in things, Gordie drinking himself down to the Bis-
marck hospitals, or Aunt June left by a white man to wander off in the
snow. How else to explain" (*LM* 195). Indeed, the sadness is vast,
ubiquitous. Isn't its trajectory the history of Chippewa and white interrelations?

Doubtless internalized oppression is not the only way to think about
the sadness, and certainly there is much more to this novel than its
sadness. William Gleason sees in the novel that "love, assisted by humor,
triumphs over pain" (51). And James McKenzie suggests that June's son
Lipsha "completes [the journey home June had begun] some three years
and thirteen chapters later in the novel's final scene" (58). McKenzie
continues:

> Having discovered and embraced his identity and delivered his newly found
> father—Gerry Nanapush, the embodiment of Chippewa life—to safety in
> Canada, [Lipsha] heads home to the reservation. Crossing the same river
> Henry Junior has drowned in (Lipsha calls it the "boundary river" (p. 27),
> which could only be the Red River, separating North Dakota and Minne-
> sota), he stops to stretch and, looking at the water, remembers the traditional
> Chippewa custom of offering tobacco to the water. This leads him to thoughts
> of June, "sunken cars" (p. 271)—clearly a reference to Henry Junior—and
> the ancient ocean that once covered the Dakotas "and solved all our prob-
> lems" (p. 272). The thought of drowning all Chippewa problems appeals to
> him briefly: "It was easy still to imagine us beneath them most unreasonable
> waves" (p. 272), but he quickly dispels this image of tribal suicide and chooses
> a more reasonable course. He hops in the car and heads back to the center of
> his tribal culture, the reservation. Lipsha's concluding words ring a change on
> the sentence describing his mother's death: "So there was nothing to do but
> cross the water and bring her home" (p. 272).
>
> (58–59)

This final scene and the novel's ending in general make me consider
again the ways I am thinking about the novel and its sadness. Lipsha
happens to be in the right place at the right time. Three-hundred pound
Gerry Nanapush, recently escaped from prison, shows up at King's
apartment where Lipsha is visiting. Lipsha helps Gerry escape to Canada, and en route to the border Lipsha's relation to Gerry is made loud
and clear when Gerry says to Lipsha: "You're a Nanapush man. . . . We
all have this odd thing with our hearts" (*LM* 271). Of course Lipsha and
readers learn Gerry is Lipsha's father a little earlier, when Lipsha tells
how Lulu Lamartine told him the truth. And as McKenzie notes, Lipsha

and Gerry each (like Lulu Lamartine, Gerry's mother and Lipsha's grandmother) "partakes in godlike qualities" (60). Lipsha has "the touch" (*LM* 190), the power to soothe pains with his fingers, and Gerry, as Gleason notes, is able to "perform . . . miraculous escape[s]." Once when he was pursued by the local police, "his [three-hundred pound] body lifted like a hot-air balloon filling suddenly" (*LM* 169). Magically he stuffs himself into the trunk of the car he and Lipsha won from King and stays hidden there until Lipsha has driven a safe distance from the law. When Gerry and Lipsha get to the border, where Lipsha will drop Gerry off, "they [hold] each other's arms, tight and manly" (*LM* 271). Lipsha then turns around and, as McKenzie noted, crosses the water that his uncle, Henry Junior, drowned in. Lipsha heads back to his reservation, to his home. Lipsha says: "The sun flared. . . . The morning was clear. A good road led on. So there was nothing to do but cross the water and bring her home" (*LM* 272).

I have trouble with all this.

Can I take this ending as a triumph for Lipsha given the ways and extent to which I see internalized oppression in Erdrich's fictional Chippewa community, in Lipsha's "home"? Has Lipsha or any of the other characters come to terms with the "blanket of sadness" in a way that they can get a handle on it, talk about it, recognize its scope? My agenda and personal experience as a reader surface again, along with all my questions about reading. I come back to myself as mirror holder, as an interlocutor with the world of *Love Medicine*.

I go home again.

Like Lipsha I traveled far to find my father, and I too headed for home.

I had to go to southern California, over four hundred miles from my family's native homeland in northern California, where I was born and raised.

I worked from a tip my mother's younger brother, my uncle, had given me. I listened to gossip, took notes, followed leads, and found my father in a Laguna Beach high school yearbook. A dark-skinned man in a row of blondes. And I saw myself in that face. Without a doubt. Darker than me. But me nonetheless.

I interviewed several people who went to school with him and my mother. It was my mother's friends who verified what I suspected. Emilio Hilario was my father. They also told me that he had died, that I had missed him by about five years.

I had to find out from others what he couldn't tell me. But now I had names, telephone numbers, addresses. I found a half brother and uncle in town. My grandfather still lived in the old house "out in the canyon" where he had moved his wife and children nearly fifty years ago when he took a job as a kitchen worker in Victor Hugo's, a glamorous waterfront restaurant.

Going to the old house was something. After all these years to find a place that was home, where my own father had grown up, where he had a mother and father, a brother and sister, where he sat at a kitchen table, where he took off his shoes at night and dreamed. Years of wondering leveled now by the sight of a small, ordinary house set back a ways from the road. I turned in the driveway, past the metal mailbox that said HILARIO.

I was amazed by Grandpa, how small he was as he held me in his arms. A small, dark Filipino with quick black eyes holding his six-foot-two, blue-eyed grandson. But I lost track of him. I forgot his first words, "the oldest son of my oldest son," and I forgot even that it was Grandpa who clutched my wrist and was leading me through the house. I was lost in the photographs. Photographs everywhere. High school graduation. Baby pictures. Family reunions. Weddings. Mostly black and white, except for the newer ones on top of the color TV. They lined the door frames, covered entire walls and the end tables on either side of the sofa. In Grandpa's bedroom there were several photos of my father and uncle in uniforms—football, Navy, Army. One of them caught my attention, a head shot of my father in his sailor's uniform. He was smiling, handsome, his white grin almost boyish. He wrote on the picture:

> Dear Mom and Dad,
> > Had fun seeing you last week.
> > > Love,
> > Your Son
> > > Emilio   May 15, 1951

He also saw my mother that week. Nine months later, February 12, 1952, he would have his first son.

Grandpa and I settled at the kitchen table. I took in other things: the faded beige kitchen walls, the odor of his pipe, the black dog at his side, his thick accent. I watched as he boiled water in an old pot, the kind that is tall with a spout and lid. "Your Grandma, she used this," he said and poured water in a cup for instant coffee. "She used this to boil her water. Only thing she drank Hobo coffee, just boil the water and run it over the coffee in a strainer." He set the pot on the stove then picked up a small stained strainer from the stove top. "This is it," he said. "She sat right there in that chair next to the stove. She smoke and drink Hobo coffee. Here's her ashtray." He held the small ceramic bowl in his hand then placed it neatly on the stove top with the strainer. He told me she died thirteen years ago. Obviously Grandpa had not changed a thing in the house.

"What happened to my father, Grandpa?"

I had heard my father died of a heart attack. But I wanted to hear it from Grandpa. Had he been sick a long time? Did he suffer?

Grandpa was at the stove watching me. I caught his eyes. He turned around and lit his pipe. Then all at once he put it down in a tin ashtray next to Grandma's ashtray on the stove top.

"Finish your coffee. Then we go to the cemetery," Grandpa said.

We got on the 405 freeway, then went east through the city of Orange. We stopped at a supermarket and bought flowers, mixed bouquets, the kind you see road vendors selling. I could see now that Grandpa lived by routine. He had probably been coming to the same market, one of dozens we had passed, for thirteen years.

"Something with his heart," Grandpa said. "All screwed up."

I was startled, caught off guard when he spoke. He had been quiet, and now the rolling green cemetery lawns were in view. It took me a minute to realize he was talking about my father.

"Yeah," he said. "Smoke too much. Fix his heart bad. Same thing with your grandmother. She smoke too much cigarettes. Get cancer. I tell 'em not to. Well . . ."

My grandmother and father are buried next to each other. The graves are close to the road. They are under a small cypress tree that marks the place for me. Grandpa performs a kind of ritual there. He leans over, and with his index finger on the raised letters of the metal grave plaque, he talks to the dead. That day, as always, he went to my grandmother first. He said: "Mom, here is your grandson. You didn't get to know him because . . ." He didn't finish the sentence. He turned to my father and said: "Son, you can rest now . . . Your boy is home."

EMILIO HILARIO   EVELYN HILARIO

In Laguna Beach I talked to more people who knew my father—friends, ex-wives, relatives. They told me he was charming, charismatic. He loved his family. He was a fine athlete at one time, a boxer who knocked down Floyd Patterson. But a few people told me that there was another side to him. The drinking and violence. He broke his first wife's jaw. In a drunken brawl he mistook a friend for an enemy and threw the friend out a second-story window. He talked badly about white people. All three of his wives were white. He was alcoholic, overweight, down on his luck when he died of a massive heart attack at fifty-two.

Growing up in Laguna Beach was not easy for any of the Hilario children. My Auntie Rita Hilario-Carter tells me that when she was in fourth grade her teacher told her to clean up another girl's urine. "She told me to do it because when I grew up I was going to be a maid," Auntie Rita said. "I was the only brown child in the class." Although the town exalted my father as an athlete, he was discouraged from dating the white daughters of the townspeople.

My father's cousin told me that near the end of his life he would call her sometimes late at night. She said he would be drunk and fighting with his last wife. "How should I kill this white bitch?" he'd holler over the phone. "Strangle her? Drown her?" My father's last wife told me that my father talked about a son he had somewhere in the world. "I want him to feel welcome if he ever finds his way home," he told her. "I want him to know us."

I thought of my mother and how she died shortly after I was born so that the truth never got back to Laguna Beach about what happened to her or me. Rumors. Gossip. No one had the full story. Auntie Rita said: "I always wondered what happened to Bunny. No one talked about it. It was hush-hush around our house. Of course I was only about twelve at the time. Bunny was so nice. I thought it was such a big deal that this older white girl would come and take me for ice cream. Hah, little did I know what else was going on!" Ironically, I was born in Santa Rosa, where my mother's mother took my mother to have me, four hundred miles from Laguna Beach, on the same land my father's mother left decades before. And I would be taken in by my father's mother's people. Where was home? Santa Rosa? Laguna Beach? The Kashaya Reservation?

Before I left Laguna Beach, I went back to Grandpa's house. I wanted to visit and say goodbye.

He was waiting for me. He had coffee ready. Two old photo albums, one on top of the other, were on the kitchen table. On a faded green cover I saw in an elaborate scroll the words "Family Album." Grandpa sat next to me and opened the top album. He started talking about the assorted black and white photos. "This is your grandmother when I met her . . . Oh, that's her sister, Juanita . . . That's your great-grandma, the old Indian from up there, Old [Tom] Smith's daughter . . ." It was truly a

miracle. Pieces of a puzzle fell together. With names, I now knew how I
was connected to everyone I knew. I could trace my genealogy. Auntie
Violet was actually my grandmother's cousin. I had dated a girl from the
reservation who was my second cousin, my father's first cousin. Grandpa
told me that he met Grandma in East Los Angeles. She had come from
northern California to stay with her sister.

"Did she speak Indian, Grandpa? Did she tell any of the old-time
stories?"

"Take what pictures you want," he said. "Maybe those ladies up there
[at Kashaya] can tell you something."

We went through the second album, and then Grandpa found a plastic
K-Mart shopping bag for me to put the photos in. I felt shy. I didn't want
to take too many, leaving gaps all over Grandma's pages. I took my time
and picked out a little over a dozen. Then I stood up and looked around
one last time before I had to go.

The house wasn't the same as when I first walked in. It was familiar
now, and not necessarily because I had been in the place before and knew
its layout. It was the photos. The smiling faces. The uniforms. Party
dresses. Sportcoats and ties. I kept thinking of what I heard from the
people I talked to during the last few days. Grandpa caught me standing
in the middle of the living room. He handed me the plastic bag of
pictures.

"It's too bad," he said. "I tell your father not to smoke. Your
Grandma, too. It done 'em in. Too much smoking . . . Heart, you know.
Cancer . . . I tell 'em not to."

"Yeah," I said and hugged him.

I had driven nearly five hundred miles by the time I reached Auntie
Violet's place. Nine hours north from Laguna Beach on Highway 101
and then the long climb from Healdsburg to the reservation on top of the
mountain. Still, I was wide awake, excited.

I told Auntie Violet and Auntie Vivien everything I learned. Uncle
Paul, Violet's husband, sat and listened for a long time too. I sounded like
Auntie Violet. I rattled off names, went up and down family trees. I knew
names. I knew my relations. I was telling Auntie Violet things she didn't
know. I knew what happened to Rienette "Nettie" Smith, my great-
grandmother, and her three children, Juanita, Albert, and Evelyn.

"Grandma Rosie knew that old lady. She knew them people," Auntie
Violet said.

I could tell in Auntie's voice that she was holding back something. I saw it in her eyes, as if she was watching for something behind her or underneath the table that might pop out anytime. She was anxious to see the pictures, and it wasn't until she had four or five of them in front of her that she let out what she was holding back, that my grandmother didn't want to be Indian. Her people were stuck-up, not good Indians. Related, yes. But so what? Auntie knew.

Auntie kept the photographs in front of her all night. Now and then she glanced at them, even after we finished talking about my trip and my grandmother. She reminded me how lucky I was to have been raised around Aunt Mabel and close to people on the reservation. "You learned from a great Indian," she said, referring to Mabel McKay. I was lucky. I was lucky to know Mabel and I learned a lot from her, things I would not have known otherwise. I wanted to tell Auntie that I agreed with her, that I was lucky. And I wanted to thank her and Uncle Paul for all they had done for me, all the love they had shown. But I was tired. I hardly remember getting up from the table and going to bed.

I woke early, before anyone else, and made my way to the kitchen. You could still smell food, the heavy odor of homecooking, but now it was cool, damp. And the kitchen was dark, the curtains pulled over the windows and across the sliding glass doors. I went to open the curtain next to the kitchen table when I caught sight of Auntie's row of my grandmother's pictures. They seemed so still. Everything else had been cleared away—the leftovers in Tupperware bowls, Auntie's pink poodle salt-and-pepper shakers. I started for the photographs. I say I started, but I didn't actually move, except to stand up straight and look around the room. Photos everywhere. Auntie's case of babies' pictures. Pictures of her Mom and Dad, Auntie Essie and Uncle Sid. In one picture Auntie Essie is standing in front of the roundhouse in her beaded buckskin ceremonial dress. And there is a picture of Auntie Violet with Robert Kennedy.

I heard birds outside. I thought of what Auntie said about my grandmother. Again I had the urge to pick up the photos left on the table. But I couldn't move. I felt as if my slightest gesture would wake the entire household.

Home, I thought. Home again.

I could be jealous of Lipsha. He got to meet his father, see him face to face. They "held each other's arms, tight and manly." Of course miracles happened for both of us. The miracle of finding our fathers. The miracle of being lucky enough to be raised and cared for by our own people, even when we didn't know about our blood relation to those people, and then the miracle of finding out. The miracle of always having been home in some way or other. But none of those miracles changes the nature of home for Lipsha or for me. There is still the drinking and violence, gossip and bickering. Indians fighting each other. Is finding our fathers and knowing our families love us as much as they can medicine enough? Lipsha observes: "The sun flared. . . . The morning was clear. A good road led on. So there was nothing to do but cross the water and bring her home." If in the novel we were to see Lipsha make it home, as I did, what would he find?

As I noted earlier, certain of Erdrich's characters sense the depth and breadth of the problems around them. Certain characters have their moments, their insights that help them come to terms with the pain. At the funeral of Grandpa (Nector) Kashpaw, Lipsha felt his "vision shifted" (LM 211). He says:

> I began to see things different, more clear. The family kneeling down turned to rocks in a field. It struck me how strong and reliable grief was, and death. Until the end of time, death would be our rock.
>
> So I had perspective on it all, for death gives you that. All the Kapshaw children had done various things to me in their lives—shared their folks with me, loaned me cash, beat me up in secret—and I decided, because of death, then and there I'd call it quits. If I ever saw King again, I'd shake his hand. Forgiving somebody else made the whole thing easier to bear.
>
> (LM 211)

Lulu Lamartine reflects on her long affair with Nector Kashpaw, Marie Lazarre Kashpaw's husband, and says:

> We took our pleasure without asking or thinking further than a touch. We were so deeply sunk in the land of our greed it took the court action of the tribe and a house on fire to pull us out.
>
> Hearing [Marie's] voice I tried imagining what Marie must have thought. He came each week in the middle of the night. She must have known he wasn't out taking walks to see the beauty of the dark heaven.
>
> (LM 231)

Later Lulu confesses: "For the first time I saw exactly how another woman felt, and it gave me deep comfort, surprising" (LM 236). Here Lulu is able to empathize with another human being, to see the limits and consequences of her needs and wants. The same thing happens for Marie Lazarre Kashpaw who attends to Lulu with the kindness of a mother in the Senior Citizens' home. As Lipsha reports, "[Marie] and Lulu was thick as thieves now" (LM 241).

These characters' insights, their moments of understanding and for-giveness, are a balm for the soul, certainly love medicine. And the fact that they are telling their stories, leading us through their pain to some resolution about it, means that they are talking, that they do in fact have a way of talking about the pain. But do their insights and stories touch upon a large cause of so much of their pain? Does their love medicine treat the symptoms of a disease without getting at the cause?

Again, the disease I am talking about, internalized oppression, cuts a wide swath. So much is unconscious, passed down through generations, family to family. So much is unrecognizable. Is Marie Lazarre Kashpaw simply an insecure woman driven to garner for herself self-worth? Isn't her insecurity, her denial of her origins, rooted in a history of which she is a part? Is King merely another male with low self-esteem who must beat his wife to feel significant and powerful? Is Gordie just another drunk, down on his luck? As I said earlier, to me much of the pain these characters experience and inflict upon one another is tied to colonialism, and ironically and inadvertently they work to complete what the colo-nizer began. Gabriele Schwab observes: "Only when the colonized's own native culture has been relegated to the political unconscious and be-come internalized as the Other, only then is the process of colonization successfully completed. As Fanon shows, the success of any cultural liberation would depend upon reaching these unconscious domains" (130). If Erdrich's characters' insights and stories, if their forgiveness and empathy, can put them in touch with that which is unconscious and historical, then the cause of the disease can be treated. I'm not sure this happens. Lipsha says "I had perspective on it all." What is "it"? If "Forgiving somebody else made the whole thing easier to bear," did forgiving expose what "the whole thing" is? Can Lipsha now name what King is afraid of? Can Lulu's empathy for another woman open the door to their shared history? Does it?

Of course readers of *Love Medicine* sense the larger historical picture. As Peter Matthiessen writes on the jacket cover of the first edition of *Love Medicine,* Erdrich "convey[s] unflinchingly the funkiness, humor, and great unspoken sadness of the Indian reservations, and a people exiled to a no-man's land between two worlds." Robert Silberman notes that "[Erdrich's] concentration on personal, family matters may be in-tentional, but the sense of being removed from political events is a powerful statement about marginality and disenfranchisement while also suggesting a preferred concern with the personal and private life of the community" (114). And given the larger historical picture and the nature of these characters' lives, there is no doubt the insights and stories of Lipsha and Lulu are triumphant. But, again, are their triumphs great enough to touch that which is a large source of their pain, at least as I see it?

And here I must come back to questions raised at the start of this chapter. I must come back to where I started, for the pain and the triumphs of Louise Erdrich's fictional Chippewa community may not be as I see them or have read them. Again, is Erdrich's Chippewa community really that similar to what I know of and read into my own Indian community? Am I merely arranging photos just as Auntie Violet did? What about the specific circumstances of Chippewa colonial history that may affect both the nature of Chippewa oppression and of Chippewa triumph over that oppression? How has Erdrich as a writer understood that history? How might I understand it?

These are just some of the questions that I should pursue regarding internalized oppression and *Love Medicine,* although I do not have space here to fully explore them. Then again my purpose was not to come up with definite answers. Rather, I hoped to raise questions, to expose my interaction with Erdrich's novel, and to extend my story of that interaction to other readers. Other readers with other stories can explore what I have said and what I have left unanswered. They can continue what I have just barely started. A testimony of the novel's power and strength is that it shocked me into thinking about my own community, and by looking back and forth at the community in the book and the one I know as Home, I found a way, however tentative, to think and talk about the pain in both places. The book raised questions for me about my own community, and it touched my own pain and the history of that pain. Reading *Love Medicine* became Home Medicine.

In closing I want to tell one last story, because I cannot stop thinking about it. It has lived with me through the writing of this essay. I want Auntie Violet and Louise Erdrich and others to have the chance to see it. So I need to tell it.

It is about Crawling Woman. She was a Coast Miwok woman who was born in the old village that was called Nicasias, near the present town of Nicasio in Marin County. Crawling Woman is not a real name. It is how she is remembered. Even her great-great-granddaughter, Juanita Carrio, the noted Miwok elder and matriarch who told me the story, could not remember a real name for Crawling Woman. She was one of my grandmother's ancestors too, though I'm not sure of the blood connection.

Anyway, she got that name because at the end of her life she became childlike, an imbecile, Juanita said. She did not know anybody or anything. She didn't talk. She only made babylike sounds and cried. And she crawled. She crawled everywhere, out the front door, up the road, into the fields. People said she was at least a hundred and ten years old by that time. She was a grown woman when the first Spanish missionaries invaded her home. She was a grandmother by the time General Vallejo's Mexican soldiers established a fort in Petaluma, and when California became a state in 1850, she was already a very old woman.

She never talked about her past. She was quiet and she worked hard. Kept her nose to the grindstone, Juanita said. She washed clothes for the Americans and she sold fish she caught herself. This was when she was over eighty years old. But people did know some stories about her. Once she ran away from the mission in San Rafael. She heard horses come up and she hid in a dry creekbed. She was on her stomach, face down, flat out and stiff as a board. It wasn't until she was home, back in Nicasias, and had opened her eyes that she realized the men who picked her up and loaded her onto the wagon bed were Indians.

No one can remember how she lost her mind, whether gradually with age or suddenly, say from a stroke. She became a nuisance. She had to be watched all the time. She would get out of the house and go great distances. She could crawl as fast as a person walked, even at her great age. She would hide and then resist coming home when she was found. Juanita's mother used to babysit the old woman. She was just a young girl at the time, and to get the old woman to behave she would put on an old soldier's jacket they kept in the closet. Crawling Woman would see the brass buttons on the coat and let out a loud shriek and crawl as fast as she could back to the house.

That coat was the only thing she recognized, Juanita said.

PART FOUR

Keeping Slug Woman Alive: Classroom Practices

CHAPTER SEVEN

Storytelling in the Classroom

Crossing Vexed Chasms

I begin my American Indian literature course by telling a story told to me by my Kashaya Pomo elders. I then ask students, usually at the next class meeting, to repeat the story as they heard it. Invariably their stories tell them more about themselves than about the story or about the speaker and culture from which the story comes. Here students can see how they are approaching the story and begin to explore unexamined assumptions by which they operate and which they use to frame the texts and experiences of members of another culture. This storytelling (about a story) engenders a reflexivity that pervades or establishes the groundwork for further study of American Indian texts. Here I present the story I tell, so that I can discuss students' responses to the story and assumptions inherent in the responses.

Now let me tell you a story. It is a story from this land, told to me by Kashaya [Pomo] elders. When I was young, growing up in Santa Rosa, just about a hundred miles north of here, I heard many of the old-time stories. In the Kashaya language they are called *duwi dici·du*, literally "telling about Coyote" or "Coyote stories," about the time when animals were still people.

Sometimes late at night the old-timers would tell these stories; sometimes just to talk, it seemed, and other times because something in the story had a particular message for us. Maybe because of something we did or said. But the stories are only to be told in winter. So now, in telling this story [during spring months], I am breaking a rule. I'll just fix the story so it's not the same.

This time Coyote was admiring the stripes on Junco's face. "How do I get stripes like that?" he was asking. He stood there looking at Junco, seeing those stripes, envious as Coyote often is of what others have. Junco—Junco is a bird, a tiny bird, grayish brown in color with face stripes—he laughed. He said, "Well, Coyote, you can't have these stripes. They are for me, they are my design." Coyote huffed. "There must be a way I can have them." "Well, if you won't tell anyone," Junco said, "I'll tell you how to get stripes. You won't want to do it anyway, not when you find out what it is you have to do."

"But I do," said Coyote. "I'll do anything."

"Well, then, this is it." Junco rolled his eyes in mock disgust, as if irritated by Coyote's persistence. "You must take the marrow from your bones and then mix it with a little water. Stir and then apply evenly on both sides of the face."

"How do I get the bone marrow?"

"Break a bone, suck it out."

And that is just what Coyote did. He hiked his leg over a thick log, and then with a good-sized rock in his hand, he came down *Swoosh* on that leg. Just like that, crushing his leg, cracking the bone wide open. "Ouch! Ouch!"

"Ha! Ha!" Junco called and flitted through the brush. "Ha! Ha! You fool. Greedy sucker, you believe anything anyone tells you." Coyote looked up, but by this time, Junco was long gone, clear over in Ukiah Valley somewhere. Coyote's leg began to swell and fester. Before long, infection set in, and a stench wafted through the air drawing the attention of buzzard, crow, and condor. Several other birds came also, all of them hungry for rotten flesh. They began to dive, swoop down on Coyote. He swung at them, fought madly, and in the end, found himself with only a handful of feathers. He found he had feathers from each bird.

"What am I going to do with these feathers?" he was asking himself. "I should sweat, pray that the birds don't haunt me with these feathers. And that way [by sweating], I can heal my infection also." So he went into the sweathouse and planted each of the feathers in a circle. He built a good fire of manzanita wood. He prayed, sang songs. Then he got too hot and went out to cool off. Suddenly, while he was lying outside under some brush, he heard voices, people all speaking different languages, coming from down inside the sweathouse. "What is that?" he was thinking. And upon reentering the sweathouse, he found the people, all different from one another, sprung from each of the different feathers. They went out [of the sweathouse] each going in different directions, destined for places all over the earth. The Kashaya people stayed right there. They are made from the feather of crow. Sometimes they are referred to as Crow Feathers, even to this day.

"My goodness!" Coyote thought. But he was so thirsty he had to go for water. He was starving, too. He stumbled upon a grasshopper den and scooped up as many grasshoppers as he could. Then, with a sharp digging stick, he began to dig a hole in which to toast the insects. Unbelievably, while digging, he hit water, causing a geyser that squirted up and went everywhere in streams and rivers, until it reached the ocean and lay still and salty. Into that water [ocean] Coyote threw a manzanita stick which became a trout; after that, a piece of madrone which became a salmon, a turtle for abalone, and for whale a bear. "Now the people will fish to eat," he said. The water looked eerie, just lying flat with whale's back up and out of the water, so Coyote caused it to ebb and flow. "Do like this," he was saying, gesturing with his arms. "Make waves."

That's how people said it was done, these things. Those who were watching and passed the story down through time. How Father God did these things. It goes on . . . Coyote did many foolish things. Once I heard a woman tell the story differently. Well, actually, it was another part of the story—about when the earth was flooded and the people ran to the highest mountain and turned into trees. Well, that's all I can say today. See you next time.[1]

I record my version of the story so that after the students have presented their versions they can hear how they rearranged and omitted certain features of the story. The version above was transcribed from the latest recording, and, during the subsequent class meeting, students' stories proved consistent with those of former students. Always most striking is the omission of contextual information. If information reporting the story's genesis, Kashaya generic classification, or rules associated with the telling itself is presented at all, it is always within a narrative that begins and ends with Coyote. Students see narrative and context of production as extricable, independent from one another, and draw lines governed by preconceived notions of narrative.

Another interesting feature of the students' stories is their assiduous

---

1. Herman James tells versions of this story in Robert Oswalt's *Kashaya Texts*. See James's "The Creation of the Ocean" (36–41) and "The Creation of the People and the Ocean" (41–45). I have heard this story several times by different Kashaya elders, including Essie Parrish and Violet Chappell.

attention to detail and plot. As they put their stories together in groups, I witness lengthy discussions about whether it was a piece of manzanita that became a trout or whether Coyote unconsciously tripped upon a grasshopper den or knew exactly where the den was. Certain details, however, are rarely acknowledged. The clause about Father God seldom appears because, according to students, "a Christian concept did not seem Indian." One consequence of students' close attention to detail is an overabundance of etiological explanation. While the students sense the story is about creation, and while the story itself contains etiological tags and does concern "creation," each action on the part of Coyote does not necessarily precipitate the formation of the world as we know it, as most of the students' stories would have one believe. On the contrary, the story indicates that Coyote was functioning, living his life, in a world that already existed, a world where people sweated, used digging sticks, and feasted on grasshoppers. As I noted in an earlier chapter, the salient feature of the Kashaya Pomo language is the verb, and if the story were told in Pomo, it would become quite clear how action and not subject becomes thematized, something suggested by a close examination of the story even as it is told in English, although it is completely ignored by the students who, I must admit, didn't have the opportunity to inspect the story until after their own retelling. What the students see, nonetheless, is that cultural biases influence interpretive acts, and when issues of language and translation are raised in the future, the students are that much more sensitive as to how a translation may itself be an interpretation. Students then continue to approach this literature dialogically, confronting, and attempting to talk across, the spaces between their world and that of an American Indian text.

I started with this example of storytelling in the classroom because it illustrates how storytelling might promote critical discourse about texts and also helps clarify the old and still pervasive misconception of critical thinking as something devoid of cultural and historical contexts.

Richard Paul, a leader in the Critical Thinking Movement, suggests that in teaching what he calls *strong sense* critical thinking, teachers must enable students "to see beyond the world views that distort their perception and impede their ability to reason clearly." Critical thinking should, according to Paul, "empower [the mind] to analyze, digest, and rule its own knowledge, to achieve fairmindedness and critical exactness" (2–3). This attractive notion is hardly new. Kant's conception of rationalism as pure thought, or as that process which Kant believed releases one from "immaturity," the state of will that makes us accept someone else's authority to lead us, assumes that rationality is in itself something transcendent, devoid of the history and subsequent bias that has largely created the subject who is using it. In reality, this rationality became inextricable from the social and political circumstances of the time. Various sciences, which had slowly been developing in the two hundred years before Kant, suddenly became legitimate and bloomed in that they had a purpose not just to explain functions of the government and human species but, more important now, to explain how government and the human species might be used for the purposes of that same government and its constituencies. Each activity in its own specific way demanded reflection on how it could best be accomplished. The prince, concerned with a well-governed polity (or, as it was called in the eighteenth century, a well-policed state), had to have a scientific—or rational—sense of his people and the environment. As we now know, what was rational for the prince was not necessarily so for the people or the environment. Although Richard Paul distinguishes self-serving critical thinking from strong sense critical thinking, his language of "rule," "command," and "critical exactness" could foster this sense of critical thinking as something separate from historical and social contingencies. Understanding and not control is the goal of critical discourse, and this understanding is dynamic, dialogical in nature. A more clearly stated purpose for critical thinking might be to foster a process or attitude which enables the individual to, as Gramsci says, " 'know thyself' as a product of the historical process to date" (324), which can only come about when that history and assumptions about it are challenged. Knowing thyself and knowing the other, then, are interdependent.

As the exercise with the Kashaya Pomo story illustrates, critical discourse and any activity that predicates interpretive acts depend largely on the thinker's tie to a given knowledge base and belief system and on the linguistic features associated with the belief system. If critical thinking or so-called rationalism does not at the same time point to its intrinsic limits, to its tie to the cultural and political realities that shape thinkers as knowledgeable subjects, then a system that excludes difference, culturally or otherwise, is likely to be perpetuated. Teachers and students are led to believe that some people think critically while others do not, so that those who have critical thinking must teach it to those who do not have it. What is taught is more likely to be a set of cultural norms associated with modes of a specific and culturally based type of critical thought, and the subjects examined are those within a given knowledge base established and maintained in very specific ways. We get

caught in and perpetuate a kind of vicious circle where those students
who don't think the way we do reinforce for us, in their inability to think
in a manner we call rational, the need for us to teach them. Intentionally
or not, critical thinking is taught as a normalizing device. All that could
engender strong sense critical thinking—that which would challenge
given assumptions and enable students and teachers "to see beyond the
world views that distort their perception and impede their ability to
reason clearly"—has been effectively excluded.

The perceived split between life experience and critical thought com-
plements a chasm that many students experience between life experience
and classroom activities. What students find in texts and from classroom
discussions often has little to do with what they know from home. Both
material and nonmaterial elements of the students' homes may be absent
from the classroom or manifested in different and unrecognizable ways.
The foreign world of Dick and Jane continues in college with a sociology
professor's definition of the nuclear family as that family comprised of
father, mother, and siblings. The culturally diverse student, and many
other students for that matter, are forced to negotiate the discrepancies
between home life and what is taught in the classroom. Too often
students become disaffected, unable to deal with the conflicts; or they
successfully learn to operate from one side of the chasm, repressing their
life experience if it interferes with what is happening in the classroom.
These latter students accept the words and ideas of texts and professors
as authoritative and tend to see their lives in terms of the texts, never
considering the possibilities of seeing the texts in terms of their lives.

Of course, much has been said lately about the disaffected and alien-
ated student. Discussions of reader response and interpretive communities, fostered by Stanley Fish and a host of others, have pointed to the
power and potential of students' subjective responses as readers. These
critics argue that the reader is socially and politically charged; what
readers bring to the text depends on the circumstances of their experience. It has become increasingly difficult to dismiss students' difficulties
as mere cognitive dysfunctions; such attributions, now more thoroughly
contextualized, have lost their objective value. A student's difficulty in
the classroom is just as likely to be social and ultimately political in
nature. In a paper presented at the 1987 MLA convention and entitled
"Literate Cultures: Multi-Voiced Classrooms," Marjorie Roemer provided a list of models that could be helpful in recognizing and incor-
porating subjective response in classroom activity. She pointed to the
work of Thomas Newkirk (1984) which, in Roemer's words, "has made

the problems we have in confronting a poem the basis for our understanding of that poem. [Newkirk] allows readers to see how their own readings enact a recessive process of revision and redefinition, amending interpretations as they proceed" (6). She also noted the work of Kathleen McCormick, Gary Waller, and Lois Fowler in the new *Lexington Introduction to Literature,* which again uses various strategies to make the reader conscious of herself as a reader. Attempting to make interpretive acts the central subject of study in her classes, Roemer described how she uses John Berger's *Another Way of Telling* to direct "students' attention at once to the 'readings' we perform in so simple an act as the recognition of an event depicted in a photograph" (7).

But in using any of these models one cannot assume that the reader's response and what constitutes that response is present or will necessarily emerge. Many people, for instance, point to dialogue, specifically dialogue of the sort Paulo Freire uses, as a basis for establishing *conscientização,* "learning to perceive social, political, and economic contradictions, and to take action against the oppressive elements of reality" (19). The "dialogical teacher" uses dialogue that enables students to reach "a perception of their previous perception" (108). But dialogue can become a circumscribed mode of discourse that excludes, often unknowingly, the student's experience, given the chasm between life experience and classroom activity, a split which is likely to be exacerbated by the perceived authority of the teacher and a knowledge base determined and maintained by dominant cultural norms. Dialogue does not guarantee *conscientização;* a dialogue can in fact just as easily be seen as an allegory, telling the story of a story of power relations between teachers and students and between certain "bright" students and other "not-so-bright" students. If students are responding, dialogically or otherwise, from one side of the chasm, that of the classroom, are we getting that which could make for a difference that makes a difference? Can all of us, students and teachers, be engaged in strong sense critical thinking?

The presence of this chasm must be considered, then, especially in light of a student population that is increasingly diverse culturally and linguistically, and indicates criteria by which we might assess or think about the models we use to foster critical thinking in the classroom. First, the model or method must engage the life experience of the students. Here, of course, much depends on the sensitivity of the instructor and precisely how the model or method is utilized in a given classroom context. Second, the model must enable students to scrutinize their experiences or what constitutes their assumptions. Eliciting subjective responses is not enough; in order for students to be conscious of what they bring to the classroom, they must be able to hold their responses up for scrutiny, say against given texts and other stories, so that they can enter into critical dialogue about their relationship to texts and other ideas. Cultural variance is a means here and not an end. An experience is not expressed to simply be validated, but so it might inform and be informed by other experiences. In satisfying these criteria two chasms are crossed, that between life experience and school experience and that between either blind acceptance or mere subjective responses to information and critical reflection about information.

People's stories can tell them so much about themselves. Stories become an important device individuals use to interpret to each other their experiences—experiences with work, school, a text, their families. Helen B. Schwartzman has observed that, within organizational settings, "stories are a pervasive social form . . . that can generate organizational activity (not just comment on it) and interpret and sometimes transform the work experience" (80). Stories are not simply representational; as representations they reveal the nature of interpretive acts. Schwartzman studied the stories of staff members in a community mental health center and found the stories to be "a form for individual interpretation, construction, and reconstruction of events [that] provides individuals and the organization with a way to create and then discover the meaning of what it is they are doing and saying" (91). In his discussion of Zuni storytelling, Dennis Tedlock illustrates that if given a fixed text and the opportunity and encouragement to revise and retell the text, people will use their individual experience as a means to interpret and comment upon the fixed text. The Zuni storyteller, recounting the oral narrative *Kyaklo an' pennane,* "The Work of Kyaklo," changes the story from one occasion to the next, as the storyteller considers his audience and what they know or do not know or realizes something about the story for the first time. As I noted in the chapter "The Woman Who Loved a Snake," Tedlock writes that "the interpreter [as storyteller] does not merely play the parts, but is the narrator and commentator as well. What we are hearing is the hermeneutics of the text of Kyaklo" (236). Likewise what I hear in my American Indian courses is the hermeneutics of the text of Coyote and Junco, and students not only see their stories as interpretations but also, in so seeing, discover what constitutes their interpretations and how that shapes the distance between their world and that of the story as I first told it. Thus, the two criteria established above have been met: students have engaged their experience, here in the mere retelling of the story, and they have been able to discover in a critical fashion what underlies their assumptions about narrative and Indian culture as my version of the story was played back against their own.

The students in my American Indian literature courses have been predominantly middle-class whites, certainly not Kashaya Pomo. Their stories, as I have pointed out, display certain kinds of assumptions associated with their experiences. What began as a dialogue across white middle-class American culture and Kashaya Pomo culture became a larger dialogue across other texts and American Indian cultures associated with those texts. The dialogue, and of course the exercise that prompted the dialogue, instill a reflexive attitude, causing students to always consider what they might be doing to texts as readers. Again, it must be remembered that this is one kind of storytelling exercise suited for one kind of subject matter. As a group, the students were generally accustomed to texts from a culture that reflected their own values and assumptions, albeit in various and sometimes foreign ways, and reading did not foster the kind of disparity between their world and that of a text of the sort they discovered between their world and that of the Kashaya Pomo that I presented. I created an exercise to hoodwink them. But in other classroom settings, such an exercise would not work, at least not in the same ways. The culturally diverse student is faced with quite the opposite scenario: what is taught in the classroom—what is read—emerges from a knowledge base and a set of cultural norms that is often quite foreign. And in the culturally diverse classroom, there may be a multitude of knowledge bases where the features and subjects of one base may or may not overlap with those of another. How might storytelling enable these students to talk back to material that is foreign in many ways? How might storytelling engage students from several different cultural backgrounds?

In the spring of 1984 I was asked to design and teach a writing course for a group of Cree students who would be selected from the Saddle Lake Reserve in Alberta to participate in a tribally funded summer educational advancement program held at the University of California at Santa Cruz. At the time, I directed the UC Santa Cruz Student Affirmative Action/Educational Opportunity Program Writing Center and taught writing courses designed for the campus's ethnic minority and low-income students. I thought material from these courses might interest the Cree students, and I sent away to Canada for public documents on native education that I thought could prompt critical discussion.

Despite my best intentions, I found that after three weeks of teaching, with only two weeks left in the program, I had succeeded in little more than encouraging personal anecdotes from the students.

The class posed many challenges from the start. The students were more homogeneous than in any class I had taught; they were from the same reserve and, in one way or another, were related to each other. At the same time, I had high school seniors and college freshmen ranging from seventeen to twenty-six years old. Most had "stopped out" of school at some point, which is not unusual on a reserve where only fifteen percent of the students finish high school, and four of the eight women in the class had children. These students were cautious, reluctant at first to speak in class. Although I felt good that we could finally talk after three weeks, it was clear that we had made little progress in terms of critical writing and reading. Their papers remained purely anecdotal and uncritical, like the classroom discussions, or full of vague, unsubstantiated claims coined in that all-too-familiar pseudo-academic prose.

I remember an eighteen-year-old woman who agreed with me that her ideas needed to be developed and that much of her language was vague. This woman was a senior who had "stopped out" twice, once when she was twelve because she "couldn't relate to school anymore," and again when she was fourteen to have a baby. She had written about alienation in the classroom, a topic we had been discussing for over a week. "I guess I need to find more stuff on it in the library," she told me, "and use a dictionary for those words." While we sat in my office discussing alienation, the student kept her experience—what constitutes her as a reader, writer, and thinker, and could illuminate any notion of alienation—far away, like something left in the dorm, locked away with the rest of her luggage. Lest a teacher jump in too quickly with suggestions about how such a student might engage her personal experience, it should be remembered that the chasm here is likely to be protective. Teenage pregnancy, poor grades, obesity, which all signal failure in some way, are difficult enough to live with let alone discuss with a teacher or in a classroom of peers. And has the cross-cultural dynamic been considered here, where assumptions and expectations that inhere in classroom activities are likely to be foreign in ways to Cree students? Yet the fact remains that this student's story could not only provide her a powerful critical tool for engaging texts and ideas but could, in the process, expose the forces which inculcate failure and alienation—the same forces that keep her experience outside the classroom.

Not long after the conference with this student, I found myself again listening to a flurry of stories about discrimination and alienation in the classroom environment. We had been discussing selections from Maxine Hong Kingston's *The Woman Warrior* and Richard Rodriguez's *Hunger of Memory,* and the students were volunteering stories, mostly second-hand accounts, providing "right examples" of discrimination and alienation. In many of these anecdotes I descried moments of conflicting cultural problems that once examined might open larger and more critical discussions. But it was at that point of contact or critical inquiry that these students would retreat from discussion. Of course, I knew that so much of what underlay the issues of discrimination and alienation in terms of the students' personal responses was morally and emotionally charged. Too much questioning, besides displaying my ignorance and insensitivity, was likely to suggest to the students a power move on my part for more "right answers."

One student then told of a teacher who sat a Native girl in the corner with a coloring pad and crayons while other students worked on computers. (These Saddle Lake Cree students refer to themselves, and to American Indian people in general, as Natives.) When this student, then a teaching assistant, asked why the Native girl was in the corner, the teacher replied, "Oh, she's not really interested. She's from out in the bush, you know. She never says much. She's more creative."

More hands shot up. We moved from one story to the next. Frustrated, I attempted to ground the discussion, at least momentarily, by returning to the story of the Native girl. I thought perhaps we could ask some questions about her circumstances in that classroom, perhaps ponder her future as a student.

"What is going to happen to that girl?" I asked.

The immediate response: "She'll drop out."

"Let's tell her story," I suggested, not knowing what to expect. "Let's take it from the time she is put in the corner to the time she drops out."

The hands went down. Silence.

"Let's just make it up, each person tell a part of her story. I'll start." I kept talking now just to fill the void I had created. "She will begin to get confused and hate her parents for sending her to school," I said, "to a place where she feels different."

Eventually, a tentative voice: "She'll feel lonely and frustrated, like she has no one to understand her."

Another student followed: "When she's about nine or ten, she'll find some other kids who feel like her. Probably Native kids. They tell each other they are OK, what they do is cool."

Then another: "By the time she's twelve, she starts skipping school."

"She's probably getting high now, too. Dope and drinking."

"She feels good she has someone like her to be with."

"But at the same time she hates school—and her parents, maybe. All of the kids are mad, pissed off mostly."

"Not when she's high. She feels good when she's high."

"She has a boyfriend by this time and might get pregnant. She's, oh, I'd say about fourteen or so now."

"Well then, she's not going to school very much and doesn't even realize it."

"So it's like nothing when she drops out. No biggie."

"She might get a job, that's if she's living in the city. Ain't any jobs on the reserve."

"Or she might stay home and take care of the baby."

"She's going to be frustrated, bummed out, either way."

"My boyfriend was frustrated. He was drinking and got killed in a car accident last Christmas. On the reserve. But I been raising our baby by myself anyway, for four years now."

By speaking in the first person, this last student—the student who had been in my office—indicated the kind of synthesis that might have taken place, not just for her, but for other students as well. Here was more than an anecdote that complemented a given idea; the anecdote, or in this case the collective story born of personal experience, informed that idea. To what extent the students were at that moment conscious of what had happened I did not know. I never attempted to interrupt the awesome silence that followed the rendering of this story.

It was at the next class meeting that I saw what had taken place. The students expressed anger. They also felt exposed. "We've been made to feel stupid all along and we believe it," they kept saying. Luckily, they trusted me and continued speaking: "Teachers make us want to drop out and they [government officials and other non-natives] say we're dumb. 'See Natives are stupid, can't take care of themselves.' They never listened to us from the start." Another student historicized the problem thus: "The first white man gave us infested blankets [with smallpox]. His people are still with us, getting our children, finishing us off in the schools." The students sensed how their own voices had been thwarted. They talked boldly now from a position of strength determined by them.

We had not yet tested what we were saying against other ideas and texts about discrimination, but I felt we were well on our way. I pointed to the power of personal knowledge in the classroom and how that knowledge can help us make connections with ideas in books, and perhaps help us to know why we may not understand ideas the way a teacher does, or why a teacher cannot understand the students.

For that class meeting, I had asked the students to read a series of government documents regarding Native education. "What do you think of the *Section V Preamble on Native Education?*" I asked in a rather quick and arbitrary shift to the day's business. I quoted the lines:

> That [deplorable state of Native Education in Alberta] is not totally the fault of the educational system.
> There are other reasons: historical, social, economic and a reluctance on the part of some Natives to fully appreciate the significance of education for their overall advancement.
>
> (Committee on Tolerance 116)

The loud excitement quieted to a mere mumbling. I pointed to another line that noted Native people suffered from "a legacy of intolerance" (151) and to the inherent irony in the lines that followed, claiming that "there is a danger that the increasing involvement by Natives in their own education may result in a growing isolation of Native people" (151). Looking back, I am certain my use of the word "irony" and other such terms did little to promote conversation.

In sheer desperation, I told a story. I played the devil's advocate. I posed as an administrator of public education and talked about my experiences with Natives and how I came to the conclusions stated in the lines above.

A woman who was older and more outspoken challenged me with a story. She did not speak in the first person—perhaps the story was not hers per se—but it was a story she knew well. She told about a Native girl's experience in school, about the books the girl had to read, and about her struggles at home where a grandmother insisted that above all else the girl remain Cree and know the language of her ancestors. Already, like her grandmother, this girl felt vulnerable before government officials and refused to talk openly about her conflicts "so it looks like we don't fully appreciate the significance of education for our overall advancement." Another student, a much younger woman, related a story about her older sister who graduated from college with a teaching credential and ended up as a hairdresser in her home. "They won't hire Natives as teachers in the school. On the reserve my sister has to wait for one of the government teachers to retire. How can I be motivated? What am I to appreciate?" "Yeah," a young man blasted, "what does 'overall advancement' mean?"

I defined "overall advancement" as I understood it from my position as a government official. "No," this last student argued, "you did not listen to the first story. How does your definition take into account our culture and our desire to keep it? When we hear our elders talk of tradition as the only thing we have left, take a look around and it's true. And then the schools want us to forget that—that and the whole ugly history of what's been done and is still being done right in the classroom. Like she [the student who spoke of infested blankets] said. Now maybe you know what a chasm is for us Natives and why we 'don't appreciate the significance of education for [our] overall advancement.' How can you know? We just told you we don't talk much to officials."

Now they were talking to an official, or at least seeing that they could. I countered again, but I was quickly losing ground. My shortsightedness exposed me not just as a proxy for a real government official, but as an American familiar with only the Bureau of Indian Affairs and other American Indian governmental institutions. The students made subtle distinctions between the two systems based on what I had assumed and projected from the American model(s). They talked openly about the discrepancies between what I assumed and how the Canadian system actually works and affects the lives of Natives. Here the students discerned assumptions inherent in a story and how those assumptions predicated thinking and decision making. Their own stories—what they knew from their lives—became the essential ingredient for critical reflection and insight. The other shoe had dropped: they had not only brought forth their stories, but now had held them up to another story for the purposes of better understanding that story and their own.

Most important here is that these students felt empowered; they found that by engaging their life experience they operated from a position of strength. They found that texts—oral stories, fiction, government documents, movies, advertisements—are alive, filled with interpretations based on certain assumptions, and that they could actively engage or, as they said, "talk back" to these texts. Storytelling became a means for critical inquiry, not just about the texts, but simultaneously about the student's relationship to them. When a text stumped us, we resorted to stories to point out the gaps between ourselves and the texts. Sometimes the stories pointed to an unfamiliarity with complex and subtle language usage. This unfamiliarity had again to do with certain kinds of experience or lack of it, and when the students understood as much, when their stories pointed to language usage in the broader academic and political context, they felt challenged to understand and make use of the various rhetorical strategies encountered.

I remember a particularly vivid story about Joan Didion, about what she looked like and about what people she wrote for looked like and how they talked, "using big words and long, long sentences." The student who told this story created a scenario where Joan Didion and a Native woman discussed the Saddle Lake Reserve in Alberta, just north of Edmonton. The Didion character discussed exteriors—the architecture and the condition of the houses, cars, the local store and gas station—in complex sentences. In simple, more direct language, the Native woman talked about day-to-day life, her concerns for her children, the struggle to make ends meet, and the excitement of winning a bingo game. Language usage told much about the speaker's world and the type of knowledge she possessed about that world. Those big words, those essays "I can't relate to," no longer provoked fear and withdrawal, but presented a challenge and aroused curiosity about a story that was yet untold. We made whatever was problematic a starting point, just as Newkirk does when teaching poetry. I noted too a smoother, more effective blending of the anecdotal and critical in their writing.

Excited by this successful experience with storytelling, I was anxious to experiment in my writing courses where I might have students from as many as ten different cultural backgrounds. That fall I had the bright idea in the middle of a discussion of Richard Rodriguez's "Going Home Again: The New American Scholarship Boy" that we should try storytelling. The students disagreed with Rodriguez's assertion that the culturally and linguistically diverse student needed to "almost mechanically acquire the assumptions, practices, and style of the classroom milieu" at the expense of the home culture in order to succeed. They argued with personal anecdotes that began with the typical, "Well, for me . . ." No one really considered how or why Rodriguez came to his conclusions, or, for that matter, how their own stories disproved his conclusions.

"Each of us tell a part of Rodriguez's story," I suggested. "From the beginning so we can see what his life was like and how he might have made certain decisions about it. Picture yourself as him, how you might have done the same." A Chinese woman started by telling a story about a Chinese girl, a story which the next student, a Chicano, had a hard time following. "We all have different stories," the students protested. Collective storytelling would not work here in the same way it had for the Cree students who shared a common history and set of cultural norms. When a Cree student told a story about Cree life, or even about a text from a Cree perspective, the other students could readily identify with the story and comment on it. Here, the Chicano student could not follow the experience of the Chinese student. I had also been wrong in assuming that, because the students disagreed so strongly with Rodriguez, a story reconciling his point of view would force them to consider their own stories in a more critical light. By making up a story, they did not necessarily have to engage their own experiences.

Improvising, I then asked the two students to tell a story illustrating how they came to conclusions different from those of Rodriguez. To ensure detailed accounts and to allow the other students time to reflect on what was being said, I suggested the two speakers tell their stories in parts, each telling the "early life" part of the story before moving on to the next part. Each storyteller and other members of the class could then listen closely to each story as it was told in parts. In this way, the stories could be held up to one another and to the original text. I encouraged the storytellers to invent from their own experiences. The following is what we heard.

First student: Ming kept thinking she sounded funny when she talked. Her voice was too soft, she thought. It was true because the teacher always asked her: "Speak up." She thought she sounded funny, worse when she tried to speak loudly. It made her accent come out. Everybody was saying the word "cool." She sounded funny saying that. She practiced at home. In front of the mirror she'd make her mouth shape [out the word] like the other kids.

Second student: No, the thing that bothered José most was the food. You know . . . what the other kids were eating at lunchtime. In those boxes, you know, the ones with Mickey Mouse painted on them . . . The other kids have sandwiches, peanut butter and jelly, stuff like that. José, he is carrying his father's old work pail and canteen and he pulls out a tamale. "What's that?" someone says. On the other side of José is a Mexican who knows what tamales are, but he does not help José. He [the other Mexican student] is a pocho; he says nothing, acts like he doesn't know what a tamale is either.

What became interesting as the two stories progressed was the ways in which they were similar to Rodriguez's story, something the students had not anticipated. A chasm did exist between home life and school life, only here the dividing mechanism was located in the company of peers, not in the teacher. The students' stories better informed them of their own positions even as the stories informed the text. Richard Rodriguez's scholarship boy sacrificed the culture of his family; at the same time, he was without the company and influence of his peers.

While the students' stories shared similarities, they were also unique. The students' cultures and individual life experiences determined how they associated with peers and mediated two different and often conflicting sets of values. The student in the Chinese woman's story maintained two separate existences. "She became a schizophrenic. Her family was very traditional Chinese. Same time, she wanted to be liked in school." On the other hand, "José rebelled against his family. They didn't understand when he didn't like school, even after he kept trying to explain. So he started hating them. He joined up with the Cholos."

These two storytellers didn't examine their stories on their own; the entire class began to speak, asking questions and commenting even before the stories were completed. "So, looking back at Rodriguez," one student said, "it is important to know what kind of relationship he had with his parents . . . From what I'm hearing, and as I think about my relationship with my parents, that [relationship with parents] is important in how a person works out this chasm problem."

As with the Cree class, storytelling, once adapted to a more culturally diverse group, enabled these students to engage texts and ideas from a position of strength. They saw that interpretive properties are inherent in any text and began to challenge texts accordingly. By bridging the chasm between life experience and classroom activity and between personal anecdote and critical thinking, storytelling opened the way for both classes to bring forth and critically explore the intercultural dynamic that constitutes our shared reality inside the classroom and out. We effected, in sum, a form of cultural critique whose purpose, in the words of Marcus and Fischer, is "to discover the variety of modes of accommodation and resistance by individuals and groups to their shared social order" (133). The Cree students unlocked forms of internalized oppression, the ways in which they had incorporated derogatory and stereotypical ideas of themselves fostered by an oppressive outside community. While resistance to school was in some ways a natural and healthy instinct given the circumstances, it perpetuated the cyclical, cross-cultural ignorance that maintained the social order that, in turn, eroded Cree culture and a sense of Cree self-worth. The UC Santa Cruz students located their problems in the homogenizing tendencies of the mass media. More conscious of themselves as mediators of conflicting cultural norms, they could discern what made for both compromise and resistance.

More and more I observed students move to historicize and politicize topics. And here I want to emphasize and illustrate how storytelling benefits not only the student unfamiliar with norms that inhere in classroom activity, but also the student whose assumptions are not regularly challenged in the classroom. One day, during a rather unproductive discussion of Judy Syfers's "Why I Want a Wife" and Gloria Steinem's "If Men Could Menstruate," a woman abruptly dismissed sexism by calling it a "dead issue." "Anyone who doesn't think women are equal is an idiot." At that point, an Arab student who had been generally quiet announced with confidence that women are mere property and that when he returned home he fully intended to have four wives. The woman could not dismiss him as an idiot, at least not openly in a class where everyone had been encouraged to consider other points of view. The woman revealed that she was Jewish, thus indicating that something else was at stake for her now. A shouting match ensued and was broken finally by the other students who wanted to know more about the wider cultural and political differences between these two students. They called for a story from each disputant.

Neither student knew where to begin his or her story. "Tell about how you came to see women the way you do," the others suggested. The woman talked about growing up in New York in a family where women were psychiatrists and university professors. Her parents had immigrated from Israel, and though she had never been to Israel, she had heard from parents and relatives that Arabs were "lunatic terrorists who keep twenty wives and kill Jews." Until now, she had never talked to an Arab. The Arab student told about his training in Islam and continued with various accounts of his strict adherence to the Islamic faith, adding that "the law of Islam says four wives is legal for one man at a time." In their full versions, these stories proved poignant examples of the degree to which a mere rendering of a story exposes what shapes interpretation and understanding. The Arab's story extolled the doctrine and practice of Islam, which in turn colored the way he interpreted the Jewish experience and the conflict between the two cultures. The Jewish woman's story was sprinkled with anecdotes of Jewish oppression. While these stories did not solve the differences these two students had with one another, they allowed the students and the rest of us in the classroom the opportunity to explore mutual prejudices in a broader historical and political framework. After class, the Jewish woman approached the Arab and said, "I do not agree with you, but I understand you better."

Storytelling has been used in a number of ways and for a multitude of purposes. Susan J. Berthouex and Robin S. Chapman used storytelling in their first-grade class at the Surabaya International School in Indonesia to integrate a non-English-speaking student into the class. The student gestured a story by flapping his arms and pointing while the others guessed what he meant and filled in the English words. And Schwartzman's study of storytelling in the work place illustrates how storytelling is an effective means for workers to interpret their work experiences to one another and thus shed light on the nature of those experiences. Telling stories as responses to texts opens up or exposes, as Gabriele Schwab suggests about reading, the manner in which the reader/teller has mediated between two more or less different cultural contexts, the text's and the reader's (110). And the dialogue that follows—the sort that I have found following storytelling in my classes—is the very sort of dialogue that is essential if we are to have strong sense critical thinking, if we are, as Richard Paul notes, to give students "intensive and continuing opportunities to construct and assess lines of reasoning from multiple conflicting points of view" (2–3).

Storytelling takes time, usually entire class periods, and there is always the risk of getting material from students that has been closely edited for what the students feel is "right." Teachers must give careful attention as to how they generate stories in their classrooms and how they balance the anecdotal and critical in what follows the storytelling(s). If students are to scrutinize their stories so that their stories might inform and be informed by other experiences as found in texts, teachers must be careful not to let difference or "otherness" be transformed into sameness. Schwab notes the tendency within interpretive communities to assimilate difference by projecting, or recreating texts to fit preconceived notions, as in the case of my students with the story of Coyote and Junco. She notes that assimilation can happen in two directions, "the assimilation of the text to the reader's subjectivity and the assimilation of the reader to the text's subjectivity" (115). In the latter instance, a reader, or in this case a listener, may identify imaginatively with a text such that the distinction between the listener's world and that of the text becomes blurred, thus barring any recognition and understanding of difference. Of course, it is hoped that storytelling and the discussions that follow storytelling will expose such tendencies when they occur, and it is here the teacher must be alert to recognize the potential of chasms between home life and school life to foster assimilating tendencies and to point up conflict and difference rather than dissolve them. Discussions that follow the storytelling event are problem-exposing in nature, not problem-solving. It is the story, after all, that can expose the differences.

What I have offered here are three stories about storytelling strategies, each suited to a different classroom environment: middle-class, non-

Indian students studying American Indian literature; Canadian Cree students reading non-Indian, American writers and Canadian government documents; and culturally diverse American students reading a host of culturally diverse American writers. Different strategies will undoubtedly be more suitable for other situations.[2] The three stories I have related illustrate, I hope, the potential for storytelling to empower and engage culturally diverse students while providing, in turn, a context for strong sense critical thinking for all of us, students and teachers alike, such that the nature of our shared reality and our relationship to it is made more visible and less intimidating. The potential is just that and no more; my stories are models of and not necessarily models for using storytelling to foster critical discourse. But it is interesting to me how even these three stories always prompt more stories.

2. And in many classroom situations storytelling may be inappropriate. Lest there be any doubt, I am not suggesting here or elsewhere that storytelling is the best or only way for students to respond to texts or to the teacher or to one another. I am showing ways storytelling can be used to foster strong sense critical thinking of the sort described in this essay, the ways it can be used to foster dialogue within and between people that can expose boundaries that shape and constitute different cultural and personal worlds. Again, as I noted at the beginning of this book, stories can be used in a number of ways and for a multitude of purposes. They can work to oppress or to liberate, to confuse or to enlighten. If storytelling in the classroom can promote critical thinking and dialogue of the sort I have described here, if it can engage many students, there is the chance that the stories told can liberate and enlighten.

CHAPTER EIGHT

Keeping Slug Woman Alive

The Challenge of Reading in a
Reservation Classroom

About four years ago a strange thing happened to my cousin. He was with his older brother and they were on their way home to the Kashaya Pomo Reservation, driving along Tin Barn Road. It was early evening and they had just turned off Highway 1, the coastal route. There is a steep grade and then the road levels along the mountain ridge. Somewhere along there, where the road levels, my cousin began looking over his shoulder. His older brother, who was driving, asked what the matter was.

"I thought someone was following," my cousin said.

His brother checked in the rearview mirror and saw nothing. But all the way home my cousin kept turning, looking. His brother said that once he jumped clear around and looked at the backseat as if someone were sitting there.

My cousin went to bed when he got home. He complained that after a long and discouraging baseball game in Santa Rosa he felt tired. "That's why you acted so weird in the car," his brother said to him. But in the days ahead my cousin began to wander. He would walk out the front door and keep on. Once he was found five miles down the road in a redwood grove. Another time his father found him sitting on a river bank, staring blankly into the waters of the Gualala River.

My cousin didn't know what was happening to him. At night he was afraid and couldn't sleep. He didn't know anything except the urge to walk, and once he was out of the house, once he was out walking, he had no sense of place or time, or where he was headed. Each morning his father or older brother escorted him to the school bus. Twice the high school principal called and asked that his parents pick him up. In the middle of class, he had gotten out of his seat and begun shuffling aimlessly up and down the halls.

His brother recalled the strange occurrence along Tin Barn Road. My aunt suspected Indian poison, that is, the work of some harmful spirit or of some evil person using such a spirit. She was raised around the old people on the reservation. She is, as she puts it, "well-versed" in Indian ways. "I've heard and I've seen; I've seen and I've heard," she says. But by this time, because of requests from the high school counselor, my aunt had taken her son to medical doctors in Santa Rosa. It was possible that my athletic cousin had suffered a blow to the head in a game. The other possibility, one that the counselor suggested, was that the fifteen-year-old had taken some drug. "You know," the counselor said, "so many of those Indian kids drink and take drugs."

After a brain scan and countless other tests, which took place over three weeks, nothing out of the ordinary showed up. The doctors, like the high school counselor, suspected my cousin had taken drugs. But my cousin, at fifteen, had never tried even a cigarette. He was obsessed with sports and played on several teams. His mother and father and brothers and sister watched him compete. They drove him back and forth to town. Because of this, he was always close to the family. The doctors told my aunt that perhaps she didn't know as much about her son as she thought she did.

My aunt called an Indian doctor, a woman from a nearby reservation. The woman prayed and sang over my cousin. After she left, he had his first good night's sleep. Before going to bed, he said, "I feel I can go to school tomorrow." But in the morning, after he left the house, he started for the woods, in the opposite direction of the school bus. He walked with the same lolling gait, the way we had seen him walking for the past six weeks. My aunt then called Mabel McKay. Mabel prayed and sang one full night. My cousin slept peacefully. But in the morning, Mabel announced that the young man would rest only as long as she was present. "This young man, something got him on that road [Tin Barn Road] out there," she said. "Something is singing in him yet, calling him to it, chasing him. I can only calm it. I can't get it out."

As a last-ditch effort, Mabel suggested my aunt take her son to a doctor woman who lived two hundred fifty miles away. "She might be able to trick it [the disease] and get it out," Mabel said. Mabel had known the woman many years before and guaranteed the woman was a fine doctor. So my aunt and uncle drove their son the great distance to find this woman. In a trance, the medicine woman confirmed Mabel's diagnosis, saying that something had met the young man along the road and followed him home. The medicine woman spoke through an interpreter who said in English: "You have many harmful things along that road: a little girl in a pink gingham dress with the face of a monkey; a sheep with eyes that leave its head and follow its victim; bearpeople trails; and a place where that small, ancient woman walks, that woman you call Slug Woman, the one who carries an empty baby cradle in front of her, as if she is begging."

The doctor began to massage my cousin's head, and they say she lifted something invisible from his brow, just above his eyes where it had planted itself, and held it cupped in her hands before she cast it away. It was the voice of a woman singing. My aunt said she thought it sounded like the woman in Healdsburg who disagreed with her in a local Indian election.

My cousin was well after that. For six months, while he regained confidence in his well-being, a home tutor helped him with his schoolwork. Then he returned to school. For a long time the family discussed the incident along Tin Barn Road and all that had happened as a result. My aunts told stories about taboo places and people suspected as poisoners. They speculated about the neighbor whose voice my aunt heard singing in the medicine woman's hands.

I listened. I recalled stories I had heard from my Kashaya Pomo elders. I thought of the stories about an old woman from a Pomo tribe in Lake County, some eighty miles east of our reservation. At the time my aunts were talking, this woman was over one hundred years old. I had heard before that she was lethal. At funerals she massaged the faces of the dead to take from the bodies whatever diseases she could so that she might use them against enemies. People claimed to have seen this. They said she possessed ancient songs and could take the form of a newt, a dog, or even the feared Slug Woman. She couldn't die, they said, until she passed on to another person whatever poisons she carried. Those were the terms of her contract with the poisons.

One night, shortly after my cousin was well, one of my aunts said she remembered hearing from somebody that the woman who had disagreed with my aunt, the woman whose voice rose from the healer's hands and was cast away, was seen coming out of a creekbed with this old poison woman. "She's training her," my aunt said. "Remember, this woman is her niece."

Last year in an attempt to foster cultural pride in the classroom on the Kashaya Pomo Reservation, the teacher Mollie Bishop introduced written, translated Kashaya stories to the students. One of the four Kashaya schoolboard members had suggested in a meeting with Bishop that it was important that the students get "Indian values" in the classroom. Bishop had been teaching the twenty-six K–8 children in the one-room schoolhouse for approximately three months. She needed to hear from the board what they wanted for the students, and she took the suggestion regarding the teaching of "Indian values" seriously. She felt it was important to integrate the curriculum with materials that the students "could relate to" so they might in turn become more interested in classroom activity. She figured if the students saw Kashaya cultural materials used in the classroom and could feel proud about their backgrounds, they might not only be more interested in school but might, at least, be more attentive. "I wanted the students to feel they could be who they are here at school," Bishop said. "I thought maybe that would help things. Something they had in common. So one day, instead of pulling out our readers, I gave them the story about Slug Woman."[1]

The older children were two to four grades behind in their reading. Two fifth graders read at a first-grade level. As Bishop said, "those two were basically non-readers." The students were behind in math also. One sixth grader could not multiply or divide. And there were significant behavior problems. One day, after Bishop had been teaching for about two months, I visited the classroom and witnessed what Bishop later referred to as "a typical infraction." Bishop and members of the Kashaya schoolboard, two of whom were my relatives, wanted any suggestions I might have after observing the class for improving the dismal state of affairs. Bishop had asked an eight-year-old to put away his crayons so that he would stop drawing and pay attention to the math she was

---

1. Bishop also gave the students the story "A Pubescent Girl Turns into a Rock," which Bishop copied directly from Robert Oswalt's *Kashaya Texts*. In this essay I will only refer to the Slug Woman story. Though student response to the Slug Woman story and to the story about the Pubescent Girl was basically the same, students did say more about the Slug Woman story. Also, the Slug Woman story is meaningful to me as I will illustrate in this essay. From here on I will refer to the Slug Woman story as one story or text, even though it is broken into two narratives, "A Description of Slug Woman" and "A Story About the Slug Woman." Bishop presented these narratives as one story. They are collected together in one pamphlet about Slug Woman published by YA-KA-AMA, a Sonoma County Indian education and resource center.

putting on the blackboard. A straightforward request. The student lifted his head, looked Bishop in the face and said, "Fuck you, you white bitch." Bishop informed the student that he was immediately suspended and she began filling out a form letter that he was to take home with him. "You better put that away, bitch," he warned her, "or I'm gonna hire someone and they're gonna find your dead ass on the side of the road someplace."

I was jolted, but not surprised. A few weeks before, a substitute teacher closed the school after she had been there one hour and wrote the school district that she feared for her life.

This typical infraction occurred shortly after the class had finished telling Bishop and me what "they wanted to be when they grew up." They wanted to be doctors and nurses and businessmen and firemen and teachers. The eight-year-old wanted to be a lawyer. They all wanted to be rich like the people they saw on TV. But the chasm between their wants and reality, like the chasm between their lives and those seen on television, would prove, for the overwhelming majority of them, too wide to cross. Again, eighty percent of California Indian school children drop out by ninth grade. Less than eight percent graduate from high school. At Kashaya the statistics are no better than the state averages.

Bishop's idea, following the ideas of many teachers working in culturally complex classrooms, was to use "culturally relevant" materials, in this case the Kashaya story, to bridge the gap between the students' lives and those of others represented elsewhere, particularly in their readers. In that way, it was hoped reading would become meaningful, and eventually students would be able to engage critically other texts and stories. They would be able to read and at the same time have a cultural base—their own—from which to work. The students would get "Indian values," as the schoolboard member suggested, which would be useful to them.

But Bishop's idea proved futile. "Most of the students hated the story," Bishop reported. "We couldn't even discuss it."

"There's no such thing as Slug Woman," one student proclaimed. "That's all devil worship," another said. The scurrilous eight-year-old shouted, "I don't want to read about no savages." The few students who didn't protest were seemingly unimpressed. "It's just like a cartoon. Not real. Something like *Peanuts*," said one girl. Another student, a sixth grader, mentioned she had heard different versions of the story from her mother. She was going to ask her mother to talk more about Slug Woman. But, according to Bishop, the girl never said another word about the subject in front of her classmates. Bishop went back to the standard reader.

How might the students' reactions be understood? Was the story unreal for the students because unconnected to anything in their lives and therefore uninteresting? For my aunts and me the story about Slug Woman had significance. For us Slug Woman is alive. She is seen and talked about in the stories we tell to understand the events of our lives. In the story I told she is associated with a neighbor. Certainly we are more cautious, suspicious, and mindful of that which may be harmful. The students are two and sometimes three generations from my aunts, and at least one from me. Still, all of them admitted they had heard of Slug Woman. Might she not also be alive for some of them, in which case their relationship to what they read was deferred or hidden in their responses? Might the context of their reading, that is, the classroom environment governed and determined by a non-Indian unfamiliar with the community, affect their verbal responses? What about the particular practice of reading in the classroom?

I want to explore these questions as a means of understanding or beginning to understand the dismal classroom situation and establishing criteria for positive change. I will center my discussion upon the students' reading of the Slug Woman text, but to discuss this reading I must consider the students' cultural and historical community, the classroom environment, their particular practice of reading, and the ways in which these facets of their encounter and response to the text interrelate. A response such as "There's no such thing as Slug Woman" might be seen beyond its stated or surface meaning. Seen in the larger cultural and historical context it can illuminate relations and patterns of relations students have with texts and school in general that cause disinterest and alienation.

In examining the various facets of the students' reading, my work becomes what Jonathan Boyarin (1989) calls an ethnography of reading where there is "a convergence between the concerns of anthropology and those of literary theory in the study of textual practices" (400). As an ethnographer, I am positioned as both participant and observer (and the observed) of certain cultural practices among my people. The story at the beginning of this chapter indicates to a large extent the reflexive stance I take as a reader of and writer about the Kashaya students' practice of reading. The details I use and the manner in which I tell the story, as well as my comments regarding how I feel about Slug Woman, reveal biases that necessarily influence my observations and conclusions. But, at the same time, my telling of the story becomes a way for me to continue its life as I come to use and understand it in this chapter. My sense of Slug Woman affects the experience of observing and reflecting on the students' reading, but the experience also enables me to see and create Slug Woman anew. Story mingles with ethnography which mingles with story, and this chapter tracks their intermingling.

In the last chapter, I discussed how certain kinds of pedagogies maintain chasms between home life, or lived experience, and school life. Such chasms make genuine critical involvement with texts impossible. Here, as I explore the Kashaya students' reading of the Slug Woman story, I am able to expose cultural conflicts and associated psychological tensions that play an integral role in the formation of chasms leading to student dissatisfaction and alienation. While my discussions and stories are concerned with one particular community, I hope they can provide a means for thinking about issues of student reading and response elsewhere.

There are today at least one thousand people known to be of Kashaya Pomo ancestry, about one hundred and ten of whom live permanently on the Kashaya Reservation located five miles inland from Stewart's Point, a one-store/gas station town on the northern California coast in Sonoma County. (Local Indians often refer to the Kashaya Reservation as Stewart's Point; the Kashaya Indians are referred to as being from Stewart's Point.) The majority of people identified as Kashaya Pomo are of mixed heritage. Intermarriage with Indians from neighboring tribes (i.e., central Pomo, southern Pomo, Coast Miwok) and with Mexicans, Filipinos, and many European groups is common. The forty-acre reservation, given to the Kashaya in 1914 by the State of California, is located on a ridgetop in the northern part of the thirty-five-mile strip of coastal land the Kashaya once claimed as their own. As noted earlier, the mouth of the Russian River marked the southern boundary between the Kashaya and Coast Miwok, while the mouth of the Gualala River marked the northern boundary between the Kashaya and central Pomo.

The climate is generally cool along the coast, foggy during the summer and damp and rainy during the winter. Inland about five miles, where the reservation is located, the weather is much fairer, with warm, sunny days most of the summer. Winters are wet with forty to fifty inches of rain. Yet seldom does it freeze. The landscape is typical of northern California: a series of coastal shelves and steep mountain cliffs line the ocean; inland, along the mountain ridges, are redwood and pine forests. Since the immense redwood forests in this region were logged at least once, sometimes twice, the trees today are second or third growth.

Linguist Robert Oswalt says "Kashaya is derived from the native term |kàhšá·ya|, which probably contains |kàhša| 'agile, nimble' " (8). He notes that other tribes refer to the Kashaya as "light (weight)" and "expert gamblers" (8). According to the tribal historian Violet Chappell, the Kashaya always referred to themselves as |wina·má·bakĕ ya|, "people who belong to the land."

Today how people think of themselves as Kashaya with a distinct history varies. As I noted in the first part of this book, the history of the Kashaya since European contact is unique in terms of the histories of neighboring Pomo and Miwok tribes. Their history with the Russians and then with a series of exceptionally strong Bole Maru leaders, most notably Annie Jarvis from 1912 to 1943 and Essie Parrish from 1943 to 1979, largely accounts for the significant retention of Kashaya language and culture to the present day. Yet the present state of affairs is extremely complex and uneasy.

In the mid-fifties Mormons made the first inroad on Kashaya religion. Ten years later the community split into two factions, those who were Mormon and those who were not. Family turned against family, sister against sister, in conflicts that were ugly and at times violent. Essie Parrish's dream flags, which flew above the ceremonial Roundhouse, were ripped down and then soaked in human excrement and placed on her porch step. Fistfights erupted between members of rivaling families. Annual community picnics were set on the same date so that friends from outside the community had to choose sides openly. It was during this period, particularly in the late fifties and early sixties, that a number of ethnographers and linguists concerned themselves with the Kashaya community, where they found what they considered vestiges of "the last true Pomo culture," where language and religion were still, as one ethnographer said, "intact." The University of California in association with various faculty members and the Department of Anthropology made over a dozen films of Essie performing "traditional activities"— making acorn mush, dancing, doctoring. She also served as principal informant for Robert Oswalt as he assembled *Kashaya Texts* during this time.

After Essie Parrish's death, a group of individuals within the Mormon faction built a new ceremonial Roundhouse where they revived various Kashaya religious songs and dances. The activity of this group angers those faithful to Essie's rules. According to Bole Maru doctrine, dances and songs brought about by the Dreamer must end with her death. Prayer songs given by the Dreamer to particular individuals for protection and health may continue after the Dreamer's death only if she has given explicit permission. Everything else associated with the Dreamer stops. (The old roundhouse was locked after Essie Parrish's death.) New or revived ceremonies must come only with a new tribally recognized prophet. There is no consensus today as to who is or is not a Dreamer. (Mabel McKay, who is Cache Creek Pomo, functions as Dreamer only for those people faithful to Essie's teachings.)

The Kashaya continue to splinter. Currently, among the one hundred ten permanent residents, there is a faction faithful to Essie Parrish, a faction of Mormons, a faction once associated with the Mormons that is reviving Kashaya religious activities, and a faction of Pentecostals preaching fire and brimstone at nightly revival meetings. Shouts of "Hallelujah" and "Praise the Lord" hang in the air along with Kashaya dance songs. But this intermingling is not necessarily convivial. Perplexed children pray earnestly for relatives condemned to hell for not accepting the Lord. Family members abandon one another because of conflicting beliefs. None of the factions has stemmed the widespread use of alcohol and drugs. None has affected the student drop-out rate.

The younger generations are not learning the language; few, if any, people under the age of fifty speak Kashaya fluently. While acorn mush, seaweed, abalone, mussels, and certain kinds of "wild meat" such as venison are still served occasionally, usually at family picnics, the younger generations show little interest in learning how to gather and prepare these foods. In the families where Kashaya singing and dancing is maintained, few young people participate. Only three households on the reservation have telephones, but many of them have televisions and stereo systems. Though TV and radio reception is limited, young people watch popular shows and listen to Top 40 radio stations. *The Cosby Show* and soap operas such as *Dynasty* and *Knots Landing,* as well as rock and roll and rap are familiar to young people in every household. They talk more openly about products of popular culture than just about anything else; indeed, popular culture appears to unite them as a group.

Many of the children in the school have lived off the reservation, mostly in the nearby towns of Healdsburg, Santa Rosa, and Sebastopol, and have attended public schools in the respective vicinities. Some families come and go, often following seasonal work in the canneries and agriculture. Children must adjust and readjust to the one-room K–8 school on the reservation. Many families are broken; children sometimes are raised by single parents, aunts and uncles, and grandparents. So Kashaya cultural history and oftentimes complicated, unstable living circumstances position students in ways within the community—and certainly with the teacher and with one another in the classroom—that make interaction of any kind complex.

It is impossible to isolate any one feature of a given student's experience as a Kashaya Pomo that influences how he or she reads and responds to a text. So far I have talked about cultural history and family life at Kashaya. Interrelated with and influencing cultural activity and family dynamics are many other issues, including the predominantly lower-class status of Kashaya residents, that affect students as readers. Few parents or guardians read regularly; the necessity of making a living takes precedence over the students' schooling and school-related activities, such as reading. Most parents have had unfavorable experiences as students, and few believe their childrens' school life will be any different. My point, though, is that the notion of culture, as it might be applied to the Kashaya Pomo, as something fixed, homogenous, and uniformly shared not only becomes obsolete and naive but also, as a result, impedes sensitive working relations with the community. As Renato Rosaldo discovered in his study of the Ilongot, this "classic concept of culture [cannot] readily apply to flux, improvisation, and heterogeneity" (208). To isolate one feature of the Kashaya culture, say that of so-called traditional learning styles, and determine how that influences the way children might read and respond to a given text and then develop a supposedly sensitive pedagogy, is to overlook how those learning styles are associated in meaningful ways with other elements of culture and how they may or may not be a part of every child's experience as a Kashaya Pomo.

The ethnographers who swarmed the reservation during the late fifties and early sixties undoubtedly sought Essie Parrish as an informant because they thought that as a "traditional" Bole Maru Dreamer she might give them "pure products" (Clifford 1988). However, it was Essie Parrish who converted and led the tribe into the Mormon Church. Her husband, Sidney Parrish, was chief of the Kashaya for over twenty years and yet he was from another tribe, the Manchester–Point Arena tribe of central Pomo, and he spoke a different language. This mixing with other religions and neighboring tribes does not mean the Kashaya have no culture. To say the Kashaya have no culture is to say they are "like everybody else," like mainstream Americans, and therefore culturally invisible, virtually indistinguishable from mainstream culture. This conclusion would enable mainstream others to claim the authority and knowledge to measure or assess the Kashaya in mainstream terms, particularly with regard to certain competencies such as reading and writing, because the Kashaya are assumed to be no different from other Americans. Granted, the Kashaya might be poorer and uneducated, in which case they are viewed in terms of what they don't have rather than in terms of what they have. To assume the Kashaya have no culture is to overlook the ways in which the Kashaya accommodate and resist other cultural influences in given social and political contexts. What, for example, might have been the cultural, political, and personal terms of Essie Parrish's acceptance and eventual rejection of Mormonism? Kashaya culture must be seen as emergent. It is heterogeneous and pluralistic and always present in a dynamic manner. What is pure or authentic is that which is complex and dynamic in the moment it is experienced. This is so, albeit in different ways, for insiders as well as outsiders associated with the community.

A Kashaya individual's ethnicity or sense of identity as a Kashaya Pomo Indian, then, is dependent on how the individual in personal and social situations, consciously and unconsciously, negotiates and mediates a range of cultural and intercultural phenomena to establish and maintain a sense of self. A Pentecostal Kashaya might internalize her mother's or grandmother's stories about poisoning and so forth as Other in order that she see herself as Christian. Indeed, that part of her Kashaya experience, and hence that part of her self as a Kashaya Indian, becomes Other. Likewise, those people reviving Kashaya singing and dancing may bury their association with the Mormon religion, or they may, as I have heard, assimilate Mormon doctrine to new Roundhouse activities. The twelve apostles become the twelve roof beams of the Roundhouse. Kashaya ethnic identity cannot be seen as uniform among the Kashaya. The individuals who make and remake the culture are complex and different; they make and remake the culture as they negotiate and mediate a range of cultural and intercultural phenomena in a variety of ways to fashion a sense of identity and self.

Tradition is often considered as that which is unchanging in a culture, that which is canonical and which governs, or at least influences in significant ways, peoples' lives. Like commonly accepted notions of culture and ethnicity, tradition, according to this view, is understood as a thing complete and still, and what is *traditional* is that which is of, or representative of, the tradition. Seen in the context of Kashaya culture, tradition is not fixed, but an ongoing process.[2] That which is viewed as tradition or traditional is subjective, dependent on the viewer. Mollie Bishop, for example, found that in the Kashaya classroom her sense of what was traditional, that is, the story of Slug Woman, was at odds with the students' sense of what was traditional. Yet the students' responses might have masked something other than mere rejection of the story as tradition, or as a relevant part of their lives as Kashaya Indians, as my brief discussion of Kashaya cultural history may begin to suggest. Yet, at this point, more can be said of Bishop's reading of the Kashaya students and their community than can be said of the Kashaya students' reading of the Slug Woman story. Bishop read the students and the Kashaya community as homogenous and fixed in time and place, to the extent she thought the Slug Woman story would be part of the students' "tradition" and "something they had in common"; she assumed that the story was familiar and so could be uniformly read and understood. The students may have had the story in common, but they did not share an understanding of it. Bishop's unfamiliarity with the community at that time obscured any challenge to her presuppositions about culture, ethnicity, and tradition that knowledge of the community might have afforded. The views of the schoolboard member who suggested that Bishop incorporate "Indian values" in the classroom were not, as Bishop supposed, representative of the entire community.

My discussion of Kashaya cultural history and diversity thus far indicates little more than the trajectory of Kashaya experience. If there was no chance that the students in their verbal responses hid or occulted their relationships to the text, I could start a matchmaking game, matching students' responses with points on an (invented) Kashaya cultural continuum. The purpose here, however, is not to unmask or read precisely each student's response, which is, I believe, impossible. Rather, it is to look at the responses in terms of what they might suggest about relations and patterns of relations with the text in the classroom that foster a breakdown in communication about the text between students and teacher and students themselves. So again, I must also consider the classroom environment and the practice of reading in that classroom; also, I must present the text the students were given to read and respond to and which I am using as a focal point in my ethnography of the students' reading and my understanding, as the subjective ethnographer, of the story itself.

---

2. Jonathan Boyarin has seen tradition in the same light in his study of reading in his "Voices Around the Text: The Ethnography of Reading at Mesivta Tifereth Jerusalem," in *Cultural Anthropology,* 1989, 399–421. I am indebted to him for his clear statement of this principle: "Tradition is not a thing but a process" (413).

A Description of Slug Woman

They say she is a woman with long hair. She is not a big woman; she is small and short.

Above the knees she wears clothes of cloth or skin or something else. From there down, her legs are bare.

She carries around a baby basket covered all over with abalone shell ornaments. She does not pack this basket on her back. She carries it in front of her. When she walks you can hear abalone ornaments jingling.

Nobody knows if there is a real baby lying in the basket.

This is all that is told about the Slug Woman. Maybe somebody else knows more about her but I have never heard it.

This is the end of the description of the Slug Woman.

A Story About the Slug Woman

There were some people living at Timber's Edge. From there they used to go to hunt deer.

One time a youth married a woman. They lived alone, not with his mother as was the custom. His mother lived close by.

The young wife had a baby. When that happened the husband's mother came to their home and admonished him.

She said, "Don't go around in the wilderness. Don't hunt deer. Don't fish. Don't even go for slugs or things like that. If you do, you will be punished."

She reminded him of the ancient Indian law that says the father of a newborn baby must not go outside until after the fourth dawn. He can't hunt deer for one month. He must not collect shore food or gather slugs. If these laws are broken the father of the baby will be punished.

The son said, "It won't happen that way to me. I don't believe that, Mother. I'm going anyway. I'm going to gather slugs." Then he set out.

When he reached the woods, he searched for slugs. He gathered a lot of them and carried them by stringing them on broken-off hazel twigs.

It began to get dark. He looked around in the forest for a place to spend the night. He walked toward a big upright tree. The tree had a hollow base. He prepared his bed there. He hung the slugs up to dry in the hollow tree. Then he lay down to sleep.

At midnight he heard something moving outside. He sat up and listened. It sounded like abalone shell ornaments tinkling along.

A short woman with long hair sat down in his living place. She carried a basket that tinkled when it moved.

After he had sat for a while the woman set the basket on the young man's knee. She said, "Hold this baby."

"Alright," he said. He clasped the basket to himself.

He began to wonder about the strange woman. Suddenly he became frightened. He didn't know what to do. He decided to leave the woman and go home.

"Here, hold this," he said. "I'm dying of thirst. I'm going for a drink of water."

He leaped outside of the hollow tree and started to run away. He ran for a long time.

He looked back and saw the woman carrying her tinkling baby basket. She was running along after him. He ran quick as a deer but she kept pace right behind him. He ran toward home but she started to catch up to him.

When he reached home, he stumbled through the doorway into the house. "Something is chasing me!" he shouted.

His mother said, "That is what I was warning you about. This is why we tell our children; so they will not be punished for breaking the law."

Slug Woman arrived right behind the man. She was clasping her baby basket covered with abalone shell ornaments.

Slug Woman said that she would not let the young man stay in the house. She would lead him back with her. "I want him!" she said. "He has become mine."

"No, save me!" cried the young man. "Make her leave me behind."

Slug Woman grabbed him and dragged him away. She led him into the hollow tree where he had been before.

The young man couldn't think much. He was already sickening. He sat on the ground. His body became weak. He couldn't run anymore. He couldn't even stand up. He became so weak he could hardly sit up.

"What's the matter with you?" Slug Woman asked. She gave him the baby to hold, but he couldn't hold it.

She said, "Is this what you wanted to see? Did you want to see what would happen to you? These are the things you were told about when your baby appeared on this earth."

The youth sat still, unable to answer.

Suddenly, a supernatural event began happening right before his eyes. He was on fire inside.

"When you don't believe," said Slug Woman, "these things happen to you. This is why you can't go home. You'll be staying with me, hereafter."

Three or four dawns later, the young man died.

After his death, Slug Woman left. Having burned up the young father she vanished.

The young man's baby was a boy. While growing up, he overheard some people talk about his father. He often asked his mother if he had a father, but she didn't tell him anything for a long, long time.

Finally she said, "You had a father."

"Where did he go?" asked the boy.

His mother didn't answer.

One day he set off into the wilderness to look for traces of something his father might have left. His mother admitted to him that he had a father and people said his father went to the woods. So he went there to find where his father had gone.

He came to a place where a big tree stood. It had a hollow base. He looked around and found an abalone shell with a hole in it. He continued to wander around in the woods but finally he returned home to his mother.

"Where have you been?" his mother asked.

"I tried to find out what happened to my father," said the child. "I went to the woods to look for traces of him and I found this abalone shell."

The mother said, "I am willing to tell you what happened."

She told her son about the death of his father. She ended her story by saying, "It was your father's punishment because he didn't believe the things his mother told him. His mother told him that hunting or gathering slugs was forbidden but he gathered them anyway. He said he didn't believe any harm would come to him. Your father was taken away to show that people are punished if the laws of our people are broken. Now you will understand that your father died because he broke the law about hunting after the birth of a baby."

"It must be so," said the boy. "I found where my father went and stayed in a hollow tree. I will never do that kind of thing."

"Remember this well," his mother continued, "as the sickness may be visited upon you when your wife has a baby. Don't go wandering around in the woods and do like your father did. Don't hunt deer, don't gather slugs and don't fish."

"Alright, I'll remember," replied the boy.

The boy cared for his mother until he was grown. He then took a wife and in time they had a baby.

The young father obeyed the rules. His children grew up to be good. They had children who obeyed the laws of the Indian way. The family lived at Timber's Edge for many generations.

This is the end of the Slug Woman Story.

(YA-KA-AMA 1974)[3]

In the early seventies, non-Indian educators working at YA-KA-AMA, a newly established Indian education and resource center in Sonoma County, collected stories from Pomo elders and various published collections of Pomo stories, such as *Kashaya Texts,* and presented the stories individually in pamphlets for school children. Each story was illustrated with drawings by Jim Blackhorse, an Indian from an East Coast tribe who was working at the center. Bishop gave the Kashaya students the pamphlet with the Slug Woman story. "I didn't know anything about the story," Bishop said. "I just found the pamphlets at the school."

I must mention, if only briefly, the ways the YA-KA-AMA educators edited Oswalt's English translation. Most apparent is their editing of Kashaya patterns of speech, such as the predominance of the verb, specifically the Kashaya verb |*mensi*|, "to do so," which is often used, as Oswalt notes, to begin a second sentence, thus tying the verb or action in

3. In September 1958, Essie Parrish gave a description of Slug Woman to Oswalt, which he titled "Description of Slug Woman" (Oswalt 139). A month earlier, Herman James told a Slug Woman story, which Oswalt titled "Slug Woman Abducts a Man" (Oswalt 139–145). In *Kashaya Texts* Oswalt presents both the transcribed version of the narratives and his English translations. The YA-KA-AMA story of Slug Woman presented in a single pamphlet was obviously taken from Oswalt's two English translations.

the preceding sentence to the second sentence (18–19). Thus, you might have in English a translation that reads: She picked huckleberries. Having done so, she continued on. Continuing on, she found a spring. Note in the YA-KA-AMA text:

> He gathered a lot of them [slugs] and carried them by stringing them on broken-off hazel twigs.

Now compare Oswalt's translation:

> He found slugs there in the woods. Then when it had grown dark, he had gathered a lot. While doing so, he strung them. Having broken off hazel twigs, he strung them on that and carried them around.
>
> (139–41)

Also, the educators at YA-KA-AMA omitted all of James's narrative commenting, most notably his lines asserting the truth(s) of the story in the present context. In Oswalt's translation James notes: "We say that the retribution is like that even now. We still remember that now. It really happens like that when those who don't believe do such things. Slug Woman would set fire to them [internally] and abandon them" (143). And again, at the end of James's narration as presented by Oswalt, James states: "Those things we still believe nowadays. . . . Therefore we still believe the things they did in ancient times. . . . These words that I have spoken are true" (145). The YA-KA-AMA version is presented without a visible narrator, a first-person speaker, nor is James identified as the storyteller anywhere on the copies of the pamphlet Bishop made and gave to the students. Sidney Parrish, who was working as a consultant and who told some stories used in other pamphlets, is listed as the storyteller on the cover of the pamphlet, even though in the case of the Slug Woman material this is clearly not the case. Oswalt is not even listed as a source by the YA-KA-AMA editors; and Bishop did not copy the pamphlet cover, so the student readers did not see any name connected with the written words. The story, subsequently, is located in an ahistorical past.

Oswalt's translation, like any translation, is not pure, without bias. A common feature of the Kashaya narrative in a variety of storytelling events is the frequent use of |mulído|, "and then, they say." In the untranslated Kashaya Pomo text James uses the phrase sixteen times. Neither Oswalt nor the YA-KA-AMA educators use it once in their translations. Oswalt suggests he kept much of the extensive repetition of verbs and the phrase "and then, they say" out of his English translation because such features of the Kashaya language, if presented as often as in Kashaya, would be annoying to an English-reading audience (19).

Before moving on to a discussion of the classroom and issues of reading in the Kashaya classroom, I have to remind the reader that Oswalt and certain well-meaning educators are not the only ones who edited the text. Both Essie Parrish, who gave the description of Slug Woman, and Herman James, who gave the story, undoubtedly edited the content and form of what they told Oswalt. Just recently Violet Chappell, daughter of Essie Parrish, again remarked: "Mom just told the stories like that for the language. He [Oswalt] wanted to collect stories to study the language and put in a book. We kids heard the stories different." I have never heard one of my elders begin a story with "Now I am going to tell about" and close with "This is the end of that." This framing device, used by the Kashaya narrators in virtually all of the texts given to Oswalt, was emergent in the context of Oswalt's recording. There is an interesting intercultural interaction or dialogue within many of James's narratives. James, a Mormon at the time, may have assimilated aspects of Christianity to various stories to impress Oswalt, a white man surely perceived as a Christian. My point, however, is that the text used in the Kashaya classroom is a text mediated by the Kashaya narrators mediated by Oswalt mediated by the educators at YA-KA-AMA. The thrice-mediated text appears with illustrations representing the characters and action of the story.

I am not suggesting the YA-KA-AMA text of Slug Woman is invalid or that it should be discarded. The text does not exist in isolation. As Boyarin (1989) observes about the rabbis' inscribed midrash, the text remains only potential without the reader (399). David Bleich notes that a text is not just a representation of interaction but also an occasion for interaction (418). And that is exactly what I am looking at: interactions with a text. I briefly discussed the text of the YA-KA-AMA Slug Woman story because the particular presentation of the text, like the presentation of any text, can affect meaning and the ways in which readers might receive or interact with the text.

When I first read the text on Slug Woman in Oswalt's *Kashaya Texts,* I was an undergraduate at UCLA. A professor mentioned the book to me. He thought I might be interested. Actually, I had seen a copy of *Kashaya Texts* in the old schoolhouse on the reservation. It was in a pile with other "Indian" books. I wasn't particularly interested, even though someone mentioned that it was "a book with Auntie Essie in it." As a child I watched the old-timers working with "the scientists" from universities. I saw how they edited information. I heard familiar stories told in new ways. I heard stories that I had never heard, and then waited for the elder's trickster wink as the scientist wrote madly, seriously. Two things seemed clear: university people weren't Indians and what was Indian wasn't in books. Since then, the matter has become less clear. I am Indian and now also a university person, and I realize now that what is in the books is Indian, even if it is Indian in contact with non-Indian.

I remember paging through *Kashaya Texts* in the UCLA library. I looked at the pictures, or plates as they are called, of Essie Parrish and others from home. I was immediately homesick. I read all eighty-two texts, which Oswalt divides into four classifications: "Myths," "The Supernatural," "Folk History," "Miscellany." I thought of stories, people, places, and the time and manner in which I heard this or that. Though I could not articulate my feelings at the time, I sensed what bothered me when reading "Indian books" for "Indian courses" at the university. Objectivism and text positivism, which influenced pedagogical practices at the time, hardly encouraged readers to think of people and places outside the actual text. I was not encouraged to engage my personal experience as I was at home when hearing stories. The text was supposedly complete, self-contained, a thing to dissect rather than to have a relationship with.

I can't think when I first heard about Slug Woman. She seems always to have been there in stories, on trails below Tin Barn Road, and in the hands and hearts of certain men and women. I don't remember what I thought when I read about her that afternoon in the UCLA library, but I must have thought of stories, just as I did the day Mollie Bishop telephoned and informed me "most of the students hated the story."

As Bishop related the various students' responses, I became agitated, then angry, not with her but with the students. Their responses hit a nerve. Their repudiation of the story was in effect a condemnation of my beliefs. As Bishop talked on, telling how she read slowly so all the students could follow, "even those who had to just listen," I thought to myself, those little no-good bastards. Well, what do you expect, I said to myself. Look at their parents. I felt sorry for the children from my family who surely were silenced, made to feel ashamed of their parents' ideas and stories. By my family I mean here those of us who adhere to Essie Parrish's teachings, those of us who are not Mormon or Pentecostal and do not participate in the new Roundhouse activities.

Then I thought of what happened to my cousin along Tin Barn Road.

Two or three of the most raucous protesters in the classroom were from a family closely connected to the woman my aunts suspected of having poisoned my cousin. In fact, shortly before Bishop related her failure with the story, I had been on the reservation and seen the aforementioned woman in a neighbor's garden. I had heard that her aunt, the old poison woman, had died. I wanted to express my condolences. I was sorry. When an old person dies, a kind of relationship with the community, no matter what its nature, ends. But now I was angry. I felt insulted by the students. And yet to Bishop, just as to the woman pruning her friend's rose bushes, I said nothing.

I felt I would lose my credibility with Bishop if I said anything just then or mentioned how I felt about the students' responses. I thought I might be seen as biased, not an objective or educated observer. Still, what I could have said—what I am saying here—could help Bishop understand the community and her position in it. I was—after all my experience in the community, after receiving a Ph.D., and after countless lectures and essays about challenging given histories and texts with personal experience—assimilating my experience to what I perceived to be the expectations of Bishop and the classroom. I was an undergraduate at UCLA again. I uttered some platitude to Bishop regarding the importance of active engagement with classroom materials for students. I was, nonetheless, silent.

Bishop comes from the East Coast, where she was raised and educated. She is a Quaker. She came to California with her husband and young daughter "to find peace, tranquility," which is not exactly what she found among the majestic redwoods at Kashaya. Her background positions her in certain ways; her history and education account in large part for her lack of knowledge regarding the Kashaya community and the ways in which the community may see her.

To the Kashaya, Bishop is an outsider. She is white and she is the teacher and principal of the Kashaya reservation school. Students and parents may respond to her differently, but she is still seen in the seventy-year history of the school as the latest representative of the dominant society, who has come with authority to teach and reinforce that society's values. As suggested earlier, the students' elders' experiences with the school have not been particularly good. There was a time when students were physically punished for speaking their language. The Kashaya became so quiet about their lives and culture that one teacher worked for fourteen years without ever knowing the Kashaya spoke a

language besides "substandard" English. Some teachers have been more
sensitive than others. Bishop wants to turn the situation around; she
wants the students to feel empowered. Yet the only thing that seems to
have changed, at least when I visited the classroom six months ago, is
that students now manifest their discontent openly and disrespectfully.

The classroom at the reservation today is typical of any contemporary
grade school classroom. It is in a relatively modern building constructed
in the early sixties (the old schoolhouse building was deemed unsatisfac-
tory by the county school district). The building contains the one-room
class complete with teacher's desk, tables and chairs, blackboard, maps,
calendars, and so forth. There is also a teacher/principal's office which
serves simultaneously as a library. Books, student records, and school
accounts are kept locked in this room. Outside the building are recre-
ational facilities: basketball courts, swings, a slide. Nothing in the classroom or on the school premises reflects in any way the Kashaya people.
Books and other materials about Indians, such as the Slug Woman
pamphlets, are kept with other books in the teacher's office.

Until the fall of 1990 when a second teacher was hired, grades 1–8
functioned as one class. A teaching assistant from the county school
district taught the kindergartners separately. Now Bishop teaches K–2
students and the second teacher teaches 3–8. The older group functions
just as they did with Bishop: students read together and then are given
individual assignments related to their respective competencies as readers. (Math is taught the same way; the group works together and then
each individual is assigned a project.) The K–2 students work primarily
as one group without much individual activity.

Bishop uses a phonics approach to teach reading. There has been
much debate regarding the merit of such an approach in comparison to
others, yet most approaches I know of are the same in terms of what
students are eventually asked to do as readers. One approach may work
faster or more efficiently than another, but most get students to read in
certain ways. As C. Jan Swearingen notes about our schooling in general,
the practice of reading, in association with other classroom activities,
"tends to teach children, among other things, to decontextualize language, spell out the implicit and assumed, formalize explanations, transform the 'impersonal' into the 'communicative,' the interactive contextual 'meaning' into the autonomous iterated 'sense.' Children are
taught to distinguish what was said from what (they think) was meant"
(152). This practice begins or at least reinforces that chasm-forming
process where the students, if they are to succeed in the classroom, must

shelve personal experience, the necessary ingredient for "interactive contextual meaning," and adapt the norms and definitions prescribed by the teacher and classroom activities. A certain kind of approach to reading yields a certain kind of response to the text(s) being read, and the students are expected to learn the former in order that they might give the latter. By establishing a chasm between the readers' personal experience and classroom norms, most methods of teaching reading rob students of the means to interact with the text in a way that enables them to contextualize it, and, hence, rob them of the means to criticize or remake the text as they see fit.

The teaching of reading, then, can be an effective colonizing device. Gabriele Schwab observes: "Only when the colonized's own native culture has been relegated to the political unconscious and becomes internalized as Other, only then is the process of colonization successfully completed" (130). Reading can encourage readers, particularly those from backgrounds different from the dominant society, to internalize life experience as Other. The first teachers at Kashaya were strict. They beat students. They preached Protestant values of cleanliness, orderliness, and clear thinking. Unbeknownst to them, their pedagogy, especially their teaching of reading, might have been as effective, if not more so, than the content of their speeches in breaking the Kashaya. Certainly pedagogy reinforced ideology. The Kashaya, however, had an exceptional leader during those years. As mentioned earlier, Annie Jarvis preached resistance. The students feigned acceptance with silence. They became poor readers, "too ignorant to learn" as one teacher said, and dropped out by second or third grade.

Today the situation is very different. Religious forces have succeeded in influencing and splintering the community in a number of ways. It is not only community against teacher and school but community members against one another. Now the reading process, rather than just working to break up and convert the community, fosters and maintains the breaks that exist. The content of what is read, say those representations of life in the students' readers, has little to do with the lives of Kashaya people. The story about going to the store in their *Basal Reader,* complete with its pictures, like the Dick and Jane story of old, is hardly representative of what students know from their lives. Students do not question this discrepancy since, according to the tacitly understood contract of reading, they keep their lived experience separate from what they read. Because the Kashaya students' lives are so complex and diverse, they might not only be able to inform or contextualize a story about going to the store and their own reading of this story, but in so doing, they might see what constitutes their lives as members of a single community in terms of what is similar and different about them, spoken and unspoken. Because their reading does not enable or encourage them to question and contextualize what they read, it reinforces the silence and indeed becomes a mechanism for maintaining silence about the fear, frustration, anger, and confusion experienced by a people splintering in the face of cultural flux, rather than creatively reorganizing them in a community-determined manner. Reading has perhaps never been more useful as a colonizing tool. It is safe for everyone, Indian and non-Indian.

On the surface Bishop appeared to break the tacitly understood contract that stipulates lived experience be kept outside the classroom, separate from what is being read. She introduced a story that probably was related in one way or another to the experience of many of the Kashaya students outside of the class, and then asked the students to talk about the story. The students were asked to talk about a representation of their experience as Kashaya by engaging and relating their own experiences. But the representation was created by someone other than and independent from themselves, at least as far as they could tell from the pamphlet, and it was handed to them by someone who was an outsider with perceived authority over them in a context where representations are engaged or read in ways that exclude personal experience. The students were asked to consider Bishop's idea of themselves in a way Bishop prescribed. Bishop's explicit command that students use what they know from home to discuss the Slug Woman story conflicted with the inherent commands of the classroom environment, which Bishop maintains, and with the practice of reading, which Bishop teaches.

This conflict no doubt effected a double bind for the students. Should they respond to Bishop's explicit command or to the inherent commands of the classroom and their practice of reading? Certainly the entire situation must have tweaked the sensitive nerve of their Kashaya identity for many of the students. Confusion over what to do and anxiety over the subject matter are likely to have influenced their responses to the text. Denial, conscious and unconscious, appears to be a method for Kashaya to cope with confusion and anxiety, particularly regarding how we constitute ourselves as Kashaya Indians. Failure of communication between people and different factions of people is the result of this denial. And so is anger. With remarks such as "That's all devil worship" and "I don't want to read about no savages," students denied any association with Slug Woman, whether there was any association or not,

and foreclosed the opportunity for discussion. And, as Bishop mentioned, the students' responses were angry. This particular reading activity, then, as I see it, replicated alienating, community-splintering practices on the reservation. It gave the students practice in such alienation
and splintering in the context of the classroom.

To further explore the students' responses, I must come back to the
text they read. If the students were angry, their anger had to be about
more than mixed messages and anxiety over the subject matter. Surely
their responses had something to do with *what* they read, with what the
text suggested to them as readers, which means that to some extent the
students did engage the text with their experiences as Kashaya individuals. Here I must mention that, while I have talked about chasms and
reading practices that may be chasm-causing, the notion of a chasm, or a
boundary as such, say between school life and home life, should not
necessarily imply something set, rigid, and impenetrable. Rather there
may be processes, such as those I have been describing, that people use,
consciously and unconsciously, that they may have been taught or that
they may teach, that work with varying degrees of success to keep things
fixed, or at least to create the illusion that things can be fixed and safely
stored in one place or another. Maintaining the illusion is often what
causes dis-ease both within the individual and within the community.[4]
So I am not suggesting that students do not use personal experience
when encountering a text. Home life and school life need not be mutu-
ally exclusive. As I have presumed above, school life may reinforce
patterns in home life. I am suggesting that there may be patterns associated with certain reading practices that make for limited engagements
that are ineffectual in terms of positive change. As I stated, I do not have
the knowledge or power to unmask each student's reading or response,
but I can suggest processes associated with the students and their reading
that I think influence certain reactions that impede change.

I was first struck by the flat language of the text. Note the persistent
subject-verb-object sentence structure: "It began to get dark. He looked

4. This reminds me of what Gregory Bateson noted many years ago in his study of
culture contact patterns. Gabriele Schwab sums up his observations thus: "In *Steps to an
Ecology of Mind* Gregory Bateson reveals a tendency of the mind retrospectively to project
epistemological independence onto those partialized closed systems of thought. General
interaction patterns show, according to Bateson, that all forms of culture contact that tend
to rigidify boundaries in order to maintain an unchanged internal coherence lead to an
increase of external conflict and hostility ultimately destructive for all agents involved"
(134). See Gabriele Schwab's "Reader Response and the Aesthetic Experience of Otherness," *Stanford Literature Review* (Spring 1986): 107–136. Also see Bateson's "Culture
Contact and Schismogenesis" in his *Steps to an Ecology of Mind*.

around in the forest for a place to spend the night. He walked toward a big upright tree. The tree had a hollow base. He prepared his bed there." Again, the educators at YA-KA-AMA omitted features of Oswalt's English version that suggested Kashaya patterns of speech. For whatever reason—perhaps the notion that school children can read only simple sentences—they used an insipid English.

Another feature of the text that I noticed immediately and have noted earlier was the absence of a first-person narrator. Except for the line "Maybe somebody else knows more about her but I never heard it" found in "A Description of Slug Woman," the text appears without any sense of a speaker, a distinct voice. This line probably remains because of an editorial oversight on the part of the YA-KA-AMA editors. As I also noted earlier, Herman James's narrative comments in Oswalt's version of the story have been cut in the YA-KA-AMA version, and neither Essie Parrish (who narrated the description of Slug Woman to Oswalt) nor Herman James is identified as a storyteller on Bishop's copies of the YA-KA-AMA pamphlet. (And, again, Bishop did not copy the cover of the pamphlet where Sidney Parrish is wrongly identified as the storyteller.) Parrish and James were related in one way or another to most of the Kashaya students; certainly the students would recognize the names. Of course the absence of a voice, or rather the presence of an anonymous storyteller, would not seem unusual to the students. Who is telling the story about going to the store in their *Basal Reader?* And isn't the language there flat also? There is, in fact, someone telling the story; what seems a void, an absence of voice, is really a ubiquitous presence. The voice, or language if you will, in the story of their *Basal Reader,* is from the world of some Other people, the world of the classroom teacher, the world of the dominant society. The voice in the text is that of the adult in the room, of Bishop, the teacher. As they are presented, the words are authoritative, without a distinct, identifiable speaker. To question the text is not merely to question Bishop but to question the context of the text's presentation and the text itself, and such questioning is not encouraged in the classroom or in the practice of reading. The students would need to use their personal experiences to question in a way that promoted rather than foreclosed discussion. Since the Slug Woman story is written in the same manner as their other reading material and was given to the students in the same context as their other studies, the students were probably further perplexed. The story as such complemented the double bind where the students were caught between Bishop's explicit command and those that inhere in the classroom and established reading practices. The story was about them in a way that was not them.

To what extent the students were conscious of the paradoxical situation in which they were placed, and to what extent their verbal protestations of the story were associated with the situation, is not clear, nor can it be. What is likely to have bothered them on a more conscious level, and what in turn may have provided them the opportunity to express a more general frustration and dissatisfaction, were the representations of Kashaya Pomo Indians and the moralizing associated with those representations. The students may not have been able to sense consciously the ways in which the voice of the text was not a Kashaya voice. They could understand, and apparently did understand, that Indians who search for and eat slugs and sleep in hollow trees are not Indians they know. Further, the drawings, which illustrate the written text, depict Indians in loincloths running about the woods. Note that admonitions regarding the breaking of "ancient Indian laws" are repeated throughout the story. The story is a moral tale. It opens with a warning. The protagonist disregards the warning and is punished. His son hears the story, heeds the warning, and lives happily ever after. James's version in *Kashaya Texts* is moral also, but at least the speaker who admonishes is identifiable, someone the students might more easily respond to.

The YA-KA-AMA version closes with an abrupt frame: "This is the end of the Slug Woman Story." No questions. No discussion. Presented in the classroom context, the story tells the students what an Indian is (i.e., a person in a loincloth who eats slugs and has rules about the birth of babies and hunting) and that if they are not like this Indian they "will be punished." The story's authority is associated with Bishop, so perhaps in a variety of ways the students may have been challenging and denouncing Bishop at the same time they were masking their connections with Slug Woman. No, we won't obey you. No, we won't be savages. No, we know nothing about Slug Woman. And that was the end of Slug Woman in the classroom. That was the end of the Slug Woman story. No questions. No discussion.

I said I think of stories whenever I hear or read about someone or something at Kashaya. The stories mix and mingle. I make sense of them, and this sense, of course, has much to do with my experience, my family, and my education. Sometimes I fancy myself a distanced observer, a fantasy that is strengthened by my education. I believe I see things for what they are at Kashaya. I believe I can move beyond my limitations as a person so deeply rooted in the community.

After I heard that the old poison woman had died, I kept thinking of the stories people told about her, not just about her poison work but about her life and history. I won't tell the stories here, lest the woman be identified. The stories are remarkable, and they say much about our people. I thought I would cover the stories in fiction, in a novel, so I would not have to cross boundaries. I would not identify the woman. I would not have to talk to her family. But who would read the novel? The conventions of contemporary fiction and the sheer length of a novel would prohibit most Kashaya from reading my book. If I am a distanced observer, if I see certain things about my people as a result, I cannot talk with all my people about what I see. I would, for the most part, be talking to others, to non-Indians who read books. So much for my distance. Silence, again. Like my cousin under a spell, like most everyone on the reservation, I move about unable to talk about what is happening. Slug Woman.

As I mentioned in an earlier chapter, little is known about so-called pre-contact storytelling among the Kashaya Pomo. Essie Parrish and other elders maintained that certain stories, especially those about Coyote, those from the time when the animals were still human, could be told only during winter. Essie Parrish remembered an old man who told stories "in the old way," full of songs, and who impersonated the various characters in the stories. He called the children to his home on winter nights and asked them to lie down in the dark before he began his stories.[5] Violet Chappell says of her mother, Essie Parrish: "Mom used to imitate the characters in the stories, too. She'd make her voice sound different ways." Many stories surely had to do with *šaba·du,* "teachings." Many stories, then, were moral. But how they were rendered moral, how they were told, received, and understood must have varied according to the individual storyteller, the listener(s), and the storytelling context. It is no different today. Mabel McKay, a Cache Creek Pomo, tells stories that are *šaba·du,* but not in a way that the story or the moral that may be associated with it is fixed, understood on the spot. "Don't ask me what it means the story," Mabel McKay says. "Life will teach you about it the way it teaches you about life."

Neither Essie Parrish nor Mabel McKay is a pre-contact Indian. In looking at how the Kashaya students read stories as opposed to how they hear stories, a scholar might want to compare and contrast pre-contact storytelling events with reading events, particularly in terms of oral versus literate dynamics. However, there is no way of *knowing* a pre-

5. Remember I noted in "The Verbal Art of Mabel McKay" that Parrish also related this about storytelling to Oswalt (Oswalt 119). There the old man is identified as Salvador (ca. 1840–1915) (Oswalt 119).

contact situation, and the current practice of oral storytelling and associated learning styles varies so greatly from home to home on the Kashaya reservation that it would be impossible to generalize about it. In addition, orality is not necessarily distinct from or incompatible with literacy. Something may be written, or printed, and something may not be. Any other distinction becomes debatable. The work of many scholars (Tannen 1982; Erickson 1984; Scollon and Scollon 1984) suggests there are different kinds of nonliteracies, just as there are different kinds of literacies.[6] Further, there is often an "interplay in spoken and written discourse in various settings" (Tannen 1982, 4), which is particularly true in situations where written texts may influence the form and presentation of oral texts and vice versa (Heath 1983; Swearingen 1986). And as Boyarin (1989) has pointed out, "there is no reason to assume *a priori* that forms of authority grounded in an interaction between text and speech are any more repressive than those which are exclusively based in orality" (401). My aunts' oral storytelling and dialogue about people and events surrounding the poisoning of my cousin did not encourage open, nonrepressive exchange with community members outside our family. Rather, whether the woman was guilty of poisoning my cousin or not, my aunts' talk framed her in given ways and thus sustained political and religious rivalries between our family and friends and hers. The younger Kashaya students listening to the story, those who could not read well or at all, were in many ways hearing in the same way as the other students who were reading. The classroom situation with Bishop as authority figure was the same for both readers and listeners. These younger students had not quite learned the practice of reading, but they already knew to keep life experience separate from what they do in the classroom. The questions that should concern scholars and others should be about the nature of the relationship students have with texts of any kind, whether written or oral, or any combination thereof. Is the text and its presentation authoritative? Can the student talk back, reinvent, exchange with others?

Of course discussions of what constitutes orality or literacy in particular cultural, social, and political contexts are likely to consider these questions in some way. Boyarin (1989) suggests that the dynamic, dialogic relationship Jewish people can have with biblical texts enables

6. Again, Scollon and Scollon note: "We feel that this [Northern Athabaskan] oral tradition is strikingly unlike the bard-and-formula oral tradition [i.e., the Homeric tradition studied by Parry and referred to by Ong via Parry] so often advanced as the representative of oral traditions" (182).

them "to dispute and recreate what Judaism is" (414). They are able
to interpret their lifeworld in a way that "satisfies their desire for personal integrity, their sense of belonging to the group, their connection to
past and future, and their place in the world" (414). Likewise, Michael
M. J. Fischer, in his study of contemporary ethnic minority autobiography, points out that for the autobiographers "ethnicity is something reinvented and reinterpreted" (195). Boyarin notes that "the means of
appropriation of the ongoing tradition is reflective" (413). The Jews
Boyarin discusses are empowered as disputants; they can talk back,
challenge the text. The ethnic minority autobiographers Fischer discusses are writers, likewise empowered, partly because of their educa-
tions, to reflect upon and dispute given notions of their ethnic identities.

The Kashaya Pomo schoolchildren are not empowered disputants. In
the classroom and, I would argue, in other parts of their lives, they
cannot actively invent or reinvent their identities as Kashaya Pomo
Indians, at least not openly, not away from their immediate families, not
with others in the classroom. Reading, as I have described it in terms of
the students' cultural and historical community, the classroom environment, and the particular practice of reading in the classroom, separates
the students from their ongoing histories and traditions and the processes of identity formation associated with their histories and traditions. Instead of engaging the students, instead of empowering them
with a cultural base—their own—from which to work, as Bishop had
hoped, the Slug Woman story served to further distance the students
from their cultural base and identities. Here, as Boyarin (1989) observed
in a healthier context, "the strategies employed in reading [were] part of
the general strategies of personhood in a world of multiple and conflicting cultural demands" (402).

My family and members of the Kashaya school board wanted any
suggestions I might have for improving the state of affairs at the school.
Instead of making suggestions, I have described some of the impediments
to positive change, particularly as I see these located in the students'
reading of the Slug Woman story, and I will offer criteria for what
reading and other classroom activities should work to accomplish. First,
reading must engage the students in a way that encourages them to feel
they have power equal to that of the text they are reading and to that of
the teacher who has given them the text to read. This sense of power does
not mean that the students should be in any way disrespectful. Rather,
they must feel knowledgeable and able in an encounter with a text and
when responding to it. Second, reading, like all classroom activity, must

be seen and promoted as something that continues and recreates culture both in the ways its practices alter and maintain previous methods for continuing and recreating culture and in the ways it helps individuals negotiate personhood "in a world of multiple and conflicting demands." Reciprocally, reading should evoke responses from the students that in given ways will inform, continue, and recreate its practice, classroom pedagogy, and the teacher's notions of logic, critical thought, and so forth. Finally, the practice of reading must work to engage the parents and the entire community. If the parents are not involved, if they do not know or understand what is going on in the classroom, another chasm forms across which there will be limited communication. So teachers must get out of the classroom if they are ever going to gain a clearer sense of the community. In both the classroom and the community at large they must position themselves as learners, and in a way students and parents can tell.

AFTERWORD

Victoria Kaplan Patterson has worked with Indian students for over fifteen years. Specifically, she has worked with the central Pomo tribes of Ukiah and Hopland in Mendocino County. She knows the Pomo people of the area well. (Her late husband, Scott Patterson, was an ethnographer and photographer who worked with these and other Pomo tribes and was well respected by them.) As a teacher and consultant for the Ukiah Unified School District, she saw Indian students' dissatisfaction with and alienation from the public schools, and her ideas and programs to rectify the problems associated with this dissatisfaction and alienation are encouraging.

One project that is particularly interesting to me is the *Pomo Supernaturals Coloring Book* created by the students of the sixth, seventh, and eighth grade Title VII classes at Pomolita School. Title VII is a state-funded program for Indian students who wish to work with teachers and others on education-related projects, such as tutoring for basic skills development. "I wanted to do something more," said Patterson. "Something that would be more than a job of catching these students up with the non-Indian students."

Patterson copied several stories from S. A. Barrett's *Pomo Myths,* a collection of stories recorded and gathered by Barrett in 1933. The stories taken from the central Pomo tribes are often about "mythic" figures such as Coyote. The students were given the stories and asked to make drawings that could be colored in with crayons. The purpose was to create a reader and coloring book for the younger Indian children. Patterson gave no other instructions. The students could choose whatever story they wanted. They could work together or individually. They could ask their parents, grandparents, or anyone else in their community for help.

The students organized themselves. They were responsible for their own re-creations of the stories. Patterson said the students divided the work, consulted family and friends, and then brought their illustrations back to the group. They examined one another's work and checked that the illustrations would be accessible to the younger Title VII students. As Patterson noted, "the students were responsible for continuing these stories, for keeping them alive for others, in whatever way they wanted." And that is what they did. One illustration depicts Coyote as a low-rider, a hoodlum, with an accompanying story about Coyote's tricky ways and the comment, "You never know where he will turn up or what he will do." In the introduction to the book Patterson writes: "We never know when the Supernaturals will reveal themselves. To be safe, we must always act courteously to our environment and take good care of it."

As Patterson observes, "the illustrations extended into other stories that are modern stories. The students told them in a way that called up the present, in a way the students could see the stories in the here and now, as real. Fire has power. Water has power. You could burn or drown. These things are real. Coyote can be seen in a low-rider." The older students' illustrations became the texts for younger students who in turn would begin remaking the texts by reading them and coloring in the illustrations as they saw fit. And of course the next step was to have the older students write the text for their illustrations.

Here it seems the criteria I set forth have been met. The students felt empowered; they were responsible for making sense of what they read based on what they knew or could find out. The drawing continued their culture in a way they determined, and it was done as a community project with one another, family, and friends. Unfortunately, funding was cut and the project ended. Perhaps the spirit remains for the students. Perhaps in the Ukiah Unified School District there are Indians who are empowered disputants.

It is important for Kashaya Pomo people to know stories and to keep the stories alive. We talk with stories; we know things about one another with stories. We can know things about ourselves with stories.

Throughout the writing of this chapter I have been thinking about Slug Woman. Earlier I said that for my family and me Slug Woman is alive. She got into my cousin, poisoned him so that he did not know what he was doing or where he was going. The medical doctors could not detect her. We had to take care of the problem our way.

Slug Woman is alive on the Kashaya Reservation. In the writing of this book, both in telling my stories and in my academic analysis, I found her in us. I found her in our silence. She has lured us there, so we don't know what we are doing as a people, where we are going, so we can't talk with one another about our confusion and pain. Will we come home? Or will we be trapped, left out in a hollow tree with our insides on fire?

This study is my attempt to doctor and to heal. Can it sing medicine songs? Can it lift Slug Woman up, singing, right before our eyes?[7]

7. I am grateful to the people who tell me stories, especially Mabel McKay, Violet Chappell, and Anita Silva. Without them I could not have written this book. I am also grateful to Judy Bare who listened to this chapter over and over again and offered helpful suggestions each time.

Works Cited

In addition to the sources cited in this section, I would like to acknowledge my indebtedness to the following individuals: Mollie Bishop, Tim Buckley, Juanita Carrio, Violet Chappell, Great-Grandma Nettie, Emiliano Hilario, Rita Hilario-Carter, Mabel McKay, Kathy O'Connor, Old Auntie Eleanor, Essie Parrish, Victoria Kaplan Patterson, Mary Louise Pratt, Anita Silva, Vivien Wilder, numerous unnamed Pomo Elders, family members, and friends, the Kashaya students at the Kashaya Reservation School at Stewart's Point, California, and the students in my Saddle Lake Summer Course and Writing I class at the University of California at Santa Cruz.

Aginsky, B. W. "The Socio-Psychological Significance of Death among the Pomo Indians." In *Native Californians: A Theoretical Retrospective*, edited by L. J. Bean and T. C. Blackburn, 319–29. Socorro, New Mexico: Ballena Press, 1976.

Allen, Paula Gunn. *The Sacred Hoop*. Boston: Beacon Press, 1986.

Apes, William. *A Son of the Forest. The Experience of William Apes, a Native of the Forest. Comprising a Notice of the Pequot Tribe of Indians. Written by Himself*. New York: published by the author, 1829.

Apess, Mary (variant spelling of Apes, above). "Experience of the Missionary's Consort, Written by Herself." In *Experience of Five Christian Indians of the Pequot Tribe*. Boston: published by William Apess (variant spelling of Apes, above), 1837 [1833].

Bahr, Donald, J. Gregorio, D. I. Lopez, and A. Alvarez. *Pinan Shamanism and Staying Sickness*. Tucson: University of Arizona Press, 1974.

Bakhtin, M. M. *The Dialogic Imagination*. Austin: University of Texas Press, 1981.

Barrett, S. A. *Pomo Myths*. Milwaukee: Bulletin of the Public Museums of the City of Milwaukee 15, 1933.

Barrett, S. M., ed. *Geronimo's Story of His Life*. New York: Duffield, 1906.

Basso, Keith H. "Stalking with Stories: Names, Places, and Moral Narratives among the Western Apache." In *Text, Play, and Story*, edited by Edward M. Bruner, 19–55. Berkeley and Los Angeles: University of California Press, 1984.

Bataille, Gretchen M., and Kathleen Sands. *American Indian Women: Telling Their Lives*. Lincoln: University of Nebraska Press, 1981.

Bateson, Gregory. "Culture Contact and Schismogenesis." In *Steps to an Ecology of Mind*. New York: Ballantine Books/Random House, 1972.

Bauman, Richard. *Verbal Art as Performance*. Prospect Heights, Illinois: Waveland Press, 1984.

Bean, L. J., and D. Theodoratus. "Western Pomo and Northeastern Pomo." In *Handbook of North American Indians*, vol. 8, edited by Robert F. Heizer, 289–305. Washington, D.C.: Smithsonian Institution, 1978.

Ben-Amos, Dan. "Analytical Categories and Ethnic Genres." In *Folklore Genres*, edited by Dan Ben-Amos. Austin: University of Texas Press, 1976.

Benjamin, Walter. "The Work of Art in the Age of Mechanical Reproduction." In *Illuminations*. New York: Schocken Books, 1969.

Berthouex, Susan J., and Robin S. Chapman. "Storytelling: A Way to Teach Non-Native Students." In *Non-Native and Nonstandard Dialect Students*, edited by Candy Carter, 37–43. Urbana: National Council of Teachers of English, 1982.

Bleich, David. "Intersubjective Reading." *New Literary History* 27, no. 3 (1986): 401–21.

Boyarin, Jonathan. "Voices around the Text: The Ethnography of Reading at Mesivta Tifereth Jerusalem." *Cultural Anthropology* (1989): 399–421.

———. "Reading Exodus into History." Unpublished paper, 1991.

Brumble, David H., III. *An Annotated Bibliography of American Indian and Eskimo Autobiographies*. Lincoln: University of Nebraska Press, 1981.

———. *American Indian Autobiography*. Berkeley and Los Angeles: University of California Press, 1988.

Campbell, Maria. *Halfbreed*. Toronto: McClelland and Stewart-Bantam, 1973.

Castaneda, Carlos. *A Separate Reality: Further Conversations with Don Juan*. New York: Simon and Schuster, 1971.

Christian, Chester C., Jr. "The Analysis of Linguistic and Cultural Differences: A Proposed Model." In *Report of the Twenty-First Annual Round Table Meeting on Linguistics and Language Studies*, edited by Chester C. Christian, Jr. Washington, D.C.: Georgetown University Press, 1970.

Clifford, James. "On Ethnographic Authority." *Representations* 1, no. 2 (1983): 118–46.

———. *The Predicament of Culture*. Cambridge: Harvard University Press, 1988.

Colson, Elizabeth, ed. *Autobiographies of Three Pomo Women*. Berkeley: Archeological Research Facility, Department of Anthropology, University of California, 1974 [1956].

Committee on Tolerance and Understanding. *Public Policy—Statements on Native Education*. Edmonton: Government of Alberta, 1984.

Copway, George. *The Life History and Travels of Kah-ge-ga-gah-bowh*. Albany: Weed and Parsons, 1847.

Crapanzano, Vincent. *The Fifth World of Enoch Maloney: Portrait of a Navaho*. New York: Viking, 1969.

———. *The Fifth World of Forster Bennett: Portrait of a Navaho*. New York: Viking, 1972.

———. "The Life History in Anthropological Field Work." *Anthropology and Humanism Quarterly*, no. 2 (1977): 3–7.

DuBois, Cora. "The 1870 Ghost Dance." In *The California Indians*, edited by R. F. Heizer and M. A. Whipple, 496–99. Berkeley and Los Angeles: University of California Press, 1971. (Originally "The 1870 Ghost Dance" was published by University of California Publications: Anthropological Records, 1939.)

Dundes, Alan. "Texture, Text, and Context." *Southern Folklore Quarterly* 29, no. 4 (December 1964): 251–65.

Eakin, Paul John. *Fiction in Autobiography: Studies in the Art of Self-Invention*. Princeton: Princeton University Press, 1974.

Erdrich, Louise. *Love Medicine*. New York: Bantam Books, 1984.

Erickson, Frederick. "Rhetoric, Anecdote, and Rhapsody: Coherence Strategies in a Conversation among Black American Adolescents." In *Coherence in Spoken and Written Discourse*, edited by Deborah Tannen, 81–154. Norwood: Ablex Publishing Corporation, 1984.

Fabian, Johannes. *Time and the Other: How Anthropology Makes Its Object*. New York: Columbia University Press, 1983.

Fischer, Michael M. J. "Ethnicity and the Post-Modern Arts of Memory." In *Writing Culture*, edited by James Clifford and George E. Marcus, 194–233. Berkeley and Los Angeles: University of California Press, 1986.

———. *Debating Muslims: Cultural Dialogues in Postmodernity and Tradition*. Madison: University of Wisconsin Press, 1990.

Fish, Stanley. *Is There a Text in This Class? The Authority of Interpretive Communities*. Cambridge: Harvard University Press, 1980.

Freire, Paulo. *Pedagogy of the Oppressed*. New York: Seabury, 1970.

Gleason, William. " 'Her Laugh an Ace': The Function of Humor in Louise Erdrich's *Love Medicine*." *American Indian Culture and Research Journal* 11, no. 3 (1987): 51–73.

Goffman, Erving. *Frame Analysis*. Cambridge: Harvard University Press, 1974.

Gramsci, Antonio. *The Prison Notebooks: Selections*. Trans. and ed. Quinton Hoare and Geoffrey Nowell Smith. New York: International Publishers, 1971.

Heath, Shirley Brice. *Ways with Words*. New York: Cambridge Univ. Press, 1983.

Hopkins, Sarah Winnemucca. *Life among the Piutes: Their Wrongs and Claims*. New York: G. P. Putman's Sons, 1883.

Hopper, Paul J. "Discourse Analysis: Grammar and Critical Theory in the 1980's." *Profession* 88 (1988): 18–24.

Hymes, Dell. "Breakthrough into Performance." In *Folklore: Performance and Communication*, edited by Dan Ben-Amos and Kenneth Goldstein, 11–74.

The Hague: Mouton, 1975. (Later reprinted in Dell Hymes's *In Vain I Tried to Tell You*, 1981.)

——. *In Vain I Tried to Tell You: Essays in Native American Ethnopoetics.* Philadelphia: University of Pennsylvania Press, 1981.

JanMohamed, Abdul R., and David Lloyd. "Toward a Theory of Minority Discourse: What Is to Be Done?" *Cultural Critique* (Fall 1987): 5–17.

Kaplan, Victoria Dickler, et al. *Sheemi Ke Janu (Talk from the Past).* Ukiah, California: Ukiah Title VII Project, Ukiah Unified School District, 1984.

Krupat, Arnold. *For Those Who Come After.* Berkeley and Los Angeles: University of California Press, 1985.

Lavie, Smadar. *The Poetics of Military Occupation: Mzeina Allegories of Bedouin Identity under Israeli and Egyptian Rule.* Berkeley and Los Angeles: University of California Press, 1990.

Leighton, Alexander H., and Dorothea C. Leighton. "The Life Story." In *Gregorio, the Hand-Trembler: A Psychobiological Personality Study of a Navaho Indian,* edited by Alexander H. Leighton and Dorothea C. Leighton. Papers of the Peabody Museum of American Archaeology and Ethnography 40, no. 1 (1949): 45–81.

Lowenthal, Leo. "The Triumph of Mass Idols." In *Literature and Mass Culture.* New Brunswick, New Jersey: Transaction, 1984.

McKenzie, James. "Lipsha's Good Road Home: The Revival of Chippewa Culture in *Love Medicine*." *American Indian Culture and Research Journal* 10, no. 3 (1986): 53–63.

Majnep, Ian, and Ralph Bulmer. *Birds of My Kalam Country.* Auckland, New Zealand: Auckland University Press, 1977.

Marcus, George E., and Michael M. J. Fischer. *Anthropology as Cultural Critique.* Chicago: University of Chicago Press, 1986.

Momaday, N. Scott. *The Way to Rainy Mountain.* Albuquerque: University of New Mexico Press, 1969.

——. *The Names.* New York: Harper and Row, 1976.

Mooney, James. *The Ghost Dance Religion and the Sioux Outbreak of 1890.* Chicago: University of Chicago Press, 1965.

Murray, David. *Forked Tongues.* Bloomington: Indiana University Press, 1991.

Neihardt, John G., ed. *Black Elk Speaks.* New York: Washington Square Press, 1972 [1932].

Newkirk, Thomas. "Looking for Trouble: A Way to Unmask Our Readings." *College English* 46, no. 8 (December 1984): 756–66.

Occom, Samson. "A Short Narrative of My Life." In *The Elders Wrote: An Anthology of Early Prose by North American Indians, 1768–1931,* edited by Bernd Peyer, 12–18. Berlin: Dietrich Reimer Verlag, 1982.

Ong, Walter. *Orality and Literacy: The Technologizing of the Word.* London: Methuen, 1982.

Oswalt, Robert. *Kashaya Texts.* University of California Publications in Linguistics, vol. 36. Berkeley and Los Angeles: University of California Press, 1964.

Parry, Milman. *The Making of Homeric Verse: The Collected Papers of Milman Parry.* Ed. Adam Parry. Oxford: Clarendon Press, 1971.

Paul, Richard. "The Critical Thinking Movement." *National Forum* (Winter 1985): 1–5.

Pomolita School Title VII students. *Pomo Supernaturals Coloring Book.* Ukiah, California: Ukiah Unified School District, 1983.

Ricoeur, Paul. *Interpretation Theory: Discourse and the Surplus of Meaning.* Fort Worth: Texas Christian University Press, 1976.

Rodriguez, Richard. *Hunger of Memory: The Education of Richard Rodriguez, an Autobiography.* Boston: Godine, 1982.

Roemer, Marjorie Godlin. "Literate Cultures: Multi-Voiced Classrooms." Paper presented at the Modern Language Association, San Francisco, California, December 1987.

Rosaldo, Renato. "Ilongot Hunting as Story and Experience." In *The Anthropology of Experience,* edited by Victor W. Turner and Edward M. Bruner, 97–138. Urbana: University of Illinois Press, 1986.

———. *Culture and Truth.* Boston: Beacon Press, 1989.

Said, Edward W. "Opponents, Audiences, Constituencies and Community." *Critical Inquiry* 9 (1982): 135–59.

———. "Representing the Colonized: Anthropology's Interlocutors." *Critical Inquiry* 15 (Winter 1989): 205–25.

Sarris, Greg. "A Culture under Glass: The Pomo Basket." In *In Writing,* edited by Paul Khoo and others, 44–53. Stanford: Stanford University Press, 1987.

———. "Storytelling in the Classroom: Crossing Vexed Chasms." *College English* 52, no. 2 (1990): 169–85.

Schwab, Gabriele. "Reader-Response and the Aesthetic Experience of Otherness." *Stanford Literature Review* (Spring 1986): 107–36.

Schwartzman, Helen B. "Stories at Work: Play in an Organizational Context." In *Text, Play, and Story: The Construction and Reconstruction of Self and Society,* edited by Edward M. Bruner. Washington, D.C.: American Ethnological Society, 1984.

Scollon, Ron, and Suzanne B. K. Scollon. "Cooking It up and Boiling It Down: Abstracts in Athabaskan Children's Story Retellings." In *Coherence in Spoken and Written Discourse,* edited by Deborah Tannen. Norwood: Ablex Publishing Corporation, 1984.

Shostak, Marjorie. *Nisa: The Life and Words of a !Kung Woman.* New York: Vintage Books, 1983.

Silberman, Robert. "Opening the Text: *Love Medicine* and the Return of the Native American Woman." In *Narrative Chance,* edited by Gerald Vizenor. Albuquerque: University of New Mexico Press, 1989.

Silko, Leslie Marmon. *Ceremony.* New York: Signet Books, 1977.

———. *Storyteller.* New York: Seaver Books, 1981.

Standiford, Lester A. "Worlds Made of Dawn: Characteristic Image and Incident in Native American Imaginative Literature." In *Three American Literatures,* edited by Houston A. Baker, Jr, 168–96. New York: The Modern Language Association of America, 1982.

Swearingen, C. Jan. "Oral Hermeneutics during the Transition to Literacy: The Contemporary Debate." *Cultural Anthropology* 1 (1986): 138–56.

Tannen, Deborah. "The Oral/Literate Continuum in Discourse." In *Spoken and*

Written Language: Exploring Orality and Literacy, edited by Deborah Tannen, 1–16. Norwood: Ablex Publishing Corporation, 1982.

Tedlock, Dennis. "The Spoken Word and the Work of Interpretation in American Indian Religion." In *The Spoken Word and the Work of Interpretation*. Philadelphia: University of Pennsylvania Press, 1983.

Theisz, R. D. "The Critical Collaboration: Introductions as a Gateway to the Study of Native American Bi-Autobiography." *American Indian Culture and Research Journal 5*, no. 1 (1981): 65–92.

Toelken, Barre, and Tacheeni Scott. "Poetic Retranslation and the 'Pretty Languages' of Yellowman." In *Traditional Literatures of the American Indian: Texts and Interpretations*, edited by Karl Kroeber, 65–116. Lincoln: University of Nebraska Press, 1981.

Tyler, Stephen A. "Post-Modern Ethnography: From Document of the Occult to Occult Document." In *Writing Culture*, edited by James Clifford and George E. Marcus, 122–40. Berkeley and Los Angeles: University of California Press, 1986.

Velie, A. *Four American Indian Literary Masters: N. Scott Momaday, James Welch, Leslie Marmon Silko, and Gerald Vizenor.* Norman: University of Oklahoma Press, 1982.

Vizenor, Gerald. *Interior Landscapes.* Minneapolis: University of Minnesota Press, 1990.

Wallace, A. F. C. *The Death and Rebirth of the Seneca.* New York: Knopf, 1970.

YA-KA-AMA Indian Education and Development Inc. *"A Description of Slug Woman" and "A Story about the Slug Woman"* (pamphlet). Santa Rosa, Calif.: YA-KA-AMA, 1974.

Index

Library of Congress Cataloging-in-Publication Data

Sarris, Greg.
    Keeping slug woman alive : a holistic approach to American Indian texts /
Greg Sarris.
        p.   cm.
    Includes bibliographical references and index.
    ISBN 0-520-08006-8 (alk. paper). — ISBN 0-520-08007-6 (pbk. : alk. paper)
    1. Pomo Indians—Folklore.   2. Miwok Indians—Folklore.   3. Folk literature,
Indian—History and criticism.   4. Oral tradition.   5. Storytelling. I. Title.
E99.P65S27   1993
398.2'089975—dc20   92-1680

Compositor: Keystone Typesetting, Inc.
Printer: Maple-Vail Book Mfgr. Group
Binder: Maple-Vail Book Mfgr. Group
Text: 10/13 Sabon
Display: Sabon